Middle Schools

MIDDLE SCHOOLS

ORIGINS, IDEOLOGY, and PRACTICE

A. Hargreaves and L. Tickle (editors)

Harper & Row, Publishers
London

Cambridge		San Francisco
Hagerstown		Mexico City
Philadelphia		Sao Paulo
New York		Sydney

First published 1980
Harper & Row Ltd 28 Tavistock Street, London WC2E 7PN

British Library Cataloguing in Publication Data

Middle Schools. – (Harper education series).
 1. Middle schools – England
 I. Hargreaves, A   II. Tickle, L
 373.2'36   LA635

 ISBN 0-06-318134-7
 ISBN 0-06-318135-5 Pbk

Typeset by Inforum Ltd, Portsmouth
Printed and bound by A. Wheaton & Co, Ltd, Exeter

CONTENTS

PREFACE AND ACKNOWLEDGEMENTS

Although middle school research emerged rather late and developed rather slowly, its production has accelerated in recent years. It now has an important outlet in the journal *Education 3–13*, which is devoted to the discussion of primary *and* middle school education, and several books based on systematic research are either in press or in preparation.[1]

It is in this context that a group called the Middle Schools Research Group (MSRG) was formed in March 1977. The roots of the group lay in a spontaneous expression of interest in sharing discussion about research into middle schools by school, college, and university teachers and a number of local authority advisers. A little more than a dozen people attended the first meeting. Membership is now in excess of one hundred and fifty. Conferences on a one-day or residential basis are held twice a year, a newsletter is circulated, and a bibliography of current writing and research on middle schools has been compiled. The group has no formal constitution, but acts in the main as a forum for the discussion and promotion of research into middle schools.

Perhaps the most concrete outcome of the group's endeavours to date is this reader. The possibility of producing a book of this kind was explored because, while many members of the group were engaged in research projects of various kinds, little of their own or other research on middle schools had been published, and nowhere was there an accessible collection of such research at hand in a single volume. This reader is intended to represent the diversity of work now to be found in the area.

In producing this book, we have been ably and consistently supported by fellow members of the Middle Schools Research Group (MSRG). In 1977, members of the MSRG appointed an editorial group to take responsibility for putting together a volume of readings on middle schools. In addition to ourselves, the members of that editorial group initially comprised Colin Richards, Mark Ginsburg and Professor Alan Blyth. At a later date, Maurice Galton was invited to join the group. We owe a great debt to these four individuals for they have expended substantial amounts of time and energy in producing, with us, a format for the book, and in reading and commenting, often in very great detail, upon various drafts of chapters that have been sent to us by contributors as well as on our own introduction. The final responsibility for the book, the introduction and introductory sections is, of course, ours.

The book is divided into four different but complementary sections: the historical and administrative context of middle schools, the rationales which have been advanced to explain and promote them, their curriculum and organization, and the features of interaction and interpersonal relations that are to be found among their members. Summaries of the chapters are provided in the introduction to each section, the major issues and themes are discussed in the general introduction and some implications of middle school research for educational policy are raised in a brief conclusion.

In the overall selection and organization of contributions, we have sought to strike a balance between those arguments addressed in the main to broader patterns of events at national or LEA level which are pertinent to middle school policy and have implications for middle school practice, and interpretations which are very much concerned with particular schools, their teachers, and pupils. The growing concern of many educational researchers to link the study of educational practice to an analysis of the economic and political constraints on educational policy is reflected in the organization of this book and in some of the chapters within it, and while the first half of the book might be said to place the emphasis on policy and the second half on practice, the links between them should not be forgotten.

As the theoretical approaches adopted within the papers differ, so do the research methods employed. Among the techniques used are the interpretation of documentary sources, textual analysis, questionnaires, sociometric tests, observation schedules, interviews, participant observation, etc. While each technique has its own particular strengths and weaknesses, some 'findings' recur irrespective of the particular techniques that have been used to elicit them. The identification of common 'findings' is a strong argument for the employment of diverse methodological techniques within studies as well as between them. We have tried to represent that diversity within this reader.

Note

1. Amongst the contributors to this volume books are either in press or preparation by Hargreaves and by Meyenn.

NOTES ON THE EDITORS AND CONTRIBUTORS

Editors

Andy Hargreaves is a lecturer in Educational Studies at the Open University. He has also taught in a primary school and a college of education, and spent three years researching into middle schools at Leeds University. This research has been published in various articles and in a forthcoming book.

Les Tickle is deputy head at Oldfields Hall Middle School, Uttoxeter. He has held various posts in comprehensive and bi-partite schools, and in the middle school. He recently completed research in classroom interaction in middle schools for a higher degree of the University of Keele.

Contributors

Professor W. Alan L. Blyth, Sydney Jones Professor of Education, University of Liverpool.

Christopher Bornett, Year Tutor, Westley Middle School, Bury St. Edmunds, Suffolk.

Kenneth A. Bryan, Senior Lecturer in Education, Chester College of Higher Education.

Sara Delamont, Lecturer in the Sociology of Education, University of Cardiff.

Ray Derricott, Senior Lecturer, School of Education, University of Liverpool.

Maurice Galton, Lecturer, School of Education, University of Leicester.

Mark B. Ginsburg, Assistant Professor, Foundations of Education, University of Houston, Texas.

Andy Hargreaves, Lecturer in Educational Studies, Open University.

James Lynch, Head of the School of Education, Newcastle College of Advanced Education, New South Wales, Australia.

Colin A. A. Marsh, Headmaster, Boney Hay Middle School, Staffordshire.

Robert J. Meyenn, Research Fellow, Department of Educational Enquiry, University of Aston in Birmingham.

Jennifer Nias, Tutor, Cambridge Institute of Education, University of Cambridge.

Colin Richards, Lecturer, School of Education, University of Leicester.

Paul R. Sharp, Lecturer, School of Education, University of Leeds.

Les Tickle, Deputy Head, Oldfields Hall Middle School, Uttoxeter, Staffordshire.

Gwen Wallace, Research Student, Department of Educational Enquiry, University of Aston in Birmingham.

Dennis Warwick, Lecturer, Department of Sociology, University of Leeds.

INTRODUCTION

EMERGING ISSUES IN MIDDLE SCHOOLS

A. Hargreaves and L. Tickle

In January 1968, there were no middle schools in the United Kingdom. Ten years later, there were 1690. By that time, over six hundred thousand pupils were being educated in schools with the designation 'middle' or 'first and middle'.[1] In 1973 alone, as many as 526 middle schools were newly established. Clearly, the development and expansion of English middle schools has been one of the most remarkable events in the recent history of the British educational system.[2]

The development of middle schools

Until 1964, transfer to secondary education at the age of eleven was fixed not only by convention but also by law. As long ago as 1907, regulations were laid down requiring local authorities to provide twenty-five % of their grammar school places free, the places to be allocated on the basis of competition by examination at age eleven. In 1926, the Hadow Report lent educational legitimacy to this increasingly accepted practice when it identified the age of eleven as the starting point of adolescence. An age distinction, which was actually the product of administrative arrangements, was thus claimed to reflect natural divisions between stages of human development. In section 8 of the 1944 Education Act, this convention was fixed by the stamp of legal authority in so far as *primary* pupils were defined as those who had not yet reached the age of twelve. This meant that any future schemes of secondary school provision incorporating an age of transfer of twelve or thirteen would be ruled out as illegal. In consequence, educational reorganization in the immediate post-war years, which was mainly based on separate provision for grammar, technical, and secondary modern school pupils in line with the recommendations of the Spens (1938) and Norwood (1943) Reports, firmly institutionalized the dividing line between primary and secondary education at the age of eleven. In legal and practical terms, this arrangement was to prevail for two decades. At times, in one or two localities such as Worcestershire and the West Riding of Yorkshire, alternative solutions were considered, but in view of the legal constraints they quickly subsided and only later made an impact at the level of public discussion.

With the advent of comprehensive school reform in the late 1950s and early 1960s, the orthodox pattern of secondary education received a thorough reassessment. Of crucial importance here was the question of how existing school buildings were to be used. As the tripartite system grew and was consolidated after the Second World War, many new and relatively small buildings were constructed to house what was, in effect, a segregated school population. Later, when proposals for comprehensivization were being considered, the Ministry of Education repeatedly insisted that those existing buildings deemed to be of good quality must be fully incorporated within any scheme of reorganization. And yet, in view of their limited size, such buildings were in most cases quite unsuitable for the purpose of providing education on a massive scale to comprehensive school pupils of 1500 or more in number.

Out of ingenuity and desperation, some authorities for whom this dilemma was particularly acute devised schemes which would enable comprehensive education to be provided in other than all-through eleven–eighteen schools. Split-site schools were proposed in some cases. In others, it was argued that the secondary stage of education could be divided into junior and senior substages, either at thirteen (this leading to the creation of eleven–thirteen junior high schools), or at fourteen as in the Leicestershire plan devised by that county's Chief Education Officer, Stewart Mason. In many quarters, however, these apparently ad hoc measures were regarded with great scepticism. Disquiet was expressed about split-site schools because of the chaotic trudging between premises which they entailed on the part of teachers and pupils, and because of the resultant difficulties of establishing an identifiable school community. This latter reason also accounted for much of the hostility directed against junior high schools, all of whose pupils were either entrants or leavers. Furthermore, there were doubts about the capacity of such schools to attract sufficiently qualified staff to provide specialist teaching in particular subjects such as French and Latin.[3] Finally, unease was expressed about the Leicestershire plan because it was felt that pupils transferring into the senior high school at fourteen would have inadequate time to prepare for external examinations. In addition, some peculiar features of the Leicestershire plan were seen to violate the central tenets of comprehensive schooling. Singled out for special criticism here was the practice of selecting pupils for the senior high school at fourteen by parental choice, thus leaving a residuum of predominantly working-class pupils in the junior high school as a disaffected 'truncated group' whose school career would be terminated at the minimum leaving age (then fifteen).

For those LEAs whose impulsion towards comprehensive educational reform remained strong and who also remained resolutely opposed to the pragmatic solutions then available, matters seemed to be at an impasse. Some new and dramatic initiative was urgently required. Such an initiative first emerged publicly in 1963, in the form of a proposal advanced, though arguably not devised,[4] by Sir Alec Clegg, Chief Education Officer for the West Riding of Yorkshire LEA, to reorganize education on three-tier lines; five–nine, nine–thirteen, and thirteen–eighteen. Fully aware of the illegal nature of what they were proposing, Clegg and others sought to persuade the Minister of the desirability, indeed the necessity of such an innovatory system of middle schools, and therefore of the urgent need for a change in the law regarding the age of transfer. Various educational arguments were advanced in support of the middle school case, including their capacity to extend the best practices of primary education, their potential for assisting pupils during a critical transitional stage of their personal development and educational career, and the possibility they held out of alleviating the pressures on upper school education incurred by their sheer size. But at this early stage of discussion, priority was attached to the claim that without an official sanctioning of middle schools, many areas, contrary to their wishes, would simply be unable to provide a viable system of comprehensive education.

Shortly before the end of his Government's term of office in 1964, the Minister of Education, Sir Edward Boyle, donated what he called his 'parting gift' to the Ministry: the Education Act of 1964.[5] This legalized a change in the age of transfer and granted limited experimental status to the middle school. From here onwards, progress was swift. Circular 10/65 'requested' LEAs to submit their plans for comprehensive reorganization and listed a system of middle and upper schools either of nine–thirteen and thirteen–eighteen or eight–twelve and twelve–eighteen types as one legitimate way of implementing change. In the next year, circular 13/66 announced the raising of the school leaving age. Given the extra load of pupil numbers on secondary school facilities which this would entail, the circular's warning that no extra money would be made available for new building projects placed further constraints on the ways in which reorganization might be achieved. Not surprisingly, the demand for schemes such as those incorporating middle schools which made adequate use of existing accommodation intensified.[6]

The Plowden Report added its own weight to the argument for middle schools by advocating that transfer should occur later than eleven. However, it displayed less decisiveness in choosing between eight–twelve or nine–thirteen middle schools as the preferred mode of reorganization. Only after considerable deliberation over much conflicting evidence and opinion did it come down in favour of the eight–twelve pattern. By the time of the Plowden Report's publication, the prospect of the first middle schools opening in 1968 in Bradford and the West Riding was very close. This kindled considerable interest in middle schools as a whole, and large amounts of time and energy were devoted to discussing the particular character that these schools should develop and the kinds of curricula that were appropriate for them. During the late 1960s and early 1970s several definitive conferences were called by the Schools Council and other bodies.[7] In accordance with guidelines set down in circular 10/65, teacher working parties were also set up in those LEAs where middle schools were being considered (as indeed in all LEAs contemplating comprehensivization), and on occasion the discussions were published and disseminated as reports.[8] Local authorities, most notably the West Riding, published their own views on middle schools,[9] and the Department of Education and Science (DES) did not hesitate to intervene in the debate.[10] Finally, a few headteachers and teacher-educators published what were on the whole prescriptive and favourable statements about middle schools in short texts,[11] and in the pages of educational journals such as *Forum*.

By April 1974, when there were over 1200 middle schools distributed (after local government reorganization) between forty-four LEAs, there was still virtually no material available which, on the basis of rigorous academic research, offered a critical evaluation of the emergence and practice of English middle schools. Edwards' (1972) shrewd and caustic critique of the administrative underpinnings of the middle school experiment did

provide a welcome corrective to the unbridled optimism which was characteristic of most other documents and reports. But his critique was based
more upon his inside knowledge as a chief education officer than on
academic research. Valuable though such knowledge is in generating
insights and possible lines of inquiry, it eludes independent assessment and
is therefore no match for the scholarly endeavour of educational research.
The remaining fragments of critical work were tucked away in little known
journals (e.g., Marsh, 1973) or in relatively inaccessible theses and disser-
tations submitted for masters' degrees (e.g., Holness, 1973). Furthermore,
the object of these critiques was, perhaps because of the middle school's
recency, largely confined to aspects of the middle school's historical
development rather than its curriculum and practice.

The rhetoric and reality of middle school provision

Given the fact, as Warwick acknowledges later, that the rise of middle
schools was both forced and rapid, it is in retrospect understandable that
most accounts and commentaries produced in the first years of their establishment took the form of elaborate and rather generalized justifications for
their existence. The middle school was an innovation that cried out for
legitimation.[12] The fact that the theory of middle schools which emerged
tended, in many respects, to distort the actuality of middle school practice is
therefore not surprising, given that it was strongly persuasive in both tone
and content.[13] Written into that theory were some of the most deeply
cherished symbols of social democratic discourse. Thus it was claimed,
amongst other things, that middle schools would provide a 'nice balance'
between the different approaches of primary and secondary education, that
they would lead to the natural elimination of educational inequality, that
they would cater for the needs of children as individuals, and indeed that
they would develop a unique identity which would enable them to respond
to the developmental needs of a whole new phase of childhood – the middle
years. Balance, egalitarianism, individualism, service, innovation, and professional responsibility; this was the optimistic language enshrining the
highest aspirations of social democracy in which the hopes for middle school
education were expressed. In some cases this theory has generated high and
unrealistic expectations of what middle schools and their teachers ought to
be achieving. One extreme example appeared as an advertisement in a local
newspaper. Note the discrepancy between the qualities sought and the scale
of responsibility offered.

Required for September 1979, an experienced teacher for this purpose-built middle school designed for 420 pupils aged from 8 to 12 years. Applicants should be able to innovate flexible grouping and individualised teaching programmes incorporating perceptual-conceptual development, functional linguistics, levels of comprehension and study techniques. Scale 1.

Against this background of middle school rhetoric, there was a growing concern amongst many of those involved with middle schools during their formative years, most especially among teachers, teacher-educators, administrators, and researchers, that the gap between the ideal and the real was substantial.[14] For many of those experiencing this educational change at first hand, it seemed that the potential of middle schools to stimulate widespread curriculum innovation and to develop their own unique identity was seriously hampered by all manner of constraints. Although not addressed in much of the widely distributed literature on middle schools, these initial misgivings have begun to be confirmed by subsequent research. We would wish to stress, however, the provisional character of its findings, given the scattered and small-scale nature of such research.

Factors affecting middle school practice: issues and research

One particular set of problems in middle schools derives from the staff and buildings they inherit. The housing of many middle schools in converted premises initially designed for the education of older pupils, has seriously restricted the options available to teachers for grouping children on lines other than the conventional class with its single teacher. In addition, open-plan extensions to some buildings have tended to be allocated to the younger age-groups, thereby reinforcing the tendency for styles of teaching and patterns of pupil grouping to differ markedly at the top and bottom ends of the middle school. The difficulties have further been compounded by the fact that in the sudden flurry of reorganization, many teachers found themselves employed in new types of institutions about which they had little knowledge, and to which they often had no definite commitment. Perhaps because of the ambiguities and uncertainties experienced by middle school teachers as to how they should perform their role in such schools (Ginsburg et al., 1977), they have been prone to cling on to their previous 'primary' and 'secondary' identities and practices with the consequence that the primary-secondary split has frequently been imported into, rather than transcended by the middle school (Hargreaves, 1978). The notion of a unique identity of the middle school looks somewhat precarious when matched against such difficulties. Other problems such as how middle schools relate to the third, upper school tier of the educational system have been widely noted (Ginsburg et al., 1977; Blyth and Derricott, 1977; Burrows, 1978) though barely researched.

Patently, most writing on middle schools has failed to address in any systematic way the peculiar problems which middle school teachers and headteachers confront in their everyday practice. Yet there is another absence in such documents, the implications of which are equally marked. In certain respects, as we have seen, middle schools are different from other schools and contain their own special problems and possibilities. But in other important respects, they share much in common with other schools. It is these features which most middle school literature, by focusing upon those qualities pertaining to the middle school's unique identity, consistently ignores. One of the most important but neglected of these common influences is that of social class. In their study of five Worcestershire middle schools, Ginsburg and his colleagues concluded that there was no reason to believe that class differences were any less prevalent in middle schools than in other sectors of the educational system. Their observations in one middle school with a predominantly working-class intake that the teachers were concerned to 'clamp down' and 'keep the lid' on 'a simmering pot' undercut many of the more idealized representations of middle school practice to be found elsewhere. Hargreaves (1979) reaches similar conclusions in his study of a social priority area middle school, where teachers adopted the strategies of policing and avoiding confrontation in order to cope with the problems they encountered. The comment by Ginsburg et al. (1977) that 'one cannot divorce what goes on in schools or in homes and workplaces from the broader features of society' (p.4) deserves close attention, and should serve as a reminder that when middle schools are investigated it is important to retain a sense of their wider social context. Several chapters in this book do precisely that.

Other studies have tended to employ the middle school as a site for more general research, without addressing themselves to the special character of middle schools as such. Thus, studies have been made of middle school teachers' conceptions of the Great Debate (Ginsburg et al., 1979), and of the tensions between their status as professionals and as union members. In the case of pupils, Pollard (1979) explores some aspects of deviance, what the pupils call 'getting done', in middle schools. He pays special attention to the processes by which understandings, routines, procedures, and standards of behaviour are negotiated between teachers and pupils, and examines the criteria according to which pupils perceive teachers to be 'fair' and 'reasonable'. In contrast to Pollard, Meyenn (1980) looks more closely at the implications of his research on pupils for middle schools in particular. Richly exemplifying his argument with transcript data, Meyenn identifies four girls' cliques in a middle school and concludes that contrary to popular assumption, belonging to an identifiable group rather than pairing off is very important for such girls. However, he does note that group membership may, for girls, be an age-specific phenomenon given that many of his respondents anticipated that they would probably begin pairing off when they transferred to the upper school.

With case-study work there are always methodological problems about how comparable the different cases are, whether they are typical or idiosyncratic, and so on. For this reason, it is particularly valuable if case-studies can be cross-referenced with large-scale surveys. Even given the methodological problems of survey research (for instance, it tends to record what people say their institutions are like rather than what they are actually like), it is useful to get an indication of how widespread and typical the problems raised by case-study research are. Unfortunately, few survey-type studies of middle schools have been published. Some teachers' unions have administered questionnaires to their own members on this topic, but the samples have either been very small[15] or the evidence has hardly been discussed except by the most oblique of references.[16] Important work of this kind is being carried out, however, at the University of Keele by Mervyn Taylor and Yvonne Garson and, not least, at the Department of Education and Science.

Historical studies of middle schools and middle schooling are more readily available, and there are useful accounts of the development and distribution of middle schools in Bryan and Hardcastle (1976, 1978) and in the early chapters of Blyth and Derricott (1977), where some empirical substantiation is provided for Edwards' (1972) view that middle schools are very much the outcome of administrative convenience. Burrows (1978), reviewing similar evidence, argues that the factors accounting for the emergence of middle schools have been remarkably diverse. He perceives this educational diversity as being a response to local needs rather than, say, the constraints of buildings and catchment areas as they differ between LEAs. Finally, accounts have now been written not only of the history of middle school provision but also of the history of the middle school curriculum (Blyth, 1979) and of associated development projects (Blyth et al., 1977).

Middle school research, then, although patchy and barely developed, has begun to map out some of the problems of the middle school either as a particular kind of school with its own peculiar features, or as simply just another school. As a result an understanding, at present somewhat inchoate, is emerging of the possibilities and limitations of middle school education. The problems which middle school research has begun to identify have by no means been universal, and exciting developments have taken place in a number of newly created middle schools. Even so, those problems have been sufficiently widespread to lead to an accumulation of interest and concern amongst many of those involved in middle schools. Accordingly, there has been a desire for a precise evaluation of and detailed research into their origins and practice.

The importance of middle schools

We have reserved for the final part of this introduction what appears to us to be the most vital question of all: why bother? There are, we feel, at least three answers to this question.

1 *As a sizeable, if minority component of the educational system, middle schools are worthy of study in their own right.*

There are many aspects of middle schooling about which very little is known. If practice is to be grounded in more than rules of thumb and unexplicated experience, it is important that research into middle schools is fostered so that those involved with them as headteachers, teachers, student teachers, advisers, and indeed as parents and governors might more adequately formulate, reformulate, and implement their ideas. In this book, the issues discussed include the nature of the transition in curriculum, learning experience, and patterns of organization such as 'setting' between the lower and upper ends of the middle school (Meyenn and Tickle), and therefore more general questions about curriculum continuity (Derricott and Richards), the relationships between middle school teachers and their first and upper school colleagues (Ginsburg and Meyenn), and the career options which are available to them (Bornett), the problems of transfer into and out of the middle school (Galton and Delamont, Bryan), and the characteristics of peer group cultures in such schools (Meyenn). The argument that middle school practice is constrained by architectural factors is pursued by Wallace, whereas much of the material in Part I explores the historical roots of these building problems (Marsh, Sharp, Blyth). Lynch points to some of the implications of a contracting educational system for middle school practice, and at a time when 'accountability' has become a keyword of educational discourse, Warwick discusses questions of participation and control in the governing of middle schools.

Most contributors address themselves to varying degrees to the central question of whether middle schools do indeed possess what has often been claimed for them; a unique identity catering for the specific needs of children in the middle years. The ideological aspects of this claim are discussed in different ways by Hargreaves and Nias. At the level of practice, Meyenn and Tickle suggest that various features such as the relative distribution of specialist and generalist teaching and the incidence of setting, change sharply between the second and third years of nine–thirteen middle schools. Middle schools, they propose, are more often characterized by sharp breaks than by smooth transitions. From a different standpoint, Bryan too challenges the 'unique identity' thesis of middle schools, suggesting that at least in terms of pupils' perceptions of transfer into the final tier of compulsory education, middle schools 'are just schools like any other', possessing no special character of their own.

In summary, we feel that the research contained in this book begins to shed some light on the problems of middle schooling and the roots of those problems.

2   *Because of their recent appearance on the educational scene and the contentious nature of their establishment, the study of middle schools highlights broader aspects of the educational policy-making process.*

Patterns of educational decision making and the values that underlie them are magnified through the lens of middle schools. By focusing on middle schools, we are able to clarify some of those issues and questions which have concerned students of educational policy for many years; whether educational change is the outcome of powerful historical forces or of the inspired actions of great men, whether new institutions emerge by accident or necessity, whether educational innovations are locally inspired or nationally imposed, and whether policies are determined by single factors (such as administrative convenience) or a multiplicity of factors. Most of these possibilities are represented in the contributions to Part I and Blyth provides a neat summary of the main interpretations that have been advanced.

In short, we feel that the study of middle schools provides empirical grounding for and lends a dynamic quality to the study of educational policy making in recent times.

3   *Middle schools are the pulse point of the educational system.*

Middle schools occupy a central position in the educational system not only chronologically but also sociologically, since they are situated at the point where pressures from the upper and lower ends of the educational system meet, where tensions and contradictions which beset the educational system as a whole become the subject of conflict and debate, and where different educational ideologies rooted in the primary and secondary sectors of schooling clash. The fate of middle schools therefore tends to be bound up with and indeed to be an indicator of the fate of the educational system in general. The legitimacy of regarding them as the pulse point of the educational system can be seen by comparing the issues of middle schooling in times of educational expansion and contraction.

In the late sixties and early seventies, middle schools grew up in the context of comprehensivization and the growth of educational progressivism, when egalitarian and individualistic educational ideologies held the stage and when there was an atmosphere of optimism and enlightenment about the possibilities of educational and social reform. These ideologies were compatible with an expanding economy and the perceived need to draw deeply on hidden reserves of talent, and to produce workers of sufficient flexibility and responsibility to cope with the problems of economic and technological change. At this time, as we have noted, there was a similar optimism about the middle school innovation and to the extent that their problems were recognized, these tended to be derivative of the gaps and inconsistencies between the educational ideologies mentioned. In the main, they were problems of how innovation was to be managed and of how the allegiances of 'reorganized' teachers to this new educational concept were to be secured. The questions did not strike fundamentally at the purpose of middle schooling, but were mainly of a technical character concerning innovation and its management. While economic growth lasted, the optimism was, with a few exceptions, unyielding.

In the late seventies and early eighties, at a time of economic stagnation and tight fiscal policies, which have included severe cutbacks in state expenditure on education, middle schools have come to highlight a mounting tension between rising expectations (i.e., the concern for standards) and falling rolls and budgets. Quite rapidly, from the mid-1970s onwards, there has been a dissipation of the cherished hopes of social democracy into empty slogans, and even these are quietly disappearing from social and educational debate. Who now speaks with seriousness about equality of opportunity? Retrenchment is instead the strident theme and the educational injunction to go 'back to basics' is a metaphor for the society as a whole. Middle schools have been caught up in these intensifying contradictions. While the demands increase for more specialist teaching, many middle schools are being forced to develop a more generalist approach as staffs shrink with falling pupil numbers and tightening budgets. More and more is being expected of middle school teachers while less and less is being offered to them in the way of material supports so that they might meet these escalating demands.

In summary, we feel that the problems of middle schooling are an indication of the wider problems to be found in the educational system as a whole. Studying them therefore provides useful access to these important wider issues.

Conclusion: the future of middle schools

The contradiction between rising expectations and falling rolls and budgets constitutes one threat to the middle school's existence. Another derives from the development of sixth-form colleges in some LEAs as a solution to the problem of shrinking sixth forms. In view of the overall consensus that thirteen–sixteen schools are educationally undesirable, nine–thirteen middle schools are not felt to be compatible with sixth-form colleges. The outcome of these twin pressures may be that middle schools will be wound up in some LEAs, or that the age of transfer will be lowered from thirteen to twelve (Fiske, 1979; National Union of Teachers, 1979). The likelihood of these outcomes might be increased by the pressure to raise the age of transfer out of first schools to ten, in order to preserve viable first schools in the context of falling rolls. Razzell's (1978) judgement that 'the concept of first and middle schools seems dead' is probably an overstatement and certainly premature, particularly in view of the restoration of an increase in the birth rate during 1978 and 1979 with its potentially alleviating effect on falling pupil numbers. Nonetheless, the threats to the middle school are very real and in many senses are indicative of the economically and politically induced threats faced by the educational system as a whole. Ironically, if such pressures do not meet with substantial resistance, the middle school may, in the absence of any explicit party political support, turn out to be no more than it was initially intended to be, an experiment, and a failed one at that. Once this small anomaly has been ironed out, then the 'real' issues can be returned to; the 'basic' issues of standards, accountability, the core curriculum, and the relationship between education and industry, etc.

Consequently, we feel there is a great need to understand the contradictions and conflicts of middle schooling in their full complexity (which includes their political and economic context), for if the only explanations available take the form of those contained in the present theory of middle schools we referred to earlier, which remain at odds with the experience of those connected with middle schools, then all that will be left will be a diffuse sense that they have somehow failed, and that it must be the middle school 'method' that is wrong. An understanding of the reality and context of middle schooling may well prove essential for its preservation. We would be disappointed if this book did not contribute to such an understanding.

Notes

1. The defining characteristic of middle schools is that they straddle the conventional age of transfer point at eleven plus. In the DES booklet *Statistics in Education* middle schools are defined as those catering for age-ranges of eight–twelve, nine–thirteen, and ten–thirteen. First and middle schools combined have an age-range of five–twelve. There are no five–thirteen schools.
2. In Britain middle schools are very much an English phenomenon. With minor exceptions, as at Grangemouth in Scotland, there are otherwise no middle schools in Scotland, Ireland, or Wales.
3. These are documented by Gosden and Sharp (1978), Sharp (in this volume), and Hargreaves (forthcoming).
4. Evidence that Clegg was not the creator of the middle school idea is provided in the chapters by Sharp and Marsh (in this volume).
5. Quoted in Kogan (1971).
6. Data supporting the argument for the influence of RSLA in the expansion of middle schools are provided in Hargreaves (forthcoming.).
7. The best known is the Middle Years of Schooling Conference, held at Warwick in 1967, from which the Schools Council Working Paper No.22 is derived.
8. See, for example, Worcestershire Education Committee (1968).
9. West Riding Education Committee Reports (1963, 1965, 1967).
10. As for example in Department of Education and Science (1970(a), 1970(b)).
11. See Culling (1973) and Gannon and Whalley (1975) for examples.
12. This is the point made by Lynch (in this volume).
13. This argument is advanced by Hargreaves (in this volume).
14. See Nias (in this volume).
15. As in the survey carried out by the Assistant Masters' Association (1976).
16. As in the report of a survey conducted by the NUT (1979).

Part I

THE HISTORICAL AND ADMINISTRATIVE CONTEXT

INTRODUCTION

No educational institution can be fully understood without some consideration being given to its origins and its location in the wider context of society. This is because the practices to be found in educational institutions are often restricted by constraints, and based upon assumptions which are themselves grounded in historical legacies, that past conflicts and decisions about education have left to the present. School buildings are one repository of these past conflicts and assumptions, and serve to impose considerable constraints on present day educational practices, as Wallace points out for middle schools in Part III.

The historical and administrative context of middle schools is therefore much more than an interesting backcloth to the present day practices of middle schooling, for that context has influenced the particular forms that middle schools now take. Yet, ascertaining the precise details of how middle schools emerged has so far proved somewhat problematic, and the general reasons for the development of such schools have been the subject of substantial disagreement.

In one sense, middle schools can be construed as being hurled into existence by the innovatory and proselytizing zeal of various educational reformers such as Sir Alec Clegg, who might be seen to have conducted an educational crusade in the pursuit of openness and change. But the argument has also been advanced that the more earthy reasons of pragmatism, economy, and administrative convenience necessitated their development. Furthermore, middle schools have been cited in the name of many different educational causes. They have been advocated as the 'natural' way of bringing about comprehensive education, they have been put forward as a vehicle for extending the desirable aspects of primary school practice to older age-groups, and they have been hailed as a completely new educational concept – as institutions with their own unique identity.

Blyth's account opens this section and gives a flavour of this diversity of historical interpretation. After the first part of his chapter, where he provides a useful overview of the historical antecedents of the middle school and sketches some of the major features in their development, Blyth then reviews various interpretations of why middle schools became established within the English educational system, and relates these interpretations to the values seemingly held by their exponents. The position taken by Blyth is very much like that of Carr (1964) who argues that:

> The historian is necessarily selective. The belief in a hard core of empirical facts existing objectively and independently of the interpretation of the historian is a preposterous fallacy. (p.6)

Blyth then concludes by giving some indication of the current diversity of middle school provision and of the uncertain future of middle schools in the context of falling rolls and economic cuts.

The next two chapters take a narrower but more detailed view of the establishment of middle schools. Each chapter focuses upon the emergence of middle schools in a particular locality. These are the West Riding of Yorkshire and Worcestershire. Using the internal memoranda and correspondence of the West Riding, Sharp analyses the detailed negotiations that took place between that LEA, several of its divisions, and the Ministry of Education, firstly over the establishment of eleven–fourteen junior high schools and secondly, where these proved impracticable or undesirable, over the inauguration of middle schools. The capacity of middle schools to enable certain divisions to 'go comprehensive' by using their existing building stock is given particular emphasis by Sharp, who then speculates that without the introduction of middle schools and the contribution that the West Riding made to that change, many LEAs may well have been unable to provide comprehensive education.

Marsh studies a set of parallel though less well publicized negotiations that took place in Worcestershire at about the same time. Drawing on Education Committee and Sub-Committee minutes as well as interviews with headteachers and officers of the Authority, Marsh, like Sharp, deduces that pragmatic considerations were of great importance in the development of middle schools although, in contrast to the West Riding, these had as much to do with problems of transportation of children to schools in rural areas as with school buildings. One of the most interesting points raised in Marsh's account is that middle schools were first considered, though subsequently rejected, by the LEA as long ago as 1959, thus casting doubt on the conventional wisdom that the idea of middle schools did not emerge until Sir Alec Clegg first aired it in 1963.

In the final chapter of Part I, Warwick discusses participation in and control of the organization of middle schooling in terms of the composition and functions of governing bodies. He relates the role of middle school governing bodies to a wider tension between increased demands for participation in society's institutions on the one hand, and to the development of corporate management styles of administration, with their tendency to concentrate power and decision making amongst the few, on the other. Thus, in recent years, while the base of participation in governing bodies has widened to include parental and other representatives, the sorts of decisions made by these bodies do not seem to have had any substantial relevance to or effect upon school policy. In Warwick's language, it seems that middle school governing bodies, like most others, are still hot on kitchens and waste disposal but not on new curricula and programmes of in-service training for middle school teachers. Accordingly he suggests that, despite efforts to the contrary, most of the business of school government remains a 'stagnant ritual'. Echoing the sentiments of other contributors, Warwick calls for a 'revitalisation' of the debate about middle schools and their purposes, and suggests that the widening of discourse in governing bodies and the increase of genuine participation in school government are appropriate means for achieving such a 'revitalisation'.

CHAPTER ONE

MIDDLE SCHOOLS AND THE HISTORICAL PERSPECTIVE

W. A. L. Blyth

The establishment of middle schools constitutes one of the strangest stories in the history of English education. A new kind of institution has appeared, and has become partially established as a minority organization,[1] without any consistent political support or opposition. The chronology of its emergence will be presented in bald outline, followed by an attempt at interpretation, and finally some comments will be offered on the type of institution which has emerged.

The origins of English middle schools

The age-graded structure of the English educational system is itself a twentieth-century development. As for the eleven-plus transfer from primary to secondary education, and even the definitive establishment of primary and secondary education themselves, they are barely half a century old. These phenomena originated through a combination of two circumstances: the establishment of systematic transfer from elementary schools to aided grammar schools and rate-supported secondary schools, and the definitive raising of the leaving age to fourteen in the Education Act, 1918.[2] Eleven gradually became the convenient age for this transfer, which could then be followed by a five-year course leading to the School Certificate. The majority who were not transferred spent three more years in the elementary school. The Hadow Reports of 1926 and 1931 gave official approval to this procedure, as well as to the definitions of successive stages in education. They also went considerably further, advocating transfer to secondary schools for all, a separate four-year junior school to precede it and to follow the separate infant school, and a four-year modern school, with a leaving age of fifteen, for those whose transfer did not take them to one of the grammar or secondary schools. In characteristically Shakespearian phraseology, the 1926 Report claimed that there was 'a tide which rises in the veins of youth. It is called adolescence' (Hadow Report, 1926). Less rhetorically, but more dogmatically, it was postulated that adolescence began at eleven or so, and that the change of school ought to coincide with its onset. The proposals were accepted.

However, these transfer ages were not universally adopted. Technical and commercial schools admitted pupils transferred at thirteen, until the recommendations of the Spens Report (1938) and the provisions of the Education Act of 1944 caught up with them. Most boys' independent schools, fed by eight–thirteen preparatory schools, did likewise. Selective central schools, recruiting at eleven, usually kept pupils only until fifteen. Meanwhile, during the Depression years, the reorganization of the all-age elementary schools proceeded sluggishly.

The legal position was amended by the Education Act of 1944.[3] A clear distinction was now drawn between primary pupils and secondary pupils and was rigidly enforced, although the 1948 Act subsequently introduced a slight easement for those whose development (usually equated with their academic achievements) entitled them to accelerated promotion into the 'secondary' category.[4] Each local education authority was required to draw up a development plan which would conform to these provisions. Nevertheless, some of them made reference to other possible transfer ages, and suggestions from various sources[5] had kept alive the idea that the age of eleven was not divinely ordained for this purpose, as was in any case apparent from the educational systems of other countries; twelve was the usual age in Scotland. However, in the late 1940s, attention was not focused on the age of transfer so much as on the nature of secondary schooling and, in particular, on whether it should embody selection.

In fact, it was this latter issue which led to the reopening of the other. Stewart Mason, the Director of Education for Leicestershire, reached the opinion that it might be possible to avoid what were increasingly seen as the drawbacks of the selective system without entirely abolishing grammar schools or establishing monster comprehensive schools (Mason, 1964). He aimed to do this by introducing a two-tier secondary system of eleven–fifteen high schools and fourteen–eighteen grammar schools, with voluntary transfer from the first to the second. Once this suggestion had been translated into action, other LEAs began to reconsider the age of transfer.

Prominent among these was the West Riding of Yorkshire, an authority whose development plan had embodied the possibility of a different age of entry to secondary schools. There, the Chief Education Officer, Sir Alec Clegg, aimed to introduce a system less selective than Leicestershire's, equally free from oversized comprehensive schools, and also capable of providing for children of nine and ten a more demanding intellectual content than could be expected from the traditional class-teacher organization within primary schools for children under eleven. His LEA developed, for carefully chosen parts of the West Riding, a five–nine, nine–thirteen, thirteen–eighteen scheme, which introduced in England, for the first time officially, the term 'middle school' which had until then been an Americanism. In order to implement this plan, it was necessary for the education acts themselves to be amended. By the Education Act, 1964, and the subsequent circular 12/64 piloted by Sir Edward Boyle (as he then was), who was keenly interested in the West Riding plan, it became legal to build new schools for this purpose, although not yet to convert existing schools. The 1964 Act also empowered the Secretary of State to 'deem' middle schools either primary or secondary with financial disadvantages for the former.[6]

Meanwhile three other developments combined to elevate the introduction of middle schools from a local to a national issue. The first of these was the commitment of the Labour Government, elected in 1964, to the reorganization of secondary education on nonselective lines. Circular 10/65, the administrative instrument which expressed that commitment, mentioned middle schools somewhat grudgingly as one of six devices which might be introduced for this purpose and indicated, quite shrewdly, some of the issues which they might pose. Grudgingly or no, they were at least included, and successive circulars referred to middle schools with increasing cordiality. The second new development, which may itself have influenced this change of climate (Bryan and Hardcastle, 1977, 1978), was the task concurrently assigned to the Central Advisory Council for Education (England), under the chairmanship of Lady Plowden, 'to consider primary education in all its aspects and the transition to secondary education'. This placed all aspects of transfer on the national agenda and it became apparent, even before the publication of the Plowden Report itself, that the *age* of transfer was to be given specific attention. In the event, the Council recommended in 1967 that there should be middle schools, within a restructured national system, undertaking some work hitherto denoted as secondary but also embodying 'the best of primary education as we know it now' (para. 383, p.146). On balance they preferred middle schools not with the Leicestershire ten–fourteen age-range, nor the West Riding's nine–thirteen, but a still lower age, eight–twelve, the one which under the 1964 Act has conventionally come to be 'deemed primary'. The third development was the firm commitment of Government and Opposition alike to implement section 35 of the 1944 Education Act which required the eventual raising of the school leaving age to sixteen, thus allowing the possibility of substantial secondary education for all pupils beyond the age of twelve or even thirteen.

The Plowden Council's recommendations were never officially accepted, nor rejected, either by the Labour Government before 1970 or by the Conservatives afterwards. Instead, each proposal by a local education authority was treated on what were deemed to be its merits. However, for those whose plans were accepted, the 1968 Education Act explicitly legalized the conversion of other schools into middle schools,[7] and guidelines for the conversion as well as the building of middle schools were published (DES, 1970(a)), accompanied by suggestions for organization and curriculum (DES, 1970(b); Culling, 1973; Gannon and Whalley, 1975; Burrows, 1978). These suggestions, further developed, have been reflected in the emergence of characteristic features within many middle schools, notably the 'horizontal' organization by year groups, the doubling up of academic and pastoral roles and the necessity of some form of power sharing and mutual advice among the staff, and the introduction of an element of specialization in the final year (twelve plus or thirteen plus) as a preparation for transfer into the upper schools. Little by little the numbers of middle schools have increased, with the proportion of schools 'deemed primary' also increasing.

As for the junior high schools pioneered by Leicestershire, they found few imitators and became a tiny minority among middle schools 'deemed secondary'. I suspect that they were regarded as both expensive and inimical to 'real' comprehensive education – at least until interest came to be focused on the sixteen–nineteen age-group and until eleven–sixteen schools, similar in some respects to junior high schools, began to develop almost by default.

Meanwhile, the position of middle schools remains anomalous. They cannot be 'deemed middle'. Education must still be primary, secondary, or further, even though a school may, in the words of the 1964 and 1968 Acts, provide both primary and secondary education.

Interpretations of the origins of English middle schools

Some more general interpretations of these developments have been suggested. The first is of the kind presented in the Plowden Report itself, and duly echoed in educational circles up and down the country. It is based on arguments drawn from child development. First, a general phase of stability in physical development can be identified between eight and thirteen, although at the upper end many girls and some boys are palpably outgrowing it. Then, the 'stage of concrete operations' derived from Piaget and his school has frequently been cited as grounds for a separate school, usually intended to coincide with that 'stage' but sometimes, and more accurately especially for nine–thirteen schools, to cater for transition to the 'stage of formal operations'. A further, more instrumental, justification frequently advanced for a middle school is that it starts just after most children have attained primary reading competence. Alongside this there is a more general claim that these middle years, eight to thirteen, are associated with a distinct stage in social and emotional development, one for which the family atmosphere of the first school and the youth culture of the high school are both inappropriate. The Schools Council endorsed this set of claims by establishing its project on the whole curriculum in the middle years of

Table 1.1: *Numbers of Middle Schools in England and Wales*[8]

Year (1 Jan)	First and Middle	Deemed Primary	Deemed Secondary	Total
1969	0	1	14	15
1970	4	31	105	140
1971	84	118	147	349
1972	86	137	186	409
1973	143	242	302	687
1974	304	505	404	1213
1975	331	578	473	1382
1976	348	645	509	1502
1977	383	685	564	1632
1978	387	702	601	1690
1979 (provisional)	390	754	620	1764

schooling, which in turn produced two reports concerned with this age-span (Schools Council, 1972, 1975). Interestingly, the designation of the years eight–thirteen as the 'middle years' enabled the Council and the project to avoid having to decide, even on balance, whether to opt for eight–twelve or nine–thirteen, or indeed for middle schools at all.

There is indeed a lack of firm evidence, and even a lack of the means of establishing firm evidence, about the educational advantages of middle schools, or for that matter of any alternative age-pattern. It is however my subjective impression that the social atmosphere of those middle schools that I have known is somewhat less strident than in many schools with an eleven-plus entry. It also appears that some other chapters in this volume may point in the same direction.

The first interpretation, then, of the growth of middle schools is that they represent the planned introduction of a pattern of schooling based, somewhat idealistically, on developmental considerations. Other writers about middle schools have been quick to challenge such an interpretation. Different explanations have been advanced for their origins. The one most frequently heard is that middle schools constituted little more than a relatively cheap, convenient, and inoffensive means of introducing comprehensive secondary education, or of earning the new school places needed for the raising of the school leaving age which would, under the Labour Government, only be made available by the Department of Education and Science if a nonselective system were introduced. Existing buildings, usually small ex-secondary modern schools, could be converted into middle schools, while medium-sized grammar schools could become, without great disruption or expansion, thirteen–eighteen comprehensive schools. Edwards (1972), Lynch (1975), and Bryan and Hardcastle (1977, 1978) are among those authors who have put forward arguments along these lines and, in the last case, there are further indications of how national policy itself came to be based largely on economic criteria. Local studies, including those by Marsh in Worcestershire (Chapter 3) and Sharp in West Yorkshire (Chapter 2) have substantiated this kind of interpretation in detail.

Others have advanced a still more general type of explanation. Blyth and Derricott (1977) comment on the apparent paradox that middle schools, which present an image of determined harmony and optimism, are in fact the by-products of social conflict, an incidental consequence of major movements of the 'tectonic plates' affecting education as a whole, and that their happy-school image is deliberately developed in order to counteract this underlying conflict, in the absence of any social group or political party committed to their cause.[9] A less metaphorical and impersonal, although politically more identifiable, interpretation has been advanced by Hargreaves and Warwick (1978), by Hargreaves (forthcoming), and to some extent by Ginsburg and his colleagues (1977). According to this perspective, middle schools are necessarily unable to fulfil the idealistic role posited for them by the proponents of the developmental arguments simply because they, like any other educational institution, are subject to the tensions and restrictions implicit in English society as constituted at present. By prolonging 'the best of primary education as we know it now', it could be said that society has avoided the costs of even the average level of secondary education while appearing to adopt a child-centred approach.

All of these analyses recognize that middle schools are a new phenomenon, and that their nature is unusual. Each explanation can have validity in its own terms, but ultimately they cannot all be entirely compatible. However, taken together, they indicate how essential it is to seek explanations at more than one level if any real understanding is to be achieved.

The varieties of middle schools

To discover, in any one instance, reasons for the establishment of middle schools may help to throw further light on their emergence as a whole. Now that plans for their introduction have been considered, and in part implemented, for twenty years, it is possible to identify several patterns of development, each sufficiently often encountered to merit recognition as representative of widespread trends.

The first of these, the most radical in character, is the total conversion of schools in an area to a five–nine, nine–thirteen, thirteen–eighteen (or nineteen) pattern, as has been introduced for example in the Isle of Wight, or the London Borough of Merton. It is the most radical because not only does it involve total conversion but, by opting for the Clegg age-range of nine–thirteen rather than the Plowden one of eight–twelve, it requires a more thoroughgoing rethinking of curriculum and organization. This will be termed type I.

Type IA can then be identified as a partial conversion to the type I pattern. Here, nine–thirteen middle schools exist in considerable numbers, alongside others whose transfer age continues at eleven. Northumberland and Leeds are instances of this pattern, which can in its turn be distinguished from type IB, typified by Shropshire, Wiltshire, or Cambridgeshire, which have only a few, scattered middle schools.

Type II is based on twelve-plus transfer, the pattern officially endorsed 'on balance' by Plowden. In its simplest form it involves a mixture of first schools (five–eight) and middle schools (eight–twelve), with combined schools (five–twelve),[10] followed by comprehensive schools (twelve–eighteen or nineteen). For historical reasons there is no instance of an LEA in which existing buildings made it possible to dispense with combined schools altogether, and it is difficult even to find instances where transfer at twelve plus and twelve–eighteen schools are universally introduced, although the London Borough of Ealing is a case in point.

In view of the rarity of this 'pure' type II pattern, it is not surprising to find that many variants have been introduced. They include:

Type IIA – the 'pure' pattern alongside schools with eleven-plus transfer, as in Sheffield.

Type IIB – also a mixture but with very few eight–twelve or five–twelve schools in a predominantly traditional pattern, as in Cheshire.

Type IIC – the 'pure' pattern five–eight, eight–twelve, or five–twelve, but with twelve–sixteen comprehensive schools and sixth-form colleges, as in the London Borough of Harrow.

Type IID – similar to type IIC but with this pattern confined to part of the LEA as in Bedfordshire, Hampshire, and Staffordshire, all of which find themselves in this position through absorbing cities which had previously adopted type IIC.

Still further permutations, largely resulting from local government reorganization and from attempts to preserve an element of selection, would permit the extension of variants of type II through most of the alphabet.

Type III is much more restricted. Its distinguishing feature is the presence of some middle schools which are the nearest to a junior high school pattern, with a ten–thirteen or ten–fourteen age-range, but these are virtually confined to Rochdale, Wigan, and the former county borough of Wallasey, now included in Wirral, together with a small number elsewhere that are attributable to incomplete reorganization.

A further category, type IV, should also be introduced as an umbrella classification covering all the distributions in which eight–twelve and nine–thirteen middle schools are both included, almost always as a result of the establishment of new local education authorities in 1974. Dorset is a clear instance of this. Needless to say, many type IV authorities also have five–twelve schools, five–eleven schools, five–seven and seven–eleven schools, indeed almost every conceivable combination. One or two nine–twelve schools appear in Buckinghamshire and Hereford and Worcestershire. Wirral even has five–twelve, eight–twelve, and ten–thirteen schools alongside the traditional eleven-plus transfer ones.

Indeed, no previous event in the history of English education has done more to increase its administrative diversity still further than the introduction of middle schools. A further complication is added by the fact that differences in transfer age exist in some LEAs between county and voluntary schools, as in Wigan. Yet another variant appears where selective schools have survived, as in Buckinghamshire. However, what appears at first sight to have been a bonanza of permissiveness owes almost as much to the vagaries of local government reorganization as it does to the lack of central direction. Any student embarking on a local study of middle school development is bound to need to examine the effects of this administrative restructuring, as well as the resources and intentions of the authorities who first embarked on reorganization of the education system itself.

It is noteworthy that none of the major political parties have taken a stance about middle schools, although the Liberals twice came near to espousing them.[11] It is not difficult to understand why there should be a lack of political alignment on this issue. Conservatives have sometimes viewed middle schools as a means of retaining a measure of selection; by deferring the age of separation, its unpopularity and divisiveness might be lessened. On the other hand, the consequences of restricting the length of full secondary school life have been regarded by some Conservatives as inimical to standards of attainment. Labour, meanwhile, has sometimes welcomed middle schools as new, democratic institutions, while sharing some of the Conservative worries about the consequences for secondary education and also sometimes suspecting that middle schools might turn out to be a subtle obstacle to the full implementation of the comprehensive principle. The Liberals have at times shared all the views of the other parties but at others have warmed to the notion of middle schools as a means of combating the excessive size of eleven–eighteen schools. However, in practice the introduction of middle schools in particular places has rarely been the result of simple political choice. Detailed studies of bargaining in committees and outside have suggested that negotiations within parties have often been as important as negotiations between parties.

For example,[12] a local education authority, with a Conservative (or Conservative/Independent) majority might be confronted with the need to find more secondary school places, when the child population was still rising, particularly in the green shires to which the population was moving and where such majorities were likely, and of course just at the time when the school leaving age was to be raised to sixteen. But, as was indicated earlier, under a Labour Government permission to provide additional places depended in practice on acceptance of the nonselective principle in secondary education. The chairman of the education committee, perhaps more aware than some of his colleagues of these pressures and constraints, held informal discussions with the senior administrators and came to the conclusion that a scheme including middle schools could be made acceptable both to his own party and to the teachers, on whose goodwill it eventually depended. It might also appeal to the handful of Liberals on the committee and could scarcely be opposed head-on by the Labour Party either, since they could not deny that it aimed to abolish selection. In Labour-controlled authorities a different set of developments took place, but here again a close cooperation between chairman and chief officer, and a positive enlisting of support from teachers, usually figured somewhere in the process.

It is difficult to escape the impression that this involvement of teachers was sometimes intended as an exercise in public relations rather than a genuine process of consultation. That does not imply that it was of no importance. It identified teachers with the impending changes in a constructive manner, as a part of what Lynch identifies as the legitimation of innovation (Lynch, 1975), and it also ensured that in one area, that of curriculum making, genuine initiatives did come from the professional teachers. Yet despite the obligatory rhetoric, based on developmental arguments, that teachers' working parties produced,[13] the reality of the decision to 'go middle' was not theirs.

Subsequent developments in middle schools

Since the majority of middle schools were established, several new factors have begun to operate. First, the dramatic fall in the birth rate has completely altered the circumstances which, in the 1960s, were impelling LEAs to earn school places by submitting middle school plans acceptable to the DES. Again, the consequent fall in demand for teachers and therefore also of opportunities for promotion has replaced the earlier idealism and optimism of middle school teachers with a growing mood of frustration (Ginsburg et al., 1977). Thirdly, the general loss of confidence in the progressive innovations made by the early middle schools, coupled with cuts in some forms of educational expenditure, have further curtailed the capacity of the schools to undertake the very innovations which have characterized their culture at its best. The climate captured in books published as late as 1977–78 is already changing.

Each of these new trends works to the disadvantage of middle schools. In addition, they have begun to pay the penalty both for their lack of overt and explicit political support and also for the way in which they have come to symbolize the Plowden era, with its optimism, its assumptions about economic expansion, and its adherence to a child-centred approach which disregarded political and many social realities. The dramatic alteration in circumstances leaves the historical perspective on this strange episode in the recent history of education looking even stranger still. For that reason alone, it is all the more essential to consider that historical perspective when making any appraisal of English middle schools.

Notes

1. A fuller account of the advent of middle schools is given in Blyth and Derricott (1977). In the final chapter, an interpretation of their minority status is suggested.
2. 8 and 9, Geo.V, c.39, sec.8(1). For a sketch of the parallel development of secondary education as a concept, see Higginson (1973), pp.165–177.
3. 7 and 8 Geo.VI, c.31, secs.7, 8.
4. 11 and 12 Geo.VI, c.40, sec.3.
5. e.g., Clarke (1940), who had suggested a scheme with a transfer age of nine.
6. *Statutes*, 1964, c.82, sec.1. The financial handicaps of the middle schools 'deemed primary' are related to staffing and to capitation allowances for equipment, etc.
7. *Statutes*, 1968, c.17, sec.2.
8. Data from *Statistics in Education*, supplemented for the most recent years by hitherto unpublished data kindly provided by the Department of Education and Science. 1969 is the first year for which these data are available.
9. It is noteworthy that in the General Election campaign of 1979, virtually no reference was made nationally to middle schools as such.
10. The statistics issued by the Department of Education and Science refer to these, in a phrase slightly reminiscent of cricket, as 'first and middle' schools. The Plowden term, at least as often encountered in current parlance, is 'combined school'.

11. In a report from its education committee in 1962, and again at the Party Assembly in 1973.
12. This is a representative, though fictitious example based on confidential data concerning a number of actual instances.
13. For a discussion of the role of working parties, see Blyth (1979).

CHAPTER TWO

THE ORIGINS OF MIDDLE SCHOOLS IN THE WEST RIDING OF YORKSHIRE

P. R. Sharp

Before considering the origins of middle schools in the West Riding, it is necessary to explain briefly the setting in which they emerged. The West Riding was a large county with an extremely diverse economic and social structure. Moreover, in the post-war era some parts of the county were staunchly Labour, some strongly Conservative, and others consistently marginal. In consequence, for most of this period there was a fairly even balance between the two major parties on the County Council and political control changed no fewer than five times in twenty years. To avoid continual changes in policy as political fortunes fluctuated, it was agreed in 1949 to allow each of the twenty-eight administrative divisions of the county to choose its own pattern of secondary school organization (Gosden and Sharp, 1978). This arrangement was upheld by both parties until circular 10/65 completely transformed the situation. During the late 1950s several Labour-controlled divisions asked the Education Committee to devise comprehensive schemes for their areas. Walter Hyman, the Chairman of the Committee, keenly supported these divisions as he had advocated this form of secondary organization for more than a decade. Alec Clegg, the Chief Education Officer, was also sympathetic, but he realized that important practical problems had to be faced in some of the districts concerned.

Clegg knew that the Ministry would not approve of the establishment of brand new eleven–eighteen comprehensive schools in some of these districts, since the existing secondary school buildings there were quite serviceable. Many of these buildings, moreover, were not suitable for conversion into eleven–eighteen schools as they were relatively small and on sites where physical constraints made it impossible to add large extensions. The

Chief Education Officer agreed that if there were two secondary schools within a quarter to half a mile of one another they could be combined in a comprehensive scheme as an upper and a lower school, but he came out strongly against: (i) the union of units which were several miles apart, (ii) the federation of buildings in bad physical condition, (iii) the combination of two or more schools under a mediocre head.[1] Clegg realized as early as 1958 that if comprehensivization was to take place at all in some districts, radically different approaches would have to be adopted. He told Hyman that he thought the Committee ought to be prepared to consider systems of junior and senior high schools on the understanding that both types of schools were nonselective.[2] At this juncture he expected children to enter the junior high schools at eleven and to move to the senior high schools at fourteen, but he maintained that the timing of the transfer would be determined by the accommodation available in specific cases. It was, of course, much easier to rearrange and adapt existing buildings with comprehensive schemes which divided children into different units according to age.

In Clegg's view, one of the crucial issues which had to be faced in schemes involving junior high schools was the provision of adequate teaching for abler children.[3] In 1958 Clegg maintained that it was essential for every child of appropriate ability in junior high schools to take Latin, a modern foreign language, science, and mathematics. He thought that it might be necessary to employ peripatetic teachers based in the senior high schools to cover some of this work, especially in relation to Latin and the modern language. He stressed that Latin was still an entrance requirement for Oxbridge and the arts faculties of most other universities, and he strongly believed that the curriculum available in junior high schools should not restrict the opportunities of their pupils later in life. More positively, the Chief Education Officer soon informed the Committee that he saw certain advantages in junior/senior high school schemes.[4] The problems posed by sheer size in eleven–eighteen comprehensive schools were avoided, and it was hoped that the best current primary school methods would be introduced into the junior high schools. It was also claimed that a one-year course in a senior high school could be a profitable experience for even the least able pupils as it could be used as a valuable springboard to launch young adults into employment.

The administrators in the West Riding were, of course, well aware of developments in comprehensive education which were taking place in other parts of the country. Clegg took considerable interest in Stewart Mason's scheme for comprehensivization on junior/senior high school lines in Leicestershire. As early as 1959, however, Clegg came out against two aspects of the plan.[5] He opposed the accelerated movement of groups of able pupils through the junior high schools, and was even more concerned that some of the children were scheduled to complete their education in the junior high schools. When children reached the age of fourteen, parents were asked whether they wanted their offspring to move to the senior high schools or stay in the juniors until the school leaving age was attained. Clegg felt that this was likely to lead to a situation in which the bright children of feckless parents ended their education at fifteen in the junior high schools, and the less able pupils of ambitious parents went on to the senior high schools. During the next few years deputations of West Riding teachers and inspectors visited Leicestershire schools, but Clegg's opposition to the scheme hardened considerably. By 1964 he was attacking the Leicestershire plan in the press, doubting whether it could be regarded as a genuine comprehensive solution. Clegg predicted that the junior highs would become 'finishing schools for working-class children' – or, put more crudely, 'dumps' for the Newsom types.[6]

The only part of the West Riding in which a straight Leicestershire plan made much headway was the excepted district of Keighley where the influence of the county authority was weak. Nevertheless, by 1962 the Committee had accepted modified Leicestershire schemes for Hemsworth, Castleford, and parts of the Don Valley. In all of these cases it was proposed to create junior high schools for children between the ages of eleven and fourteen, and then to transfer all the pupils to senior high schools, thus avoiding selection by parental choice. In 1962 the scheme for Castleford was submitted to the Ministry, which then stalled. Eventually it became clear that officials were unhappy about the short period which would be spent in the senior high schools by many pupils.[7] With the school leaving age set at fifteen in the 1960s, the majority of children affected by the proposals would be destined to spend one year or less in their senior high schools. For some time the staff at Wakefield had realized that a break at fourteen was a terrible handicap with a leaving age of fifteen,[8] but a break at thirteen seemed to imply the existence of two-year eleven–thirteen schools in which all the pupils were either newcomers or leavers. In the spring of 1963 Clegg came up with radical proposals which avoided both the break at fourteen and the two-year schools.

In May of that year Clegg wrote unofficially to L. R. Fletcher of the schools branch of the Ministry of Education tentatively setting out a scheme for five–nine primary schools, nine–thirteen middle schools, and thirteen–eighteen high schools.[9] He acknowledged that he was flying a kite, but he wanted to know whether there was any chance of getting such a proposal accepted if it was put forward officially. A few days later Clegg met Fletcher and his colleague Morrell in London, but at this juncture the officials were sceptical as nine–thirteen middle schools were not permissible under the Education Acts of 1944 and 1948.[10] Clegg also outlined his ideas to his committee and it was agreed that he should work further on the scheme.[11] Eventually, in October 1963, Clegg presented a lengthy memorandum on the subject to the Policy and Finance Sub-Committee.[12]

The three-tier proposals remained first and foremost a means of reorganization on comprehensive lines in areas where existing buildings were unsuitable for adaptations into eleven–eighteen patterns. For Clegg, a further big attraction of the scheme was that it would be used as a means to encourage the introduction of primary school methods to the eleven–thirteen age-range. It was argued that this would give the less able children the security of more contact with class teachers, and would keep the more able free from premature specialization and examination pressures. In addition, he maintained that this form of reorganization would remove pressure from primary school accommodation and thus enable the primary sector to reduce class sizes and reintroduce nursery provision. At the other end of the scale, he wanted the high schools to develop into adult institutions and he questioned the wisdom of educating young children of eleven in the same schools as citizens of eighteen. It was also pointed out that three-tier arrangements avoided the problems of size posed by eleven–eighteen comprehensive schools. Clegg quoted the precedent of the public schools admitting pupils at thirteen, and he also made much of the fact that he had consulted 'fifteen of the ablest and most experienced teachers in the training colleges, grammar, modern and primary schools of the Riding', and they had, with few exceptions, favoured a transfer age of thirteen to the high schools.

From October 1963 Clegg was adamant that the age of transfer should not be fourteen. He argued that it was essential for the high schools to have three years to prepare for 'O' level and CSE, and he predicted that if they were given less time, the pressure imposed by external examinations would be felt in the middle schools. He maintained that with a transfer age of thirteen, any specialization which was derived from examinations, apart from languages, would be avoided in middle schools, and he was particularly concerned to prevent those teachers who were thinking of 'O' level syllabuses from 'getting at' children of eleven and twelve.[13] It is perhaps important to mention, in the light of later justifications for middle schools, that very little emphasis was placed on physiological or psychological factors. No claims were made that middle school children would be qualitatively different from other children, and such rather spurious assertions which became somewhat common in the late 1960s and early 1970s were largely avoided in the original West Riding proposals.

In October 1963 Clegg realized that his proposals for middle schools had national significance, and he ensured that they were given wide publicity. Even before his committee approved the scheme, he sent copies of his memorandum with personal comments on its importance to the education correspondents of many national newspapers and journals, to the chief officers of leading LEAs, and to several influential officials at the Ministry of Education. In October the three-tier proposals were accepted in principle by the Education Committee, and this issue never generated party political strife at county level. From the outset Clegg acknowledged that he put forward his middle school scheme in defiance of the existing law so that the Minister might be pressed to consider the issues involved.[14] He argued that if the law remained unchanged, the West Riding would be forced either to reorganize on Leicestershire lines against its better judgement, or to use two-year eleven–thirteen schools which were almost universally condemned. In the winter of 1963–64 Clegg pleaded with civil servants at the Ministry to allow reorganization on nine–thirteen or ten–thirteen lines to go forward in Castleford,[15] but they could do little without fresh legislation. A few months later, when the Minister, Sir Edward Boyle, visited the Don Valley, he told C. T. Broughton, the Chairman of the Education Committee, that he hoped an act of Parliament would be passed to enable LEAs to try experiments of this kind. According to Boyle, it seemed to him and his colleague, Chris Chataway, that 'here was a pattern of secondary reorganisation which might well fit the needs, and the existing resources, of a number of LEAs' (Boyle, 1972). At this juncture there were still some very influential figures in the educational world who were sceptical about this proposal. William Alexander, for example, was against middle schools at this stage (Kogan, 1971), and in his early drafts of the Association of Education Committees' evidence for the Plowden Committee, he suggested that the standard age of transfer from primary to secondary school should be twelve.[16] At the Harrogate conference of the Association in June 1964 however, an amendment was put that the evidence for Plowden should be changed, and it was agreed that the Association should recommend that 'secondary education should range from between 10-plus and 13, at the discretion of the LEA, to 16 on a compulsory basis and optionally to 19'.[17] Alexander continued to express certain misgivings about this during July,[18] but in that month Boyle's 1964 Education Act became law. Henceforth LEAs were permitted, with the specific permission of the DES, to vary the age of transfer from primary to secondary school on an experimental basis.

At the local level, meanwhile, the divisions which had agreed to comprehensive schemes involving eleven–fourteen junior high schools and fourteen–eighteen senior high schools had to be persuaded to switch to three-tier middle school arrangements. Hemsworth and the Don Valley eventually agreed to this change, although the divisional executive in Hemsworth was clearly frustrated by the long delay involved. Castleford, however, proved much more intractable. Clegg explained the nine–thirteen scheme to the divisional executive on the 4th May, 1964, but in July it resolved to retain the original proposals.[19] The Ministry had by this time indicated that it preferred a break at thirteen rather than fourteen in Castleford, and Clegg predicted that if the scheme was resubmitted to the DES the West Riding would be asked whether it now repudiated the arguments which it had advanced in favour of nine–thirteen schemes.[20] A further attempt to change the mind of the division failed because, according to the divisional officer, there was a strong anti-Broughton feeling within the Castleford Labour group and the nine–thirteen scheme was known to have been originated by Clegg with Broughton's strong support. At this point Clegg gave up and said that he would make no further observations on the matter until the West Riding was asked by the DES to declare its intentions for the future organization of the area.[21]

Some of those who have written about middle schools seem to imply that Clegg and the West Riding should be associated exclusively with the nine–thirteen variety of middle schools, but this is misleading. It is certainly correct that the West Riding had a preference for nine–thirteen schemes which is hardly surprising since it pioneered them, but Clegg and his committee were quite prepared to countenance other forms of middle schools as long as they did not involve transfer at fourteen. As early as May 1963, when Clegg first approached the Ministry, he mentioned the possibility of eight–twelve middle schools if they seemed more acceptable than nine–thirteen ones.[22] A few months later he proposed ten–thirteen middle schools as a possible solution to reorganization in Castleford.[23] Later, in the early months of 1965, Clegg told the Minister and the Under-Secretary of State at the DES that he did not mind very much about the actual age of transfer as long as children had at least a three-year run to 'O' levels and CSE in the high schools.[24]

When circular 10/65 was issued, it mentioned that eleven should be the normal age of transfer and stressed that the Secretary of State did not intend to give approval to more than a very small number of middle school proposals in the near future. At this juncture, Tony Crosland, the Secretary of State, explained to the local authority associations that he did not wish to encourage more than a limited number of experiments until definite decisions on the age of transfer had been reached.[25] This matter was, of course, within the terms of reference of the Plowden Committee then sitting, but both this committee and successive secretaries of state resisted pressure from LEAs for an early interim report on the age of transfer.[26] Clegg was rather concerned about the lack of flexibility implied in circular 10/65. In October 1965 he wrote an article in the journal *Education* in which he argued that if the country insisted on having one age of transfer, it would completely thwart the aims of circular 10/65. He maintained that with a rigid age of transfer it would prove impossible to develop comprehensive schools within a limited period of time.[27] He could not see how England could produce a uniform pattern of comprehensivization. These points were developed further at a meeting with Tony Crosland and several leading chief education officers in February 1966.[28] Clegg later recalled that he told Crosland that as far as the West Riding was concerned, the best scheme would be produced for each area, and regardless of whether it was nine–thirteen or eight–twelve it would be sent to the Minister. If the Minister then decided that he required something which was educationally less sound and probably more costly, that was up to him.[29] To reinforce this point, a few days later he wrote to Crosland's private secretary thus: 'I don't think there will be any shortage of cases where flexibility is almost irresistible. Although in the West Riding 11 plus may well be the transfer date for half our divisions, there will be some where I believe that we shall have no difficulty in showing that a transfer at, say, 12 will be far sounder educationally and far less costly. If we can show this beyond reasonable doubt, the Secretary is surely going to have the greatest difficulty in saying to us

"You must do a worse job at greater cost".[30] Crosland was eventually persuaded by this line of argument, for soon after the 1966 election he announced in the Commons that 'our attitude has shifted in the light of experience since the day we used the language in the circular. We would now be more willing than we were to consider, possibly 9–13 schemes. We would still ask to be shown that these schemes would produce a clear advantage in terms of teachers and buildings, but supposing they could, we should be more inclined than it appeared in the circular to approve such schemes. At any rate, I want to insist on the point that there will not be any single uniform pattern of comprehensive education. There will be variety which will be a thoroughly healthy thing for the whole country.'[31] About a month later circular 13/66 was issued and this claimed that there were now urgent, practical reasons for more flexibility.[32] Henceforth, a change in the age of transfer was to be regarded as a local option, as long as the local authority could show that the change would result in clear, practical advantages in the context of reorganization on comprehensive lines or the raising of the school leaving age or both.

The response of the West Riding to circular 10/65 was that the Committee asked the divisions to prepare reorganization schemes in consultation with the staff at Wakefield. By the summer of 1966 the Authority was ready to submit the bulk of its reorganization plans to the DES, and in its preamble to the submission explained that the individual schemes emanated from the divisions and that only in a few rare instances had the local proposals been modified.[33] It was also mentioned that the West Riding had accepted eleven–eighteen comprehensive schools, eleven–sixteen schools working in conjunction with eleven–eighteen schools, and three different kinds of middle school schemes: five–eight, eight–twelve, twelve–eighteen; five–nine, nine–thirteen, thirteen–eighteen; and five–ten, ten–thirteen, thirteen–eighteen. Clegg and his committee had certainly used the flexibility for which they had argued to the full. Statutory approval for the Hemsworth scheme was given in November 1966, but it was not until September 1968 that the first West Riding middle schools opened their doors.

One of the main conclusions which can be drawn from this account is that negative constraints contributed as much as positive choices to the emergence of middle schools in the West Riding. First and foremost they developed because existing buildings made it impossible to have eleven–eighteen comprehensive schools in some districts. Secondly, the Chief

Education Officer and his committee found the element of selection by parental choice in the Leicestershire plan unpalatable. Thirdly, initially the Ministry was sceptical of all pupils transferring to new schools at fourteen when so many would leave at fifteen, and then Clegg came out strongly against fourteen as he believed that transferring at this age would bring specialization and examination pressures into the schools catering for the younger children. With these three constraints, one of the few remaining viable and nonselective possibilities was some form of middle school arrangement. Clegg was probably convinced of this by 1963, and Crosland was eventually persuaded to take a similar viewpoint. The pioneering of middle school schemes was probably the West Riding's greatest single contribution to national educational developments in the post-war period. Without this innovation, the unsuitability of existing buildings coupled with the weakening economic position of the nation would almost certainly have provided an insuperable barrier to the development of comprehensive education in many parts of the country in the late 1960s and 1970s (Gosden and Sharp, 1978).

Notes

1. West Riding Education Committee (WREC), B.77.Co., Clegg to Hyman, 18th August, 1958.
2. Ibid.
3. WREC, M.77.Co., Clegg to Wright, 20th August, 1958.
4. WREC, Policy and Finance Sub-Committee, Memorandum, 9th June, 1959.
5. Ibid.
6. WREC, S.G. 605 Co., Clegg to Dempster, 9th November, 1964. The reference to 'Newsom types' is to those 'less able' children with whom the Newsom Report (Central Advisory Council for Education, 1963) was concerned.
7. WREC, S.G. 605 Co., Clegg to Fletcher, 15th May, 1963.
8. WREC, B.81, Deputy Education Officer to Clegg, 22nd September, 1958.
9. WREC, S.G. 605 Co., Clegg to Fletcher, 3rd May, 1963.
10. WREC, S.G. 605 Co., Clegg to Fletcher, 15th May, 1963.
11. WREC, Policy and Finance Sub-Committee Minutes, 7th May, 1963.
12. WREC, Policy and Finance Sub-Committee, Memorandum, 8th October, 1963.
13. Ibid.
14. Ibid.
15. WREC, Clegg to Ministry of Education, 31st October, 26th November, 16th December, and 30th December, 1963.
16. Association of Education Committees (AEC), Files 1057 and 1058. William Alexander was Secretary of the Association.

17. Ibid. (1058).
18. *Education*, 3rd and 31st July, 1964.
19. WREC, 511, Johnson to Clegg, 20th July, 1964.
20. WREC, Policy and Finance Sub-Committee, Memorandum, 8th September, 1964.
21. WREC, S.G. 605, Clegg to Nicholson, 16th February, 1965.
22. WREC, S.G. 605 Co., Clegg to Fletcher, 15th May, 1963.
23. WREC, S.G. 605 Co., Clegg to Fletcher, 30th December, 1963.
24. WREC, S.G. 605 Co., Clegg to Leadbetter, 12th January 1965, and WREC, notes for meeting with R. Prentice, 11th February, 1965.
25. AEC, File 1112, meeting with A. Crosland and R. Prentice, 14th May, 1965.
26. AEC, File 1112.
27. *Education*, 22nd October, 1965.
28. WREC, S.G. 605 Co., Clegg to Dempster, 3rd May, 1966.
29. Ibid.
30. WREC, S.G. 605 Co., Clegg to Litton, 22nd February, 1966.
31. Hansard, House of Commons, 1966–67, vol. 727, cols. 494–95.
32. DES, Circular 13/66.
33. WREC, Policy and Finance Sub-Committee, Memorandum, 12th July, 1966.

CHAPTER THREE

THE EMERGENCE OF NINE–THIRTEEN MIDDLE SCHOOLS IN WORCESTERSHIRE

C. A. A. Marsh

A number of writers have enquired into the emergence of middle schools in this country. Amongst them have been Edwards (1972), Marsh (1973), Bryan and Hardcastle (1977), Blyth and Derricott (1977), and Burrows (1978). Although these writers do not reach total agreement as to the paramount reason for the emergence of middle schools, they do agree that they appeared in response to local education authority initiative and pressure. Baroness Summerskill, in welcoming the introduction of the 1964 Education Act, said it was the direct result of the pressure applied by progressive local education authorities. The latter wanted to experiment in new forms of education and they saw the introduction of middle schools as an aid to comprehensive reorganization by making possible a full utilization of existing buildings. Sir Edward Boyle (1971) has stated that because of local authority pressure it became clear to those in the Ministry in 1963 that changes would have to be made in the law to allow for the development of middle schools.

This chapter attempts to show how one local authority played a significant part in building up the pressure which resulted in the passing of the 1964 Education Act. The information was obtained from the minutes of the Worcestershire Education Committee and its Planning and Development Sub-Committee. The minutes of the Droitwich District Education Committee were also examined and interviews were held with Mr. R. E. W. Saunders, Deputy Education Officer of Worcestershire and with headteachers, teachers, and officers of the Authority.

Worcestershire was, and is, a county with a number of small- and medium-sized towns, but with a substantial rural area. In the fifties, prior to the reorganization of local government, the main industrial area was in the northeast, with light industrial development taking place in Redditch, Bromsgrove, and Droitwich.

The Worcestershire Local Education Authority had accepted the principal recommendations of the 1926 Hadow Report, and in June 1929 the Director of Education produced a scheme to implement them. As in other areas steps had been taken within the county as early as 1911 to provide separate schools for senior pupils.

The first schools, designed specifically for senior pupils, were opened at Rubery and Pershore in 1931, but because of financial restraints it was not until 1936 that the next school for senior pupils was opened at Stourport. Six further senior schools were opened in 1939.

Immediately after the Second World War the stage of reorganization that had been reached varied widely across the county. Owing to government restrictions, finance was not available to build schools purely to facilitate reorganization and it was therefore only in areas with a rising school population (largely the urban areas) that reorganization could take place. As more and more urban areas were reorganized, the disparity in the educational opportunity being offered between the urban and rural areas increased.

By 1957, 88.5% of the children of secondary school age were in separate secondary schools.[1] To complete the reorganization, provision still had to be made for the children living in the Martley area.[2] The latter lies in the west of the county and is part of the sparsely populated rural area which extends over the northwest of the county with small concentrations of population at Tenbury and Bewdley. These two districts already had a two-form entry secondary school and proposals were included in the county development plan for primary and secondary schools to build a similar school at Martley. The projected figures revealed that no greater provision was required and the County Education Officer pointed out that they would be creating another 'thin' school.[3]

The problem the Local Authority had to face was how could it provide extended courses and adequate facilities in this rural area to give children an educational opportunity comparable to that being offered in the larger urban area schools. The officers of the Authority believed that in order to be able to establish a fifth-year and specialized courses, secondary schools had to be at least a four-form entry size.[4] Both the Tenbury and Martley schools were situated too far from other secondary schools and colleges of further education for it to be practicable to provide specialist courses other than in the schools themselves.

The County Education Officer believed there were three possible solutions to the problem.[5] These were:

1 A reorganization of the whole area on a three-tier basis using nine–thirteen intermediate schools. The existing and planned secondary schools would become intermediate schools with a new seven-form entry high school built at Great Witley.

2 The building of a single seven-form entry school at Great Witley for the children in the eleven–sixteen age-group and the utilization of existing secondary schools as primary schools.

3 The building of a five-form entry school for children of the eleven–sixteen age-group at Martley. The Tenbury secondary school would be used as a primary school and the Bewdley secondary modern school would remain as it was.

In his evaluation of the three plans, the County Education Officer pointed out that the first plan made full use of the existing buildings and would make possible the provision of a wide variety of courses extending to the provision of a county college. He also expressed the view that it would be an interesting experiment and would have the added advantage of giving better facilities to the older primary school children.

Whilst they agreed with the County Education Officer that the three-tier plan offered many advantages and solved the problems presented by this particular area, the Planning and Development Sub-Committee recognized that it contravened the law and might well be ruled out by the Ministry of Education.[6] This, in fact, proved to be the case as the County Education Officer received a communication from the Ministry rejecting the plan. At their June meeting in 1959, the Sub-Committee decided to lodge the plan with the Ministry.[7]

Plans for three-tier reorganization with nine–thirteen intermediate schools were shelved but they were certainly not forgotten. Evidence of the continuing interest amongst the officers of the Authority was provided by Mr. R. L. Portman. In 1961 he was headmaster of Chawson County Primary School, Droitwich, and in that year he was asked by the Deputy Education Officer for his views and ideas on a school for nine–thirteen-year-old children.[8]

In January 1963 the County Education Officer presented his thoughts and ideas for future developments in the rural areas to the Planning and

Development Sub-Committee.[9] He pointed out that they had a relatively stable county population and that the existing national building policy ruled out any substantial development involving the construction of new schools. He added that in areas such as Droitwich, which had been scheduled for expansion, a refashioning of the whole secondary school system might be required. The academic requirements, such as the provision of a wide range of subjects and the need to create viable groups, favoured the provision of large schools. However, the County Education Officer felt that after a certain point the sheer size would destroy the community spirit in a school and he suggested that a maximum figure for a school should be 1600 pupils. Various forms of viable school organization for varying concentrations of population were exemplified, and the point was made that in some rural areas schools were below the minimum viable size, and were likely to remain so under the current organization. Such areas required special consideration and perhaps a radical solution.

In the early sixties several of the Worcestershire rural primary schools consisted of three classes or less, whilst many of the secondary schools had only a two-form entry.[10] In both it was felt that it was the older children who were suffering. In the primary schools the lack of numbers restricted the older child's opportunities in games, physical education, and craft, and they did not have the challenge of working in groups of children of equal ability. In the secondary schools the lack of numbers restricted the formation of groups based on ability or options, whilst the variety of work was seriously limited by the accommodation and staff. To overcome these problems, larger groupings of children were required but this would necessitate more travelling which in turn would raise serious social problems.

The solution suggested by the County Education Officer was the introduction of a three-tier system utilizing nine–thirteen intermediate schools. The existing primary schools would cater for the first stage, the smaller secondary modern schools for the intermediate stage, and the larger secondary schools, or new schools, would become the upper or high schools.

The Sub-Committee agreed with the County Education Officer[11] that his plan would provide a sound educational organization offering the advantages of making full use of existing plant, increasing educational opportunities for older children in the junior stage, extending the period of general education, improving the range of educational choices for children in rural areas, and making little demand for additional staffing. Despite the fact that the plan contravened the 1944 Education Act, the County Education Officer stated that in his opinion it was well worth pursuing in discussion with the Ministry.[12]

At that time (1963), a decision had been made to develop the town of Droitwich, increasing its population from eight thousand to thirty thousand over a period of fifteen years. The Education Committee had to make plans to cope with this expansion. To assist the Planning and Development Sub-Committee in their task, the County Education Officer stated that they should bear in mind the educational needs of the rural periphery, that in new towns the number of children is high in relation to the total population, and that they should keep in mind the national discussion and debates that were taking place on the issue of the age of transfer.[13] He said that he was confident that the law relating to the age of transfer would be changed before 1981, and that they should draw up a plan which was sufficiently flexible to take advantage of any changes in the law that might occur.

In drawing up their plan, the Sub-Committee were influenced by certain factors. Firstly, it had been decided that all the new buildings required for the provision of secondary education in the expanded town would have to be in the same area. This gave the opportunity for some form of unified organization or at least for the establishment of a related group of schools. The Sub-Committee considered such possibilities as a single comprehensive school, and separate comprehensives for boys and girls.[14] A second factor that had to be borne in mind was that the projected number of children above the age of eleven that had to be catered for was 2600. This was a thousand in excess of what the County Education Officer and the Education Committee felt was a maximum acceptable figure for a single school. If the group were divided vertically according to sex, this would give two eight-form entry schools, but it was felt that this would not provide sufficient numbers to support academic elements of the required quantity. To obtain viable groups it was felt that there would be a need to mix the sexes probably after the age of thirteen and certainly at the sixth-form level. It was pointed out that if the Local Education Authority were to be allowed to introduce nine–thirteen intermediate schools catering for the eleven- and twelve-year-olds, then the number on roll of the upper school would be reduced by approximately 1000 giving a projected and acceptable number on roll of 1600 pupils in the high school.

A third factor that influenced the planning was the policy of the Authority when building large schools to make provision for a separate lower school building for the eleven–thirteen-year-olds. It was felt that this practice should be continued with the proposed Droitwich school in order to break down the large organization into workable units which would also give the necessary flexibility to make possible a change to a three-tier structure if a change in the law should so permit.

The plan that was suggested was for a single organization with separate heads for the various departments and with communal facilities.

Fig. 3.1

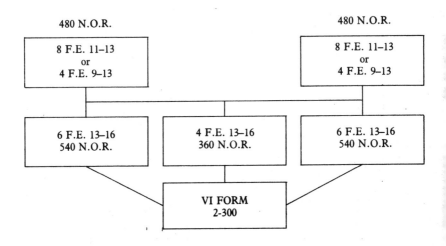

Abbreviations   N.O.R. = Numbers on Roll
F.E.   = Form Entry

(It should be noted that if this plan had been implemented and then changed at a later date to a three-tier structure, two more schools for the nine–thirteen-year-olds would have been required.)

Before this plan was put to the Education Committee, in December 1963 the Planning and Development Sub-Committee requested the County Education Officer to make further representations to the Ministry concerning the possibility of utilizing a three-tier structure of organization containing nine–thirteen intermediate schools.[15] When the plan was brought before the Education Committee in January 1964,[16] it was pointed out that the county had accepted the comprehensive principle to avoid the rigid differentiation of schools and their firm belief that sufficient pressure was building up to force a change in the law relating to the age of transfer.

The 1964 Education Act was passed on 31st July, 1964 with circular 12/64 being published on 27th August. The new act made it possible for local education authorities to submit schemes for reorganization in their areas with transfer ages other than that stipulated in the 1944 Act. Speaking to the Planning and Development Sub-Committee in December 1964,[17] the County Education Officer pointed out that the possibility now existed for adopting their original three-tier plan. The Sub-Committee asked the County Education Officer to discuss their original three-tier plan with the officers of the Department of Education and Science as directed in paragraph 4 of circular 12/64 to see if it would be approved.[18] These discussions took place but they did not go well for the Authority. The DES proved to be hesitant, and in May 1965 the County Education Officer reported that he did not believe that the Sub-Committee would get even an informal indication from the DES within the near future.[19] All that he had been able to obtain was an acknowledgement that Droitwich seemed to be the type of area for which three-tier organization might be possible.

Despite this lack of encouragement it was decided that planning should continue. At their meeting in October 1965, the Planning and Development Sub-Committee discussed circular 10/65.[20] They criticized its mandatory nature and the short time limits it imposed, but they agreed to begin consultations prior to a revision of the county development plan. They foresaw that reorganization would be complicated because of the varying character of the county, the uneven distribution and lack of any large concentrations of population, and the uncertainty that existed about the age of transfer.[21] During their discussion in March 1966,[22] the Chairman stated that he felt that a three-tier system appeared to be the best plan when considered on educational grounds, but he expressed the view that such a plan would not be suitable for all areas of the county. The County Education Officer agreed,[23] and stressed the need to make full use of existing facilities and to keep costs down to a minimum. After much discussion the Sub-Committee agreed to assume that secondary education would begin at thirteen.

On the 20th April, 1966, the County Education Officer informed the Planning and Development Sub-Committee that the reorganization plan for Droitwich, which incorporated nine–thirteen middle schools, had been approved by the Secretary of State for Education.[24] The Chairman, Sir Hugh Chance, suggested that the plan should be published and that it should be emphasized that this was the plan that they had devised long before the passing of the 1964 Education Act or the appearance of circular 10/65.

Following consultations with the various district education committees, the County Education Officer reported in November 1966 that there had been general agreement that the proposed three-tier system was the most suitable for most areas of the county.[25] A draft reorganization plan was drawn up and this was approved by the Education Committee and then published and circulated to all interested parties for discussion and constructive criticism.[26] It was accepted by Worcestershire County Council on 8th May, 1967.[27] In September 1969, the first Worcestershire middle schools were opened.

Thus, a reorganization plan incorporating nine–thirteen middle schools, which had originated about a decade earlier as a possible solution to the problems of education in a rural area, became the basis for the reorganization of education in almost the whole county of Worcestershire.

Notes

1. Worcestershire Education Committee, Minutes of the Planning and Development Sub-Committee, 14th October, 1957.
2. Worcestershire Education Committee, Minutes of the Planning and Development Sub-Committee, 28th February, 1955.
3. Worcestershire Education Committee, Minutes of the Planning and Development Sub-Committee, 21st January, 1959. Memorandum submitted by the Chief Education Officer.
4. Worcestershire Education Committee, Minutes of the Planning and Development Sub-Committee, 22nd June, 1959. Report of the Chief Education Officer.
5. Ibid.
6. Worcestershire Education Committee, Minutes of the Planning and Development Sub-Committee, 22nd June, 1959.
7. Ibid.
8. Interview.
9. Worcestershire Education Committee, Minutes of the Planning and Development Sub-Committee, 7th January, 1963.
10. Worcestershire Education Committee, Minutes of the Planning and Development Sub-Committee, 7th January, 1963. Memorandum from the Chief Education Officer on the organization of secondary education.
11. Ibid.
12. Worcestershire Education Committee, Minutes of the Planning and Develop-

ment Sub-Committee, 7th January, 1963. Memorandum from the Chief Education Officer on the organization of secondary education.

13. Worcestershire Education Committee, Minutes of the Planning and Development Sub-Committee, 4th November, 1963.

14. Ibid.

15. Worcestershire Education Committee, Minutes of the Planning and Development Sub-Committee, 2nd December, 1963.

16. Minutes of the Worcestershire Education Committee, 6th January, 1964.

17. Worcestershire Education Committee, Minutes of the Planning and Development Sub-Committee, 9th December, 1964.

18. Ibid.

19. Worcestershire Education Committee, Minutes of the Planning and Development Sub-Committee, 17th May, 1965.

20. Worcestershire Education Committee, Minutes of the Planning and Development Sub-Committee, 18th October, 1965.

21. Worcestershire Education Committee, Minutes of the Planning and Development Sub-Committee, 10th December, 1965.

22. Worcestershire Education Committee, Minutes of the Planning and Development Sub-Committee, 21st March, 1966.

23. Ibid.

24. Worcestershire Education Committee, Minutes of the Planning and Development Sub-Committee, 20th April, 1966.

25. Worcestershire Education Committee, Minutes of the Planning and Development Sub-Committee, 7th November, 1966.

26. Minutes of the Worcestershire Education Committee, 9th January, 1967.

27. Minutes of the Worcestershire County Council, 8th May, 1967.

CHAPTER FOUR

THE LOCAL GOVERNMENT OF MIDDLE SCHOOLS: GOVERNING BODIES AND THE PROBLEMS OF MIDDLE SCHOOL IDENTITY

D. Warwick

Introduction

Explanations for the introduction of middle schools in the late 1960s and 1970s in England and Wales have suggested on the whole that we should stress economic and demographic rather than educational reasons. In many Western capitalist states after the Second World War, periods of economic expansion and population growth were accompanied by a process of comprehensive reorganization of schooling. This relatively popular and apparently progressive mode of educational reform required, however, not only the ending of selective tests for pupils, but also the adaptation of many existing buildings. Although new housing schemes and suburban developments entailed some new school buildings, most schemes of reorganization required the new wine to be poured into old bottles. Middle schools in a three-tier form of full-time nonselective provision often offered the cheapest and surest way of using existing schools and ending eleven-plus selection in a number of localities in England and Wales.

The often forced and rapid innovation of middle schools has created a number of consequences which this book is attempting in part to outline. A number of different solutions to organizational and curricular problems have been tried but, despite the emergence of an ideology which attempts to provide a basis for overcoming contradictions and conflicts in middle schools, the identity and legitimacy of middle schools remain in doubt (Hargreaves, in this volume). Threats to the continued existence of middle schools, and suggestions of a return to the more traditional break at eleven plus have been made as the numbers of children on roll decline, and educational expenditure is axed in attempts to deal with an economic crisis (NUT, 1979).

Economic and demographic reasons are therefore very significant in accounting for the rise and possible fall of middle schools. It is important, however, not to overlook the way that economic and demographic trends are variously interpreted by political parties, professional groups, parents, and community associations. In particular, as several chapters of this book stress, the way that decisions have been taken in different localities has depended very much on the varying balance of power between these groups, and the way that each group has defined its own situation. In that case, we should recognize that there need be no inevitability about middle schools becoming victims of a social system out of control.

It is vital therefore to analyse the processes which take place in what Cockburn (1977) has called the 'local state', as well as at a national level. Other chapters deal with this analysis, but what this one seeks to do is to look at these local processes from the point of view of one statutory agency at the local level. In many ways this agency remains a shadowy entity. It exists in law, but teachers, parents, and other community groups who have interests in schools are sometimes only slightly aware of its presence and function. The agency in question is the school governing or managing body. Do such bodies have any power to influence the outcome of the problems of identity and continuity which beset middle schools?

The functions of governing bodies

The recent Taylor Report seemed convinced that by more effective representation of interest groups on governing bodies, thus ensuring wider participation, educational concerns could be more effectively served. Despite, or even because of, increasing tendencies to professional and bureaucratic control in local authorities, under the presently growing influence of corporate management, we should be aware, the report claims, 'of the value of the governing body as a distinctive means of ensuring proper consideration for the education interest in local government' (DES and Welsh Office, 1977, p.9).

If the education or school interest can be enhanced by governing bodies as a consequence both of corporate management and wider participation, then we should consider this in relation to middle schools. They have emerged as institutions in fact, in the very same period in which moves towards corporate management and demands for wider democratic participation have impinged on local government. The political, professional, parental, and local community interests can, at least on paper, come together much more clearly in the school governing body, than in the education committee and district or county council. This is especially true in the reorganized and enlarged authorities following the 1972 Local Government Act.

Under the 1944 Education Act, sections 17–21, local authorities are required to constitute a body of governors for secondary schools and a body of managers for primary schools. In fact, as the Taylor Report suggests, there has been an ever-decreasing distinction between the function of government and management. 'Moreover, the introduction of middle schools, spanning part of the primary and part of the secondary age range has tended to blur the traditional distinction.' (DES and Welsh Office, 1977, p.18.) In this chapter it will be convenient and not disabling to forget the distinction, and refer to them all as governing bodies.

The retention of governing bodies in the 1944 Act was more a consequence of the necessary acknowledgement of the interests of churches and voluntary educational trusts in school provision, than of a desire to give some autonomy to individual schools under a relatively independent body of governors. The latter motive was not entirely unimportant, but sprang more from desires to see a local cultural elite involved in schools than from ideas about grass-roots democracy. Nevertheless this latent possibility has remained. Some local authorities, like Sheffield, even realized the possibility in restructuring their school governing bodies to take account of demands for wider participation in the early 1970s.

The powers of governing bodies may seem to be quite considerable. Ministry of Education recommendations issued after the 1944 Act listed their functions as covering (i) financial estimates and expenditure, (ii) maintenance and use of premises, (iii) appointment and dismissal of head-teachers, assistant teachers, and ancillary staff, (iv) oversight of school organization and curriculum, (v) the fixing of occasional holidays, and (vi) admission and removal of pupils. Local authorities were, however, allowed the right to determine the educational character of controlled schools, and to group schools for governing body purposes. Thus in many cases the links between a school and a governing body could be very tenuous, even nonexistent, depending on local authority directives. Furthermore, head-teachers were empowered to control the internal organization of the school in consultation with the governing body, but with the recent and growing professionalization of teaching, governing bodies, even where they had more than a shadowy existence, often left the agenda of consultation to the headteacher.

M.S.   F

In addition, there has been an increasing professionalization of the administration of education and local advisory services. Without a determined attempt by one or other of the parties interested in wider participation, such as parents or community groups, governing bodies' powers could be overlooked, or, less seldom, be fossilized into a stagnant ritual. Tendencies towards ritualization are enhanced by the fact that political parties in local authorities use governing body membership nominations as a local honours system for ageing party loyalists, or for 'warming up' inexperienced and aspiring young politicians and 'cooling out' those who are old and no longer usable.

The local honours system was probably a more crucial aspect of their functions than any other, especially in the period before local government reorganization and corporate management. The little research that has been carried out has suggested that governing bodies exert little real influence on educational matters (Howell, 1976; Mack, 1978). The amount of research data remains very sparse in fact, and it is necessary to remain a little sceptical of any conclusions already reached. By tracing chronologically the significant activities of the governing bodies of some middle schools between 1970 and 1978 as a case-study, it is hoped to add further to the research and to stimulate others to add their accounts, so that we may approach with greater validity answers to the questions of whether Taylor's suggestions are likely to be proved correct, and whether middle schools can usefully offer a more significant role to their governors.

Case-study

The context

It is worth stating that the governing bodies in this case-study were concerned with schools in a middle-class area north of an industrial conurbation, with which it was linked as a rapidly expanding suburban area. Throughout the period it always returned a predominance of Conservative representatives to central and local government. Before 1974 the County Council of which it was part was controlled alternately by Labour and Conservative majorities, but from 1967 to 1974 the controlling party was Conservative, and this control was continued into 1979 in the new Metropolitan District Council which replaced the County Council as the local education authority in 1974. This relative political stability is likely to stimulate further the tendencies which support more effective control by the corporate managers, since the Metropolitan District policy has always explicitly supported the idea of corporate management.

There was a period, from 1958 to 1967, when the County Council had been Labour-controlled, and during that time in several parts of the county decisions were taken to reorganize education on three-tier comprehensive lines. In the area which concerns us, a relatively autonomous local education sub-committee, part of a northern educational division of the county, voted to accept comprehensive reform on a three-tier plan, which was to be implemented with effect from September 1970. A post-war secondary modern school was to become, with additional buildings, a middle school, and an older, voluntary grammar school was to be enlarged to become the upper school, while retaining the name of grammar school. Two further new middle schools were to be built to meet the expected needs as the population expanded, and to provide enough places for all the nine–thirteen age-range pupils in the area. The initial phase necessitated that the middle school should take only the ten–thirteen age-range, in a planned capacity of 480 school places. In the event the provision of the other middle schools was delayed by central government expenditure limitations, and land purchase and building problems. Thus the original school became overcrowded, with the numbers on roll quickly rising to over 600 when it opened. These conditions placed important constraints on future governors' meetings.

At the time of school reorganization, the Divisional Education Authority took the opportunity to replace the former district sub-committee with a governing body for the middle school and its feeder primary schools, constituted in accordance with the 1944 Act and later recommendations.[1] This body first met in September 1970, with the implementation of the three-tier plan. It continued to meet monthly with occasional exceptions until April 1974, when the new Metropolitan District Council instituted a new system, in which schools were governed and managed by age-group. By now there were middle schools in our area and these were given a separate governing body which met once per term. Four of the members of the former body became members of the new body, including the man who had been chairman from 1970. He took the chair again. As a local professional, his background was somewhat typical of the Conservative members of the governing bodies. He was a solicitor, born in the area, of professional parents involved in architecture and the law. His mother had also been a member of earlier education committees. He had no children and had not attended local schools, yet assumed the right to govern them. He never pressed openly political views about education on the governors, and indeed attempted to reduce discussion of general problems of power and control in education if ever they arose. He visited the schools regularly, however, and was thought by headteachers to be generally helpful and willing to support them when consulted. He never at any time made lengthy or principled statements about the organization and content of educational provision, which he preferred to leave to the teachers and educational advisers. There was thus never at any time at his request a discussion of the aims and principles of middle schooling. Perhaps the one major innovation brought about under his chairmanship was to have those meetings of the former governing body which were convened outside the Town Hall held in the schools. He won his case for this against much voluble opposition within the Conservative ranks, no doubt because of the duties laid down in the articles of government that the body should 'from time to time inspect and keep the Local Education Authority informed as to the condition and state of repair of the school premises'.

The first four years

During the period 1970–78, the governing bodies for these middle schools met forty-six times.

Table 4.1

	Period of meetings	(a) Total member- ship	No. of meetings	(b) Average attend- ance	(b) as % of (a)
County Council Governing Body for Middle and Primary Schools	1970– 1974	19	33	12.8	67%
Metropolitan District Governing Body for Middle Schools	1974– 1978	16	13	9.1	57%

It is clear from Table 4.1 that until 1974 meetings were far more frequent and better attended. The attendance of the Divisional Education Officer or his deputy, sometimes accompanied by other county officials such as architects and building inspectors, and the frequent discussions of financial estimates and priorities for action, maintenance and equipment of school buildings, continued to give the older members the semblance of still having a fair degree of autonomy. Headteachers who asked for representation on the governing body were refused it, on the grounds that they would be consulted when necessary. The problems of reorganization, especially the difficulties of the new middle school, also loomed large, and the chairman chose to hold the first meeting of the body outside the Town Hall on its premises. The new headmaster was asked to make a report. This left the governors in no uncertainty about the difficulties of the first few weeks, with completed additional buildings, a seriously inadequate kitchen, and undelivered furniture and materials. The staff were praised for their 'commendable resourcefulness'. The headteacher also promised to set up a parent-teachers association. The report concluded: 'The middle school is taking shape and is developing a character of its own. We look forward to the future and to the part we shall play in our tier of the comprehensive opportunities available for all local children.'

The governing body continued to hear about the problems and pressed the local authority for solutions, which in due course it attempted to deliver. Some problems could not be resolved without pain, yet the governing body did not discuss, but merely noted in its minutes, the fact that the deputy headmistress, the senior mathematics teacher, and a groundsman left speedily at the end of the first year. Much of the discussion tended to concern the material rather than the cultural provision of the school. Governors tended to be hot on kitchens, waste disposal, roof repairs, and parking space, but not on new curricula, new courses for middle school teachers, and new forms of classroom organization. The appointment and resignations of staff were dealt with for the governing body either by the chairman, or a small number of governors whom he asked to be present. Decisions about staffing were merely reported to the full governing body. In general, headteachers and local authority officers were the most influential persons and their decisions were usually fully supported. The headmaster in an aside to the author at one of the governing body meetings which discussed inadequate classroom accommodation at the middle school, suggested that he did not think it was worthwhile wasting so much time in general meetings. Nevertheless meetings continued, even though most crucial decisions were probably made out of governors' meetings.

The problems of that middle school were, however, much less severe in some ways than those of the second middle school. It had been planned for a completion date of 1972. Because of the overcrowding at the initially opened middle school, the children living in the village where the second one was to be built were kept back in their primary school from 1971 to 1972. This created much dissatisfaction among parents, which turned to great anger in the spring of 1972, when it was announced that their middle school would not be ready until 1973. Staff were nevertheless appointed for an opening in 1972. The primary school site, therefore, had to cater for two schools. The use of temporary accommodation became a fact of life for the new school, and when it was made clear that the new school building could not be completed even by September 1973, temporariness almost took on the air of permanence. The reasons for the delay in completing the building were never made fully clear although the governors, the local urban district council, and an ad hoc committee of parents continually made representations to the Divisional and County Education Officers, to county councillors and members of Parliament. The local *Gazette* (14th July, 1972) reported also that the Divisional Educational Officer could not 'give a realistic report for the simple reason that he had no information from the contractor'.

The sense of impotence was thus not confined to the governing body but it was very clear that this sense was shared by all the governors. It was probably this as much as any change of basic values among the Conservative members, that led them to agree in January 1973 that henceforth 'head-teachers of the schools covered by the articles of government . . . will be entitled to attend future meetings (of the body), if they so wish' (Minutes of the governing body, 1973).

Their attendance did not make much difference to the discussions or business of the body, however, which continued to be dominated by problems of middle school accommodation, until local government reorganization in April 1974 led to changes in the instruments and articles of government. Basic questions about the developing 'character' of the new middle schools, raised in the first report of the headmaster in 1970, had been set aside.

Into the era of corporate management

By April 1974, the preparation for the take-over by the new education authority, the Metropolitan District Council, had been made. Seminars for interested parties had been held under the direction of the Chief Executive designate during 1973. It was already agreed in principle that governing bodies should have a somewhat different constitution and functions from those of the former governing body. Corporate management required that such bodies be much more involved in the flow of information between constituent parts of the system. This could only be achieved, it was theorized, by representation of all the legitimate interest groups in schools. The Council, minor authorities within the district such as parish councils covering a school's catchment area, teachers, and parents were all to be given a place on the new governing bodies. Cooptions were also agreed to cover 'other community interests'.[2] Priorities and decisions about the financing of schools were to be decided in the council, however, and the scope of governors was strictly limited. The new articles set organization and curriculum, followed by consultation as the first priorities. With a clear resonance for the previous governing body, clause 3(a) of the articles announced that 'the Council shall determine the general educational character of the Schools and their place in the educational system and the Governors through the agency of the Head Teachers shall be responsible for implementing any determination . . .'.

At the time of the change-over in 1974, and in the months afterwards, the new governors also became aware of a new vocabulary of local government, which emphasized the change in style to corporate management. Letters of appointment to the governing body were received from the offices of the Directorate of Administration in the new Metropolitan Council. Invitations to meetings came from the Directorate of Educational Services, and the office of the Chief Schools Officer. Previously they had come from the Divisional Education Officer in a town nearby, who was very familiar to the former governors. New governors learned of a new hierarchy in which schools were part of a network of educational services, again enclosed in a broader administrative context, in which the Chief Executive Officer, the Chief Secretary, and the Directors of Administration, Development Services, Finance and Social Services and the Personnel Division, seemed to act as a management team and play crucial roles in determining what happened in education. Elected councillors on the governing body, on learning the new vocabulary and their own role within what they often defined as a powerful professional hierarchy, further elaborated on the new situation in discussion at governors' meetings.

The new body was concerned only with middle schools and once it settled into normal operation it was serviced by a schools adviser for the Chief Schools Officer, who was nominally the clerk to the governing body.

Meetings were now held only once per term, and although much continued to be made of accommodation problems, which did not cease to be   portant, on account both of faults in the new buildings and of rising numbers on roll, the reports of the headteachers and of what was being done by pupils and teachers in the schools came to be a more usual element in the meetings. On one occasion in 1975, the Chief Schools Adviser came to the meeting to discuss the provision of the third middle school in the area (it was opened in 1979), and there was an attempt to create a full discussion of the theory and practice of the middle school. At other meetings members of the teaching staff presented aspects of the curriculum, and the problems of the transfer of pupils between the three tiers were discussed. Even so, this rarely led to any resolution by the body except perhaps in terms of providing a new building. Usually the minutes record only the 'thanks' of the governors. But rarely also did heads or teachers press the governors to make resolutions. They possibly really preferred to keep the governors at a distance. Appointments and resignations of staff were processed exactly as in the case of the earlier governing body. The numbers and grades of staff were determined however by the management group.

The character of the new middle schools was thus being determined to some extent in the presence of, but hardly through, the governing body. Opportunities for raising the level of discussion, for exploring the possibility of participating in the activities of the schools, for watching the schools at work, and for gaining other perspectives on that work were never taken. The commitment of members to the new governing body was not as great as to the old, at least in terms of attendance, as Table 4.1 suggests. Members also more frequently seemed to leave the meeting earlier than they had tended to do before 1974. Thus, opening the membership to other interest groups did not increase in any real sense the rate of participation.

Conclusions

If this account with its selection of facts and reported events can be taken as valid, it seems to support the view that governing bodies do not exert much influence on educational matters. In terms of the crucial question of the identity and legitimacy of middle schools, the governors only passively influenced the development of the school's character, through the ritual of listening to, noting, and thanking headteachers for their comments and reports. If local authority officials and advisors were impotent, as they were in the case of the delayed building of one middle school or in other cases concerned with the repair and maintenance of premises, the governors were even more so. One or two governors may have exerted some influence in terms of the choice of new members of staff, but this was not brought about through an openly discussed policy, and their action was clearly less important than those of the headteachers and authority officials. Much of the discussion and routine activity of the governors' meetings can be described as a stagnant ritual, played out so as to conform with local authorities' norms about the role of governing bodies. The ritual was only broken at times, such as when the governors were caught up in the general hue and cry over the delayed building of the new middle school in 1972. Headteachers and local authority officials were able, if they wished to do so, to use the governing bodies for confirming their own standpoint. Where a conflict existed between headteachers and the local authority, the governing body tended to become a sounding board for the different positions, rather than a political assembly which had the right to reach, recommend, and have executed an agreed policy, even within the limits of its instruments and articles of government.

Changes occurred over the eight years. In the later period, under corporate management from 1974 onwards, although participation was widened by the appointment of parents and teachers to full membership, the sense of involvement seemed to decline. Corporate management at a general level means the coalescence of power among groups of functional representatives (such as local authority officers – the management team, professional association members, and elected members) meeting as apparent equals, rather than among groups of democratically elected representatives served by bureaucratically appointed officers. Decision making by the management group then seems to be as legitimate as decision making by the council of a local authority. Professional and managerial expertise is as important as, if not more important than, the political beliefs and party control of a council. The sense of this developing in the local authority of which the governing body was part after 1974 was forced on the members both by some of the discussion and by the general tone of communications received by them. The distance of education officers from the governors, the new vocabulary of local government, the growing significance of the management team, and the apparent subordination of education to administration all became obvious. There was a clear sense that the governing body was a very small cog in a bureaucratic machine with a relatively distant centre compared with the previous one in the years between 1970 and 1974. The

Taylor Committee's suggestion then that the education interest might be better served through revitalized governing bodies in a corporate management system did not seem to be realized in this case.

It is possible, of course, that the governing body was not in any sense typical. It is a matter of further comparative research to establish whether governing bodies can and do have an influential role. In the case of voluntary-aided schools where the voluntary body concerned, be it church or educational trust, is contributing some resources to the provision of the school and has a majority of members on the body, a different balance of power exists and this may add a significant dimension to decision making. In the majority of schools, financial power vested in a local authority is ultimately and generally the determinant of decisions. What is crucial is who has the greatest influence on the use of financial power.

The consistency of the chairman's approach to the governing body meetings, his general unwillingness to allow discussions about contentious policy issues stemming from central or local government decisions, and his backing by a Conservative majority on the body, meant that the internal dynamics of each meeting were relatively predictable. Clearly, had the chairman wished to call for more participation by encouraging more members to develop ideas on particular themes, by arranging more visits to the schools, and by making members more aware of the educational issues in 'training' meetings, the activities of the governing body might have forced a more unpredictable response from the middle schools and the local authority. By not doing these things he certainly did not force other members to question their own roles. It would be useful to know how far a varied role performance by chairmen affects the influence a governing body has on educational interests in schools and their neighbourhoods.

Research into educational decision making has tended to overlook governing bodies possibly because of a general view that they now no longer perform more than a stagnant ritual. It could be that we should, however, encourage much more the exploration of this agency in local government. There are some possibilities for wider participation, and both school staffs and local authorities could, without much expense, encourage governors to hold greater expectations for their work through training and through legitimate demands on them made under the instruments and articles of government. If middle schools need to resolve some of their problems of legitimacy and identity, it is possibly also the case that middle school governors do, and so joint enterprise might be mutually beneficial.

Such a revitalization would, of course, seem to be essential in a society suffering a crisis of legitimacy, where the political direction of an uncertain economic future is leading to a willingness to make cuts in the public provision of services such as education, and where demographic change is merely used as one reason for accepting these cuts. There is no consensus about such political behaviour, and there is likely to be much more conflict. If we are to resolve the problems of lack of consensus without resort to force and violence, we need to use all the agencies of institutionalized authority for widening democratic discourse. Corporate management can restrict such discourse. Demands for participation should be taken seriously. Middle schools are a part of educational provision which might well be a subject for particular cuts. We must realize then that if we want to understand, to 'know how to go on', we must put more emphasis on using the immediately available means like governing bodies for reaching mutual understanding and an acceptable set of values to guide future negotiations (Bauman, 1978).

Notes

1. The constitution allowed for the membership of the Chairman of the County Education Committee, ex officio, six persons nominated by the County Council, six by the local Urban District Council, one by a nearby parish council, two by the Anglican Churches – which had interests in two voluntary controlled primary schools, one representing the grammar school governors, and two by cooption, giving a total of nineteen. Until 1974, there were never less than fourteen who had overt political affiliations, twelve of whom were Conservatives.
2. In the new body, out of sixteen members, two were teacher representatives, two were parent representatives, and one member was coopted. This left political representatives very much in the majority.

Part II

RATIONALES

INTRODUCTION

Most forms of schooling have their rationales, the relationship of which to actual practice is questionable. While the rationales most usually take the form of prescriptions about education in general, they have a tendency to be linked to particular types of schools. Thus primary schools are associated with educational progressivism, comprehensive schools with egalitarianism and meritocracy, and public schools with cultural elitism. The three chapters which comprise Part II of this book attempt, in very different ways, to define the rationale or ideology that has become associated with the middle school. They explore the process by which that ideology emerged and changed over time, and examine the various functions of an educational, social, and political kind which it has performed.

Over the years many claims, some of them rather grandiose, have been made about middle schools. They have been said to possess their own unique identity catering for the age-specific needs of children in an identifiable stage of development, the middle years of childhood. They have been depicted as being responsive to local needs, facilitative of democratic relationships amongst their staff, and supportive of egalitarian education for their pupils. How might we evaluate these claims; as accurate portrayals of middle school realities, as carefully constructed devices to gloss over some of the less desirable aspects of middle school practice, as genuine but misguided conceptions of middle schooling, or what?

Ideologies or rationales (for the purposes of this book we will not distinguish between them) possess at least four features, each of which is acknowledged in the following three chapters. Firstly, ideologies are sets of values and beliefs which are, on occasion, given fairly clear and systematic expression in documents, speeches, and so on. In these terms, they are simply like philosophies. For example, in written and oral statements about the middle school, the above-mentioned themes such as the middle years as a separate stage of childhood recur with systematic regularity. Such views of the middle school are therefore more than uncoordinated and disparate opinions but, because of their systematic character, might be said to constitute a philosophy or ideology.

Secondly, ideologies are used to bestow meaning on the world, they are sense-making devices. Thus when administrators, headteachers, and so on embrace middle school ideology, they are conferring meaning on and giving purpose to their actions. To some extent, belief in the ideology gives them a reason for continuing. For that reason, we should not be surprised when such persons passionately defend the principles contained within the ideology, for in a way they are defending their own professional commitments and identities.

Thirdly, ideologies are often employed as instruments of persuasion, as ways of gaining converts to a cause or of securing the loyalty and commitment of those already involved. Thus, the optimistic character of middle school ideology, together with its capacity to appeal to sentiments such as individualism and egalitarianism, which already hold strong currency in social democratic thinking can be seen as an aid to gaining recruits for the middle school cause when educational reorganization takes place. It is a means of smoothing the process of educational innovation.

Fourthly, ideologies have been viewed in some quarters not just as sets of values and beliefs but as distorted accounts of the world, deflecting attention away from its problems and conflicts and the power relationships and inequalities from which these arise. Thus, it has been claimed that the emphasis on a 'unique identity' of the middle school deflects attention away from the conflicts between the primary and secondary traditions which are to be found within such schools. Similarly, it has been suggested that the preoccupation with a generational problem of 'the middle years' has meant that more pervasive problems of class, racial, and sexual inequality to be found in these as in other schools have not been addressed.

Nias opens the discussion on middle school rationales by outlining six facets of the middle school image as portrayed in documents produced by LEAs, teacher working parties, HMIs and the DES, the Schools Council, and so forth. The way in which middle schools are discussed, she suggests, resonates with many positively valued features of British society. Thus, they are claimed to be imbued with qualities such as egalitarianism, democratic responsiveness to educational and social need, readiness to serve as a site for innovation, and a tendency to promote pluralistic relationships amongst their members. In addition to these characteristics, the ideal image of the middle school is reinforced by an excessive and pervasive optimism, and by a tendency to emphasize consensus and integration at the expense of conflict and difference. Nias concludes by expressing concern about the possible discrepancy between the notion of the ideal middle school purveyed as its public image, and the experiences of middle school teachers. She feels that in the event of such a discrepancy, teachers may understandably respond through guilt, cynicism, and withdrawal.

While Nias is reticent about claiming that there *is* an actual discrepancy between the real and the ideal middle school, Hargreaves, in the following chapter, suggests that the gap between ideology and practice is substantial. He proposes amongst other things that while middle schools are discussed in educational terms, their emergence has been determined in the main by administrative factors. While they are said to have a unique identity and to provide a nice balance between different educational traditions (i.e., the old primary and secondary approaches in terms of curriculum, teaching style, and the amount of setting and streaming), they still tend to be separated by the conventional eleven-plus dividing line albeit *within* the middle school, and while they are advanced as a response to local needs, these needs might more properly be construed as constraints in terms of staffing and building resources for example. Yet, Hargreaves argues, this ideology is not the outcome of a devious conspiracy on the part of headteachers and administrators, but has been built piecemeal and fairly unselfconsciously from notions which are widely accepted and highly valued in social democratic thinking. The distortive character of middle school ideology is therefore a product of the wider and usually unquestioned distortions contained in social democratic ideology. These include an emphasis on temporary generational problems rather than permanent class ones, a narrow interpretation of politics as party politics which are to be kept out of sacrosanct areas like education and sport, and so on.

Lynch, in the final chapter of this section, takes up the point that middle schools should be understood in a wider context of economic and political forces when he analyses the problem of how middle schools are to be legitimated at a time of falling rolls and standstill budgets. Charting developments since 1974, Lynch documents a series of policy initiatives and reports which have marked a withdrawal of financial support for middle schools (as indeed for all schools) alongside a tightening ideological grip on the curriculum and standards of middle schooling. Lynch warns us that in a time of contraction and constraint, the future of middle schools is uncertain. The ideology discussed by Nias and Hargreaves may have provided appropriate legitimation in the optimistic and expansionist sixties and early seventies, but now it constitutes weak defence indeed against some major economically induced shifts in educational policy. The ambiguity which was once its strength is now its Achilles heel. For example, the emphasis on the middle years which once drew attention from the fact that middle schools were an administrative convenience, can now be employed to justify the view that there is no necessity for separate middle schools as such. Insights like these lead one to conclude that any further legitimation of middle schools should be based on a detailed understanding of their practice and a realistic and critical awareness of the economic and political context within which they operate.

CHAPTER FIVE

THE IDEAL MIDDLE SCHOOL: ITS PUBLIC IMAGE

J. Nias

A traveller in Africa is reputed to have asked of a familiar brand of tinned milk: 'Is it called "Ideal" to distinguish it from real?'

In 1965 there were no middle schools. By 1976 they had not only become an established feature of the educational scene, but had also acquired a distinctive image based to a large extent upon the publications which appeared between 1966 and 1976. These include LEA and teacher group working party documents, descriptions and commentaries by HM Inspectorate and the DES, reports of national conferences, Schools Council working papers, and descriptive or analytic books by participants in, or observers of the middle school scene. A striking feature of all these publications is the degree of agreement among them about the nature of the middle school. Whatever their age-span, middle schools emerge from the printed page with the same set of characteristics. Thus their image is a powerfully consistent one. It depicts schools with a number of fissiparous tendencies – committed to egalitarianism and democratic decision making, responsive to pressures from within and without, swift to innovate, ready to espouse conflicting value systems – yet unified and stabilized by shared self-confidence and a commitment to cooperation and consensus. Whether these characteristics are 'ideal' or 'real' remains a matter for empirical enquiry, but the model which is presented to planners or administrators who turn for guidance to the available literature is a remarkably uniform one.

Egalitarianism

The first middle schools resulted from discussion among interested parties in the LEAs (West Riding Education Committee, 1967; Worcestershire, 1968), and a belief in the value of democratic decision making is reflected in the internal organization of the ideal middle school. From the start official policy urged headteachers to involve staff in discussion, and advocated substantial delegation of responsibility to the holders of 'major coordinating roles' (DES, 1970(b)). Communication and consultation soon came to be viewed as crucial aspects of the headteacher's role (Gannon and Whalley, 1975). Indeed, the authority structure of the school as a whole is collegial rather than hierarchical. The headteacher expects senior teachers to follow his example in the delegation of authority and responsibility. Gannon and Whalley (1975) recommend that specialist teachers be occupied as much in consultancy as in subject teaching, and that year-group leaders act as coordinators and communication channels rather than as heads of 'mini schools'. Even within a strong year-group structure, class teachers are perceived as having considerable autonomy (Clegg, 1967). The role compression observed by Blyth and Derricott (1977) in many actual schools ensures that few, if any, members of any middle school staff have only one function. Even the deputy head is likely also to be a subordinate member of a subject team, while a probationer may acquire institutional status either because of his expertise in a specialist area or because he has innovatory skills not possessed by his more senior colleagues. It is not that middle schools lack authority structures, so much as that these vary in response to the needs of the situation (DES, 1970(b)). Leadership is defined by competence rather than by formal role, and may pass from one member of a school team to another as circumstances dictate (Edwards, 1972). In short, the ideal middle school is a democratic institution and its head occupies a position of *primus inter pares*.

This disregard for traditional hierarchies is also felt to characterize relationships between the teaching and nonteaching staffs, between staff and parents, and between staff and children. Ross (in Schools Council, 1969) sees nonteaching assistants as an integral part of teaching teams. Culling (1973) goes further and substitutes the name 'helpers' for 'auxiliaries' or 'welfare assistants'. Gannon and Whalley (1975, p.63) urge that parents 'should be active participants in the educational process'. The Schools Council (1972, p.89) reports that many teachers in their sample of 1400 want to establish 'closer links between teacher and taught', while Cohen (in Raggett and Clarkson, 1976, p.205) praises the middle school's ability to provide 'a rational and structured form of freedom' for early adolescents.

Moreover, all the early publications, including those of the DES architects (DES, 1966), anticipated some form of vertical grouping or, at the least, of facilities shared by children of different ages. Even among the children status differences were, it seems, to be reduced.

These egalitarian expectations also permeate both curriculum planning and the organization of learning. Most writers assume that there will be unlimited access to all areas of the curriculum for children of all ages and both sexes. In both *Launching the Middle School* (1970(a)) and *Towards the Middle School* (1970(b)), the DES set their collective face against a selective curriculum. Five years later this notion had achieved the status of a principle. The Schools Council working paper on *The Curriculum in the Middle Years* (1975, p.32) stated that 'all subjects shall be seen as the vehicles for the general development of all children'. No curriculum decision must be taken which would limit a child's future, whether vocationally or in terms of personal interests. Options should be kept open for as long as possible and no doors should be closed upon individuals or groups. 'Despite the foreshadowing effects of intended destinations, differentiation within the curriculum should be kept to a minimum until 13 years.' (Schools Council, 1972, p.9.) Gannon and Whalley (1975) go further and suggest that subject and social hierarchies are interdependent so that the use of 'integrated thematic studies' will encourage egalitarianism in both areas.

According to the DES (1970(b), p.25), most middle school working parties have, for similar reasons, 'expressed a strong preference for mixed ability classes', and this view is borne out by subsequent publications. For example, Gannon and Whalley (1975, p.73) unequivocally state that 'the main teaching organisation will be based upon mixed ability groups'. Despite a growing, although largely unexplained, acceptance of the necessity of setting in some subjects, especially with older children, all the published opinion appears to be against streaming. It is also widely accepted, on grounds of social equity, that where some division by attainment or speed of learning is inevitable, equal resources will be available to children of all abilities.

Responsiveness

Middle schools are also perceived as responsive institutions. Often owing their very existence to a local response to economic or political pressure (Blyth and Derricott, 1977), they are seen as displaying in curriculum, organization, and personal relationships the capacity to adapt to the needs and demands of parents, children, and community. The fact that this readiness to respond to conflicting expectations imposes tensions upon both children and teachers, and presents the latter with impossible choices is never mentioned. The dilemmas are masked by the optimism (described below) which helps to counterbalance this and other centrifugal tendencies in the ideal middle school.

The curriculum is widely viewed as a dependent variable, built to serve children, rather than as a strait jacket into which they must all fit. 'There is no such thing as a curriculum for the middle years, but a curriculum for a particular middle years school, and within that school ideally a curriculum for each child.' (Schools Council, 1975, p.34.) The earlier Schools Council working paper (1972) also saw the children as a 'dynamic force' acting to modify a planned curriculum, whilst most other sources stress the importance of responding, within agreed school guidelines, to individual interests and catering for varying paces of learning.

Yet the curriculum is not to be without structure. Rather its aim should be the development of the actual and latent abilities of every individual. Thus teachers must promote interests, increase aptitudes, and preserve and extend the curiosity of early childhood so that children will themselves display the needs to which teachers can then respond (Clegg, 1967). To facilitate this responsiveness to individual need, every school will have a carefully devised system of tutorial care and be staffed by teachers who know not just the children or the subject, but the child learning the subject (Schools Council, 1975).

The curriculum of the ideal middle school will not, however, be responsive only to the interests and expertise of particular staff members and to the needs of children. It has also to heed a number of external constraints. From outside the school, and from within, comes the demand for achievement in the three Rs (e.g., Edwards, 1972; Schools Council, 1975; Raggett and Clarkson, 1974). From the third-tier school come pressures for the systematic, orderly pursuit of knowledge, the formation of focused tastes and aptitudes, and the pursuit of study in depth and with precision (Schools Council, 1975). By contrast, authors such as Clegg (1967), following the Plowden Report, press for the further development of 'the curriculum, methods or attitudes which exist at present in junior schools' (Central Advisory Council, 1967, para.383), advocating in semiofficial terms the pursuit of broad enquiry-based learning, and the extension of children's experience through a variety of media and forms of expression. Given an underlying dedication to the ideal of individually tailored curricula, in which the degree of specialization is adjusted to the natural abilities and rates of progress of particular pupils, it is surprising that the middle school curriculum does not break under the further strain of accommodating demands from varied external sources.

Moreover, the complex differences of children between eight and thirteen dictate a high degree of individual and group work. The organization of space, time, and specialist personnel must be flexible and responsive, both to the contribution which can be made by particular staff and to the perceived needs of individual children. It is 'the judgement of the teacher about the value of the particular activity for a particular child at a given time which is the deciding factor in determining the rhythm of the child's day' (West Riding Education Committee, 1967, p.5). Pupils will be taught in different sized groups (Badcock et al., 1972), for different lengths of time (Edwards, 1972), by different people (DES, 1970(b); University of Exeter, 1968), or teams of people (Culling, 1973), in a variety of places (DES, 1966). The structure of the building 'must recognise and respond to these needs' (West Riding Education Committee, 1967, p.4), and resources must be dispersed throughout the building (DES, 1966).

The role of individual staff members also alters with the demands of the situation. Partly because there are more adult functions to be fulfilled in most middle schools than there are available adults, staff face the challenge of changing their roles many times during the school day. In any case, such changes are consistent with the egalitarian ethos of the middle school, and are therefore implicitly encouraged by it. As Blyth and Derricott (1977), among others, point out, the status of a teacher may vary as he plays within one day the parts of class teacher, team leader, team member, administrator, resource provider, specialist teacher, specialist consultant, counsellor, and tutor, not to mention a number of extracurricular and community roles. Even simply as a teacher he must be prepared to move easily between the role of instructor and that of learning facilitator or organizer (Edwards, 1972).

Some publications (notably Clegg, 1967; DES, 1970(b); Culling, 1973) also assume that the LEA will in its turn respond to the perceived needs of the children and the external pressures upon the school by making available to teachers the help of laboratory and other technicians, librarians, and other auxiliary personnel.

The headteacher too must be responsive in the way in which he exercises his powers of leadership, both to the community which his school serves, and to the talents and objectives of his staff (Culling, 1973). He must, in short, reconcile the needs of his school with the constraints imposed from without. Gannon and Whalley (1975, p.49) describe their 'educational catalyst' as a person who 'must encourage, support, sympathise, constructively criticize, humanize, and still be able, at times, to chastise'. He must, in short, be flexible, accommodating, accessible, and versatile. A middle school headship is, it appears, no job for an applicant with a low tolerance for ambiguity or with a high score in tests of authoritarianism.

Innovation

The ideal middle school is also innovative. Indeed the Plowden Report (para.383) explicitly described it as 'a new and progressive force', while Culling (1973, p.4) wrote: 'Wherever middle schools are developing . . . they are concerned with an entirely new educational concept and every aspect of education must be rethought.'

In the first place they are seen as a new type of school, different from either junior or secondary schools. 'This is not a "transitional" stage of education; it is unique and complete in itself.' (University of Exeter, 1968, p.8.) Secondly, in their community role (Gannon and Whalley, 1975; Blyth and Derricott, 1977) they represent a move away from the concept of the school as the one provider for all the educational needs of a growing child. The Schools Council (1975, p.15) recognized that 'the curriculum is only part of the total life experience of the child', and urged that teachers be alert to the potential contribution of people and institutions outside the 'edu-. cational system as narrowly defined'.

In a less radical manner, middle schools are perceived as being open to new ideas and practices (not least to the influence of Schools Council curriculum projects, many of which have, in the past decade, been concerned with children in 'the middle years'). Clegg (1967) and Blyth and Derricott (1977) both suggest that middle schools have often attracted young teachers, anxious to try out their own ideas and ideals. The conversion of existing schools has also provided a stimulus to teachers and administrators to look afresh at old problems. Early publications suggest that middle schools will take a new took at time-tabling (West Riding Education Committee, 1967), the use of space (DES, 1966), the use of specialist staff, especially for team teaching, (DES, 1970(a), grouping and the teaching of exceptional children (University of Exeter, 1968), curriculum content (Schools Council, 1969), and the provision and distribution of resources (DES, 1970(b)). Later works have recorded the development of thinking and practice in all these areas, of the 'deliberate and planned adoption of mixed and varied approaches' (Raggett and Clarkson, 1976, p.191).

Pluralism

The ideal middle school, being collegial, adaptive, and innovatory, is almost bound to be pluralistic as well. Like comprehensive schools, although for somewhat different reasons, middle schools allow for, and sometimes even seek, the cultivation of differences. For a start, there is no unified concept in the literature of what a middle school should be. Although lip-service is continually paid to certain key propositions (e.g., the unifying nature of the developmental characteristics of the middle years), these are differently interpreted and applied in different LEAs. Within authorities too, individual schools are free to develop autonomous cultures, deriving from their distinctive past and present circumstances, and based upon differing philosophies, sizes, and forms of organization (Culling, 1973).

Moreover, within each school there is likely to be only a minimum consensus on aims, a fact which allows individual teachers considerable latitude in defining their own roles and priorities (Schools Council, 1972; Owen, 1974). Teachers are free within a collegial discipline to follow their own professional judgement, indeed 'there are compelling arguments in favour of diversity' (Schools Council, 1975, p.54). In the same way, the formal and informal organization of each school must be sufficiently tolerant and flexible to accommodate individual idiosyncracies and to encourage the development of varied talents and types of expertise.

Just as schools are seen as being free to develop their aims in response to the beliefs, skills, and interests of their staffs, so the teachers' goal will be to cater for divergence among their pupils. Different value systems are freely propagated (Blyth and Derricott, 1977). There is no single pattern of success and no single set of religious, political, or social ideas. No special status is given to any particular subject and there is no distribution of resources which favours any specific curricular or extracurricular activity. Gannon and Whalley argue that the middle school must encourage 'the unique personality of the child to develop in an all-round sense' (p.15), while the Schools Council (1975) stresses how important it is that staff should recognize talents in spheres other than the academic one. The picture which emerges from nearly fifteen years of descriptive and analytic writing is of diversity and pluralism, of schools in which teachers practise, recognize, and support many forms of excellence.

Optimism

Those schools which are characterized by an active commitment to democratic egalitarianism, to communication and response, continued innovation, and the pursuit of varied, often conflicting, goals, might be seen as unstable and divided institutions. That this is not so appears to be due to countervailing pressure within the schools from two centripetal forces.

The first, optimism, is an intangible quality. Hopeful statements abound in the literature on middle schools. They are 'bright, cheerful, colourful, exciting places' (DES, 1970(b)), producing 'happy, thoughtful children' (Schools Council, 1969). They are an 'educational experiment which . . . will bring immense benefit to many children' (DES, 1970(a)), welding together the best practices of both primary and secondary education. In them children develop at their own pace, secure in the support, approval, and encouragement of sympathetic adults (Charles, 1974).

Staff too will learn from the challenges which the schools present, their experience and vision will be broadened and team teaching will extend the influence and expertise of exceptional teachers (Schools Council, 1969). Some will be saved from stagnation by the demands of innovation and others will find new fulfilment in their collaborative milieux (Culling, 1973).

Above all, they are 'happy places' in which both learning and teaching are 'fun'. Blyth and Derricott (1977, p.89) consider that the 'happy-school' image 'bears some relation to reality as we perceive it'. Whether or not this is so in the majority of middle schools, there is no doubt that in the ideal middle school, morale is high, the present is rewarding, and the future exciting.

Integration

The second centripetal characteristic – integration – shows itself in a large number of organizational ways which themselves reflect shared values and beliefs. Together these tend to blur differences and cultivate interdependencies. In the first place the presumption that harmony exists or can be made to exist underlies all decision making. The schools themselves are posited on the existence of a developmental unity in the middle years of childhood (e.g., University of Exeter, 1968; DES, 1970(b); Schools Council, 1972). They draw from their primary roots (e.g., Clegg, 1967; University of Exeter, 1968; Schools Council, 1969) an emphasis upon the quality of personal relationships, and an insistence that children must spend a large part of each day with one teacher who will know every child, and through this knowledge ensure for them all an atmosphere of cooperative endeavour. In addition, the very characteristics which I have earlier described as centrifugal have the paradoxical effect of facilitating consensus. The egalitarianism, pluralism, and innovative zeal of middle schools reduce differences between subjects, age-groups, sexes, and roles, and make it possible to achieve communication across traditional barriers.

Belief is supported by appropriate organizational forms. Pairs and groups of teachers plan and teach together, often on a year-group or departmental basis. There is frequent discussion, much emphasis upon cooperation, and a marked willingness to share ideas, space, and resources. Coordination and communication are key organizational functions. The head too plays a unifying role, facilitating discussion, cooperation, and joint decision making. This stress upon consultation and collaboration is such a marked characteristic of the ideal middle school that every publication draws attention to it, either directly or by inference.

Buildings too often seem to have been deliberately designed to foster interdependence (DES, 1966; West Riding Education Committee, 1967). Children and teachers are encouraged by the grouping of rooms and dispersal of resources to interact across vertical and/or horizontal boundaries. Open-plan buildings and the provision of multipurpose spaces rather than specialist workrooms encourage movement around the school and the blurring of territorial boundaries.

Integration goes beyond the school and characterizes the relationship between the middle school and its lower- and upper-tier schools. The literature on the subject abounds in words such as 'bridge', 'liaison', 'continuity', 'reciprocity', and 'exchange'. Middle school staff are forced, by their position in a three-tier system, into contact with teachers from their related schools. Joint attempts to provide continuity of both curriculum and pastoral care strengthen early and tentative contacts between them (Schools Council, 1975).

Good working relations have also been achieved by collaboration between architects, administrators, and teachers over the modification and building of schools (Edwards, 1972), and by the complex process of consultation which has characterized the introduction of middle schools in many LEAs (a 'model' example is described in DES, 1970(a)). Some schools have even chosen to adopt a community role and are forging links between pupils, teachers, parents, and social workers (Blyth and Derricott, 1977).

Middle schools can thus be seen to have organizational, and sometimes architectural features which encourage both internal cohesion and links with external bodies. Integration is also a marked characteristic of the middle school curriculum. The Warwick conference, in 1967, took a cautious line over the retention of 'systematic courses in the separate disciplines' (Schools Council, 1969), but the DES (1970(b)) bluntly stated 'conventional subject teaching in specialist hands . . . is unlikely to be satisfactory' (p.15), and advocated broad groups or blocks of related subjects. This ambivalence about the role of the traditional disciplines in the education of children in the middle years has persisted to the present (Schools Council, 1975), and has often resulted in compromise arrangements for linked studies. Yet integration received further impetus from the Schools Council, who argued that 'a balanced curriculum should ensure that a child has had the opportunity of sampling all the main fields of study and modes of thought and creativity' (Schools Council, 1972). This notion of balance was grafted on to the primary roots of the middle school and encouraged the existing emphasis upon thematic study, and upon 'learning how to learn' (Raggett and Clarkson, 1974, 1976). Although the precise nature of related or integrated subjects will vary from school to school, some form of linking or blurring of traditional subject boundaries is assumed to take place in every middle school. Thus, curriculum integration serves to unite values with interpersonal relations. As an ideal it reflects and enhances the collaborative ethos of the school, while structurally it ensures that teachers are mutually dependent for specialist knowledge and skills.

Conclusion

During the past few years, the 'Plowden image' of the English primary school has been increasingly called into question. Recent empirical studies have demonstrated that progressive primary schools are neither as numerous as had hitherto been believed, nor as child-centred as both their supporters and detractors supposed. Arguably, this gap between public knowledge and the reality on which it was based has harmed the schools, inducing guilt, defensiveness, and the unthinking adoption of techniques among teachers, and polarizing over-reaction among parents and taxpayers.

Middle schools, it might be claimed, have been the victims of a similar process of myth making. To read the accumulated publications of the decade between 1966 and 1976 is to enter a hopeful, exciting educational world, full of dynamism, innovation, and social justice, a world in which conflicting value systems, individual development, and common need are joyfully reconciled by the organic processes of exchange and growth. This is not to say that individual middle schools do not have some or all of the characteristics which I have discussed above, nor to suggest that writers have deliberately distorted their perceptions of the schools which they have visited or in which they have worked. This chapter does not claim, in the absence of adequate empirical evidence, that there is a discrepancy between the ideal and the real middle school, nor does it set out to explain the consistent picture of middle schools which emerges from the literature available. It does, however, suggest that this picture exists and that its individual features can be distinguished, classified, and described in much the same way as was done for primary schools in the Plowden era.

The absence of evidence to support or challenge this picture, and the likelihood that it therefore influences lay and professional thinking about middle schools has implications for all connected with them. Where the notion of the ideal school is at odds with the personal experience of teachers, one may predict responses ranging from cynicism and withdrawal to guilt and frenetic search. It offers those outside the school, be they parents or administrators, a platform for impassioned advocacy or dogmatic attack, both equally uniformed. It is time that we moved from the blueprint and prototype into a detailed and constructively critical appraisal of the product of fifteen years of educational endeavour.

CHAPTER SIX

THE IDEOLOGY OF THE MIDDLE SCHOOL

A. Hargreaves

The origins and practices of English middle schools are closely tied up with the fact that in British society, schools tend to reproduce social inequalities as well as maintain a social, economic, and political system which is organized around such inequalities. The ideology of English middle schools, in common with most other educational ideologies, obscures this connection. In this chapter, I shall explore how that ideology has emerged, what its main elements appear to be, and the way in which it has been constructed from a much broader fund of explanations contained within social democratic ideology. It will be my contention that the distortions contained within middle school ideology are derived, albeit indirectly, from the range of conceptions that make up social democratic ideology.

Middle schools and progressivism: the extension model

It is now generally agreed that middle schools were established mainly because they were an administratively expedient means of going comprehensive (Blyth and Derricott, 1977). However, their development was also harmonious with and could be justified in terms of the child-centred, progressive ideology that was a strengthening force in the primary school sector. It would, perhaps, be an exaggeration to state that middle schools were at any time viewed as little more than an extension of the primary school. Indeed, there are many counter-instances which show that the need to create something new and original was also felt to be important even during the earliest days of their establishment. Nevertheless, in the initial stages of debate about the middle school, one of the major justifying themes was that a delay in the age of transfer could lead to an extension of primary school methods beyond the age of eleven. Certainly, middle schools were regarded as carrying over more characteristics of the primary school than of the secondary school. This extension model was expressed with full clarity in a definitive document produced by the West Riding of Yorkshire LEA and its Chief Education Officer, Sir Alec Clegg, when middle schools were first mooted.

> The advances made in the last ten years by children of all ability groups in those primary schools which have come to rely more on the exploitation of the individual's experience and less on the inculcation of subject knowledge have been so outstanding that they must be regarded as of major significance. Standards in this County have risen considerably and many who have observed this approach to education are convinced that it is wrong to cut it short at age 11. (West Riding Education Committee, 1963, p.3)

Similarly, in the evidence which they submitted to Plowden, the National Union of Teachers (1964) reached the conclusion that 'there is a balance of advantage in extending a primary-type regime for pupils to a later age than is now generally the case'. But it is the Plowden Report (1967) which encapsulates most appropriately the middle school mood of the mix-sixties:

> If the middle school is to be a new and progressive force it must develop further the curriculum, methods and attitudes which exist at present in junior schools. It must move forward into what is now regarded as secondary school work, but it must not move so far away that it loses the best of primary education as we know it now. (paras. 383–384)

Even more fundamentally, the period which preceded the establishment of the first middle schools in 1968 was one when professional educators of all kinds were able to advance what they felt to be truly 'educational' arguments in support of one particular type of middle school, the eight–twelve school, as against the nine–thirteen school which administrators tended to support for reasons of administrative convenience. Increasingly, therefore, as time has progressed, the *extension* model has become less applicable to middle schools in general than to one specific variant, the eight–twelve school. In this respect, some groups and individuals have argued vociferously against the 'administrative convenience' position, recommending instead the establishment of eight–twelve schools on 'educational' grounds. The NUT (1969), for example, suggested that LEAs who were adopting middle school plans, should opt for a transfer age of twelve as recommended in the Plowden Report, and also expressed a wish to retain the word 'primary' when referring to eight–twelve schools. It was clearly preferable to extend established favourable identities rather than to create precarious new ones. This situation, where middle schools were regarded as an extension of the best of primary school practice and as worthy of implementation only if justified by such educational reasons, was to be transformed quite rapidly towards the end of the decade.

The exclusion from the brief of the Plowden Report of those factors which normally constrain the actions of local government administrators and politicians, such as the building costs involved in catering for different ages of transfer, had led to the advocacy of an institution (the eight–twelve school) on 'educational' grounds, which many LEAs were later unable to adopt. Indeed, by the time the Plowden Report appeared, several LEAs such as Hull (Gorwood, 1978), Worcestershire (Marsh, in this volume), and the West Riding (Sharp, in this volume; Hargreaves, forthcoming) had already made the decision to reorganize on nine–thirteen grounds because of material constraints.

The nine–thirteen school, which made the greatest initial headway, is less easily legitimated as an extension of primary school practice than is its eight–twelve counterpart. Firstly, with the 'O' level year only two years distant from when the child enters the upper school, nine–thirteen middle schools are under considerable pressure to ensure that their transferring pupils possess an adequate grounding in most of the traditionally defined high-status areas of the upper school curriculum. Secondly, the legacy of previous traditions of primary and secondary education is taken on board in the form of a divided teaching staff who may, on reorganization, have found themselves in a middle school irrespective of whether or not they held any general commitment to the idea of middle schools as such.[1] There is then a problem of how these diverse factions might be cemented together. It is for these reasons that a specific ideology of the middle school emerged and that there was an overall transition from an *extension* to an *invention* model of middle schooling.

Elements of middle school ideology: the invention model

I now want to draw out some major characteristics of this *invention* model of middle school ideology, and show their connection with a range of conceptions enshrined in social democratic ideology. For most of these characteristics, of which I identify six, I do not claim that they are the sole preserve of middle school ideology. The distinctiveness of middle school ideology is rather the outcome of the particular way in which these characteristics are combined.

Education and politics

In debates about middle school reform and reorganization, one central bone of contention has been unearthed over and over again by critics; that the middle school is a consequence of administrative convenience and economic expediency and that some of the educational arguments which have subsequently been used to justify its existence are of doubtful validity. For these critics, middle schools have been implemented for administrative and political reasons, not educational ones.[2] In a conference on middle schools, for example, the Assistant Masters' Association (1976) concluded that:

> . . . in too many areas the system had been introduced basically on the grounds of administrative convenience ('the buildings fitted') and not on educational grounds. . . . Decisions taken on this basis were deprecated because the introduction of the middle school system was then seen as an administrative rather than an educational decision. (p.16)

Commentators and critics alike have viewed the production of educational justifications for middle schools as separate from and preferable to the administrative reasons which have been put forward for their implementation. Three mechanisms have been involved here. Firstly, year by year, there has been an increasing 'amnesia' regarding the 'administrative' reasons for middle school reform in official and semiofficial documents. In the 1964 Education Act, in circulars 10/65 and 13/66, and in the Schools Council Working Paper No. 22, considerable attention was paid to such questions. However, the year 1967 would seem to be a watershed here, for the Plowden Report failed to mention such considerations, HMSO Pamphlet No. 57 devoted only a perfunctory introductory paragraph to the issue, and Schools Council Working Papers Nos. 42 and 55 avoided 'administrative' questions altogether.

As the first middle schools were to be inaugurated in 1968, debates about their *general* viability were rapidly becoming redundant. To many headmasters, teachers, and parents the middle school would be presented as a *fait accompli*. The urgent economic reasons for their implementation were widely acknowledged. Now there was a need for the creation of post hoc rationales to legitimate what seemed to be quite a novel educational concept. Increasingly therefore, from 1967 onwards, advocates of the middle school have proved less willing to discuss the more earthy, pragmatic bases of middle school reform and 'educational' arguments have come to the fore. The memory of the middle school movement has instead been preserved in the writings and statements of its critics, who are ever ready to open doors

M.S.   G

on the middle school question and reveal the administrative skeleton in the closet.

Secondly, as in the case of the eight–twelve *extension* model, advocates of the middle school have frequently regarded administrative motives as culpable evils requiring replacement by more righteous educational justifications. For example, Culling (1973) poses the loaded question: 'Is it *merely* an administrative convenience or can it be related to phases of development in childhood?' (p.10).[3]

Several commentators, such as Lynch (1975), take this argument further and suggest that political expediency may prove a blessing in disguise, for the middle school might yet show itself to be educationally worthwhile. At the extreme, the emergence of the middle school is regarded not so much as the offspring of 'doubtful parentage' (as in Edwards, 1972), but of what might be regarded as an 'immaculate conception' consequent upon a dignified concern for good book-keeping on the one hand, and a humanitarian interest in what is considered to be educationally desirable on the other (as in Gorwood, 1973; Holness, 1973). The thrust of such arguments lies in playing down the significance of administrative considerations while giving greater weight to educational ones.

Thirdly, comparisons have been drawn between middle school reorganization and previous modes of educational reorganization, which reflect poorly on the latter. The arguments presented in previous education reports, it has been suggested, were little more than rationalizations of administratively expedient policies. In this respect, the Hadow Report (1926) is frequently and justifiably criticized for the poetic rather than scientific manner in which it stated the case for transfer at eleven plus to fit the needs of those commencing an identifiable stage of development known as 'adolescence' (e.g., Nisbet and Entwistle, 1966).[4] Culling (1973), for example, comments that 'the Hadow Committee not unnaturally sought to rationalise what was administratively convenient' (p.10).

On the face of it, this critique is an unimpeachable one. However, its supporters fail to recognize that while enthusiastically searching for educational justifications for middle schools, they too have become entrenched in the very same process of legitimating administratively convenient modes of reorganization. Marsh (1973), for example, has stated that:

> The main impetus for creating middle schools came from the administrative problems associated with the introduction of comprehensive education and the raising of the school leaving age. This reason for change in no way

invalidates the change in the age of transfer, as the age of 11 had also been chosen for administrative reasons. (p.37)

This is a strange equation indeed, and is tantamount to saying that two wrongs make a right. By sleight of hand, Marsh has here turned vice into virtue.

The promotion of educational justifications for the middle school at the expense of more pragmatic reasons may even convey the impression that educational reasons were the driving force behind the establishment of those schools. History then becomes inverted as in the following remarks of an ex-West Riding adviser whom I interviewed. For him, 'middle schools were originally based on an idea, a notion, and ideas of child development'. They were 'based on attitudes held about the age of transfer and child development'. For him 'the educational argument was always uppermost'.

Interestingly, this account contradicts the interpretations which the West Riding offered when first contemplating middle schools. In their first (widely publicized) document on the three-tier system, prime importance was given to the administrative reasons for the establishment of middle schools (West Riding Education Committee, 1963). Even more interesting than this, however, is the fact that the redraft of this document in 1965 showed a weakening of the 'pragmatic' arguments. Priority was instead given to various educational justifications, such as the desirability of extending a primary-type regime to older pupils (West Riding Education Committee, 1965).

Yet the manner in which proponents of the middle school have separated out educational issues from administrative and political ones is perhaps of less importance than the fact that this dichotomy has been wholly taken over by critics as well as advocates. The comments of the AMA, quoted earlier, are a good example of this. The important point here is that the treatment of education and administration or education and policy in this way, implies an acceptance of the narrow social democratic definition of politics as either party or pressure group politics, where there are observable conflicts of interest over particular policies serving explicitly articulated ends.

The conventional notion that 'education must be kept out of politics and politics out of education' (referred to in Benton, 1974), a conception which dominates official debate at all levels of educational policy, implies a tacit denial of the central fact that the schooling process is unavoidably political in a wider sense, in so far as it affects pupils' future careers through policies of educational selection and manpower allocation, and hence 'the distribution of life chances, resources and power in society' (Marsden, 1971). In this respect, middle schools are underlain by political concerns in that their emergence has, in all but a few cases (Benn and Simon, 1972), been inextricably tied to the development of comprehensive schooling, which in turn seems to have been bound up, at least in part, with the recruitment of talent for an expanding economy.

Thus, at one remove, the establishment of middle schools has been linked to economic and political forces. The acceptance of a portrayal of education and politics as discrete areas of social life leads to the misplaced view that where middle schools can be justified educationally or even implemented because of educational considerations, then this can only lead to the further liberalization of the education system. Conceiving the problem in these terms, however, entails a misrecognition of the political significance of all schooling. This 'ideology of no ideology' where educational decisions are said to be untainted by political or ideological concerns, is ideology in one of its most insidiously potent forms.

Identity and uniqueness

As middle schools have developed, the realization has dawned that they are permeated by forces of a conflictual nature. Not least of these divisive effects of middle school reorganization is the often involuntary inheritance of teachers who are trained and experienced in the divergent and, at points, opposed systems of progressive primary and traditional secondary education. This tendency for middle schools, especially nine–thirteen schools, to be no more than a receptacle for two coexisting traditions with the maintenance of a break at eleven was a foreseeable one. As a result, one of the distinguishing features of the invention model of the middle school that emerged in response to these problems emphasized the institution's uniqueness which would transcend preexistent educational categories, and its common identity which would unite a fragmented teaching body around a set of agreed-upon ends. Counterposed against this view was a discredited notion of the middle school as a 'half-way house', a simple hybrid of previous traditions (e.g., Culling, 1973). As the number of middle schools especially of the nine–thirteen type has grown, the concern for identity in the invention model has gradually eclipsed those educational legitimations derived from the principles of progressive primary education that were more typical of the extension model. The later position of the West Riding, for example, is neatly summarized in their pamphlet on middle schools

(West Riding Education Committee, 1967), which provides an interesting contrast with the more extension-based arguments to be found in earlier documents (West Riding Education Committee, 1963, 1965).[5]

> We have felt that it is important to recognise the middle schools for what they are – a *new* departure, a new kind of educational and social grouping, and *not a half-way house* between primary and secondary as we have come to use these words. . . . These schools must find their *own identity* and must develop their own form of organisation and way of working in response to the needs of their children.

Once middle schools had been instituted, had demonstrated their inevitability, and shown that their nine–thirteen variant would be considerably more than an experimental oddity, then, during the 1970s, the active strivings for an independent middle school identity became more widespread in literature produced by the Schools Council, LEAs, headteachers, etc. The emphasis on the *unique identity* of the middle school has been achieved through four mechanisms, one of which I will discuss in detail later in this chapter. The other three are as follows: firstly, the very language in which explanations and descriptions have been expressed indicates an exaltation of new and innovative educational practice.

Phrases like 'a new departure', 'fresh thinking', 'their own ethos', 'an entirely new concept', etc., are distributed liberally (in both senses of the word) throughout writings on the middle school.[6] The rhythmic regularity with which such phrases emerge over and over again, imply the equation *new = good*. However, while the word 'progress' has often connoted advance and improvement, in view of the doubt cast upon the capacity of the innovatory comprehensive school to be any more egalitarian than its grammar/secondary modern predecessor (Ford, 1969; Bellaby, 1977), for example, we should beware of seeing any proclaimed newness of the middle school as a necessary virtue.

Secondly, the emergent characterization of the middle school has been detached from previous identities where it was defined in ways that related to existing educational institutions. The Schools Council, for example, rejects the *extension* model of the middle school in Working Paper No. 42. Similarly, Gannon and Whalley (1975) have commented that:

> Experience has also shown that . . . the extended primary school philosophy, while better adjusted to the middle years child, can be as constricting of the child's development in the sense of preparedness for the next and final stage of the 'continuous process of education' as the too early specialisation and the resulting subject-based learning of the 'formal' secondary approach. (pp. 17–18)

This resistance to possible incorporation into preexisting identities has sometimes led to a total repudiation of the vocabulary and rhetoric which are attached to these traditions. The Schools Council, for example, has asserted that 'the use of such phrases as "the primary school tradition" or "the secondary school approach" can get in the way of clear thinking'.[7]

Thirdly, the image of welcome insularity has also been enhanced by symbolically freeing the middle school from the undue domination of the upper school. This constitutes an attempt to protect the middle school from the constraining effect on its curriculum and teaching styles of the upper school's role in allocating children to occupational positions through a system of examinations. In places, there have been calls for *total* insularity with the recommendation that upper schools should be the ones to adapt *their* practices and philosophies in order to cope with the type of pupils which middle schools autonomously come to produce (e.g., Culling, 1973, p.93). Where there *is* discussion of the concrete ways in which the upper school might come to exert an influence on the middle school, stress is placed on the freedom from direct examination pressures, rather than on the subtle ways in which parental pressure or liaison between schools might indirectly impose considerable constraints on teaching methods within the top years of the middle school. The claimed consequence of such liberation is that

> Teachers of middle years children are more free from outside pressures, especially when transfer is achieved without an external assessment. . . . A great measure of freedom brings with it greater responsibility for decisions about the curriculum. (Schools Council, 1975, p.11)

However, the removal of this particular constraint cannot be equated with the removal of *all* upper school pressures. Examinations are only one means by which schools integrate and channel the young into society. Differentiation also takes place within the school where different pupils are exposed to different social relations through different classroom regimes. It may be that this differential exposure assists in preparing pupils for working life; for the varying social relations of the shop-floor, the office, and the boardroom (Holly, 1977, p.186; Willis, 1977).[8]

In the comprehensive school, this differentiation usually takes the form of streaming or banding. In the middle school, more often it takes the less harsh form of setting in the 'linear' subjects such as French, science, and mathematics, particularly in the upper years where the intergrative pressures are most keenly felt. The evidence available to date would seem to suggest that, at least in the nine–thirteen middle school, setting is extremely common (Beetham et al., 1973; AMA, 1976; Ginsburg et al., 1977; NUT, 1979).

The social class-based nature of internal division within the middle school is compounded by a manifestly age-based one, linked to divergent styles of teaching. Middle schools often have to employ teachers who are attached to either primary or secondary approaches.[9] My own investigations certainly seem to suggest that where teachers belong to the former category, they are more likely to have been allocated teaching positions in the lower end of the middle school, and where they belong to the latter, they will more likely be placed in the upper years (Hargreaves, forthcoming).

Whether an increase in the number of specifically middle school trained teachers will overcome such an organizational split must remain an open question for the moment. The important point, however, is that a unifying ideology of the middle school which stresses the unique identity of that institution is doomed to failure in achieving its object – the resolution of conflict – in so far as attempts to resolve such conflicts and contradictions take the form of appeals to teachers' professional judgement and other similar sentiments, to the exclusion of rigorous critiques of and attempts to change the broader structures in which middle schools and their problems are embedded.

A question of balance

Despite the insular, autonomous strand which runs through the ideology of the middle school, there are also references to the tensions between the primary and secondary school traditions which exist within the middle school. As a response to such tensions, there is another conception which parallels and often overlaps the unique identity model, as indicated in the following quotation:

> It is to be hoped that the attention now being given to the middle years will result not in the further introduction of unnecessary breaks in the child's education, but in the creation of a *transition period* that will smooth rather than interrupt the change from what is distinctively 'primary' to work that is distinctively 'secondary'. (Schools Council, 1972, p.8)

Such a conception creates a difficulty. The idea of the middle school as a *zone of transition*[10] releases it from a wholesale attachment to any previous institutional identity, but it also threatens the very coherence of the autonomous identity which educators seek to establish for it. Therefore, although it goes some way towards expressing and coping with some of the conflicts contained within the middle school, the transition model simultaneously threatens to undermine the rationale of the middle school as an autonomous institution with its own identity, and poses the danger that it might now be seen as little more than a hybrid of previous traditions, a mere half-way house. One ideological solution has been to replace the weakness of divisiveness by seeking strength in diversity. For example, Whalley (1972) has pointed to the diversity in experience and training of middle school teachers. Elsewhere, he comments that 'such a mixture is of itself an immediate and unique advantage' (Gannon and Whalley, 1975, p.8). But he does not discuss the concrete constraints which limit headteachers' options in allocating staff and which therefore tend to perpetuate the primary-secondary split *within* the middle school, even where there have been explicit attempts to overcome this.

While faith has sometimes been placed in diversity, the most elegant manner in which the contradictions of the middle school have been ideologically glossed is in the solution of *balance*. This notion involves a portrayal of different educational alternatives as extreme and as irreconcilable if accepted in toto. Yet, it is argued, there is good and bad in each tradition and the task which lies ahead involves selecting and combining what is recognizably good. Tensions are viewed as resolvable and there is much talk of 'marriage' between different approaches and of establishing 'a "nice balance" that has to be found between these two viewpoints' (Schools Council, 1972, p.70). The outcome of this centrist characterization of the middle school is a vision of 'middle schools for the middle way' (MacLure, 1975). Such views have, of course, been expressed in educational contexts wider than that of middle school debate, and have increasingly been articulated by members of the Inspectorate and the LEA Advisory Service. A reply to the survey by Neville Bennett, *Teaching Styles and Pupil Progress*, was phrased in just these terms.

> Almost daily, I see evidence that the majority of teachers have taken and are taking a stance somewhere at the centre of a line whose poles Bennett would define as 'traditional' and 'progressive'. This middle ground is consistent with a liberal, democratic view of society and enables childhood to be enjoyed as a unique stage in its own right. (Hardcastle, 1977, p.9)

This notion of balance provides an antidote to any so-called extremist proposals for educational change, whether these are progressive or reactionary. It transforms contradiction into complementarity. Pierre Bourdieu has pointed out the conservative functions which 'balance' performs more widely in social democratic thinking. Discussing statements made by specialists in political science, he argues:

> The most common rhetorical device in use consists of setting up two extreme positions (archaic conservatism – unrealistic revolutionism) in order to produce the mean position of rational and reasonable equilibrium. This structure . . . corresponds to the structure of the dominant class, characterised by the opposition between a fraction which is ideologically retrograde because it is threatened with decline, and a progressive segment . . . ; the bureaucratic fraction having as its particular interests the general interests of the class – that is to say enlightened conservatism which is opposed both to reactionary conservatism and blind progressivism. (Bourdieu, 1977, p.119)

Bourdieu's analysis provides an interesting commentary on the assertion that 'the broad general aims of the middle school curriculum, as other curricula, should "strike a balance" between the conservative (the "transmission of the culture") and the innovative' (Schools Council, 1972, p.23). While the legitimate objection can be made that Bourdieu's discussion of balance takes place in the context of *class* questions, whereas the issue of balance in the middle school curriculum is almost totally posed in *generational* terms of age differences, I want to suggest that the drawing of a hard and fast distinction between these criteria would be misleading. Progressivism and traditionalism are, of course, very closely tied to the education of younger and older age-ranges respectively. The juxtaposition of these previously separated age-groups in the middle school therefore carries with it a potentially awkward combination of the two traditions. In that sense, the problem is certainly a generational one. However, class factors are also present. The traditional secondary view implies a model of schools as transmitters of skills and selectors of pupils for manpower needs, and as disseminators of valued and, arguably, dominant culture. Such a form of schooling, as the Plowden Report stressed, is poorly equipped to meet the needs of a technologically advanced and rapidly changing economy and of an increasingly complex political system. For that reason, Plowden, like other 'progressives', argued that schools should produce 'flexible, responsible and adaptable individuals fit to participate in such a changed society' (para.496).

What both views hold in common is the expectation that, broadly speaking, schools should support the existing social, economic, and political system. The principles of class, racial, and sexual inequality on which that system rests are hardly addressed and certainly not challenged in any fundamental way. At the extreme, even where progressivism is regarded as too individualist in emphasis and as not adequately meeting the requirements of a competitive economy (Cox and Boyson, 1975), it is criticized for being indifferent to rather than challenging the perceived needs of the existing system. The friction produced by the meeting of progressivism and traditionalism is, therefore, as much a result of disagreements about how the changing needs of the social, economic, and political order are to be met, as it is the outcome of competing views about what kinds of education are appropriate for different age-groups. These are the materials from which any resulting balance is constructed.

The point can be clarified further by drawing attention to those elements which are excluded from the progressive-traditional continuum. These elements imply some kind of opposition to the existing social order and would include, for example, those practices, publicly condemned as extreme, which teachers at the William Tyndale School sought to encourage (Ellis et al., 1976; Dale, 1979). There, teachers explicitly aimed to undermine the existing class structure by refusing to give priority to economically useful skills and by giving positive discrimination to 'deprived' pupils within the school. In other words, they challenged the view that schools should serve the economy. In addition, they also encouraged questioning among their pupils (including the questioning of school rules), and sought to convert the school into an active democracy by crediting the head with no greater decision-making power than other teachers. In other words, they encouraged active political involvement and awareness at all levels. Conceptions like these stand far outside the limits of normal social democratic debate, and as such are not part of those views and arguments from which balance is constructed. It is in this sense that progressivism-traditionalism or primary approach-secondary approach are just as much *class* issues as *generational* ones.

Balance, as derived from social democratic ideology, therefore comes to serve a basically conservative function within the ideology of the middle school. Yet it is also always in tension with the practical conflicts and contradictions of the middle school which it misrepresents. In other words, the 'happy marriage' between previous traditions may daily prove to be little more than an uneasy cohabitation of opposed practices and ideologies, progressive, primary-based ones occupying the lower end of the school, and traditional, secondary-based ones, the upper end. The notion of balance is also constantly in tension with another major feature of middle school ideology; the stress upon uniqueness and identity. Nowhere is this twofold tension more prevalent than in the peculiar conception of the middle years of childhood as an identifiable stage of development.

Ages and stages

One of the main reasons why some forms of ideology are so effective, is their capacity to translate socially and politically based distinctions into natural, unalterable differences. The interpretation of phases of childhood (including *the* phase of childhood) according to developmental principles which take no account of historical or cultural differences (like Hadow's 'adolescent' or 'the middle years child'), is one instance of the way in which categories which have an historical and social origin are presented as 'taken for granted' expressions of natural differences. Generational groups are seen to exist independently of cultural or historical determinants, and are regarded as having their own needs, requiring appropriate policies to satisfy them. This enables institutional arrangements or political policies to be presented as a response to natural requirements, instead of as a product of administrative and political constraints. The category *middle years of schooling* expresses this process, being one particularly dramatic example of how political questions are translated into educational ones. It can also be seen as one way of overcoming some of the tensions in the ideology of the middle school, which have been generated by the picture of it as little more than a transition between the first and upper tiers of the schooling system.

The focus on *the middle years* as one of the keystones of the middle school rationale has sometimes been sharpened through conscious attempts to define what will be on the agenda of any debate about the nature and purpose of the middle school, most especially in terms of limiting discussion to *how* the middle years could be seen as a separate stage of development, not *whether* such a category might be valid in the first place.[12] On the whole, however, conspiracies are rare. More usually, the characterizations of the middle years of childhood are complex, and often exhibit great caution and verbal hedging, sometimes to the point of direct contradiction. Indeed, where the category of *the middle years* is dealt with explicitly, the conclusion is often reached that 'the middle years is not a discrete phase of education' (Schools Council, 1972, p.18), or that 'there is no such creature as "the middle years child", there are only children in the middle years' (p.44).

However, in more routine discussions, the language used betrays a reification of an administrative category, the middle years of schooling, into an identifiable *phase* in the educational career and development of the child, to the point where it becomes possible to talk about 'the 11–13 stage' (Schools Council, 1972, p.21) and 'the middle years child' (p.77), a notion which the authors had earlier rejected. The repetitive use of phrases like 'the middle years' therefore indicates a taken for granted acceptance that they have a thing-like referent.

Now as Holness (1973) points out, there is a lack of hard psychological evidence which would substantiate the argument that there is a particular phase of childhood between the years of eight and thirteen when there is homogeneity in either physical, moral, emotional, or intellectual growth, and when this pattern of development differs markedly from other phases of childhood. Fortunately, no writers on the English middle school have indulged in the conceptual excesses of some of their American counterparts who have coined a motley assortment of quasi-psychological terms to refer to the middle years child such as the 'inbetween ager' and the 'transescent' (Eichorn, 1966). Indeed, supporters of the English middle school have put forward an alternative solution of far greater subtlety, one which closely resembles the procedure by which an institutional identity of the middle school has been conceptually established. In other words, the organizing theme underpinning the notion of the middle years is that of a *zone of transition*.

The intellectual aspects of this phase are, for most writers, based upon Piaget. Such writers note that the middle years of childhood constitute a period when most children move from the concrete stage of operations to the formal (abstract) stage. In the realm of emotional, social, and moral development, the evidence is less 'hard' and vague references are made to the development of powers of judgement and discernment and to the quest for self-discovery. Since these transitional qualities indicate flux and continuity, there is a very real danger that the pillar of the middle school movement, namely the separate and unique identity of the middle years, will collapse. Some ideological device is thus required to provide additional support. In the case of the middle school identity, the notion of balance was seen to be somewhat effective in this sense. For the middle years, the solution is slightly different.

One way of lending significance to a transitional phase is to conceptualize it not as one fleeting moment in a developmental progression which is no better or worse than any other fleeting moment in its implications but, like the chrysalis stage in the growth of a butterfly, as a crucial formative period upon which the quality of all further life depends. Hence:

> The middle years are *the decision years* when children not only discover themselves as people but invariably develop attitudes towards studies in general and certain subjects in particular. (Gannon and Whalley, 1975, p.15)

In this chrysalis model, the middle years become reified into a developmental stage and become *the decision years*, a crucial formative phase requiring special educational care offered within an institution specifically devoted to the needs of children at this stage.

Throughout history, definitions of childhood and of youth have always been at least partly contingent upon processes of socio-economic change within society (Wardle, 1974). The category of 'the middle years' is no exception. In so far as comprehensivization was an educational response to and the outcome of changes in the organization of capitalism, and since middle schools arose partly out of the necessity to implement inexpensive forms of comprehensive reorganization, then the creation of the middle years as an underlying rationale for the middle school can be seen as an indirect consequence of such wider determinants. At the same time, its ideology has induced a misrecognition of the nature and significance of those determinants. A political and administrative category of 'the middle school' has thus been converted into an educational category of 'the middle years'. Accordingly, a social order has been transformed into a natural order. In the broader ideology of social democracy, wherever social distinctions (such as those based on race, class, or gender) are presented as natural ones, the political, economic, and administrative determinants which underlie the emergence and shaping of institutional, educational, and social structures are hidden from view. The portrayal of the middle school as a response to the educational needs of the middle years is one more instance of the way in which the social world has been depoliticized in social democratic ideology.

Generation and class

One of the greatest class ideologies is the ideology of classlessness, since it deflects attention away from the processes according to which rewards, privileges, and life chances are unequally distributed, and focuses instead on the very real but less significant lines of demarcation such as those of generation. The argument that differences of generation have superseded differences of class is central to the perpetuation of a myth of classlessness. In this way post-war popular debates on the 'youth problem' and the 'generation gap' helped to nudge questions about class off the political agenda.[13] It is for these reasons that there is a need to develop a particularly critical approach to the study of the middle school and its attendant ideology, elaborated around the generational category of 'the middle years'. We thus need to analyse the extent to which the ideology of the middle school has occluded questions of class by stressing a generational problem of ages and stages.

At this point, I must emphasize that I am not suggesting that problems of generation are unimportant and not worthy of attention, nor that generational groups are simply figments of our imagination. But the common treatment of generational groups such as the teenager in all-embracing terms neglects the complex mechanisms by which generational problems are themselves differentiated according to criteria of race, sex, and class. Within such an approach, therefore, class questions are assumed to be irrelevant. The result is that age distinctions become detached from class distinctions or even replace them altogether. At the extreme, youth *is* the new class.[14] Attention is focused on a social grouping which is both homogeneous and transitory (in so far as everyone is a member of it for a short part of their lives only), and away from the permanent, structurally embedded system of class division in society. The growth of concern about youth culture and generational differences was therefore a crucial element which, from time to time, contributed to the eclipse of explicitly class-based questions from public discussion and debate in the social democratic arena.

The ideology of the middle school, most especially its emphasis on a homogeneous generational category, the middle years, can be seen as one example of such a powerful force. Not only its characterization as a separate and identifiable stage of development with a set of intrinsic educational needs, but also its very monopoly of the agenda in debates about the middle school has made the middle years a particularly effective conception for the dissimulation of class questions.

In posing questions of egalitarian reform for example, even if a moderate liberal 'equality of opportunity' position is taken which notes with disfavour the correlation between parental class, pupil stream membership, and pupil life chances, it seems no less than astonishing that hardly any investigations have been made of how extensive setting practices are in the middle school, or of the deleterious effects which such practices may have on the performance and self-concept of pupils. But then there is little room for egalitarian questions (even of such a limited character) on an agenda overcrowded by generational issues.

In like vein, curriculum programmes have been presented in generational terms, thus reducing their controversial character (Bornett, 1976). Titles like *Education in the Middle Years* or *Social Studies 8–13* do not contain the stigmatic and divisive implications inherent in, say, *The Education of Socially Disadvantaged Children in Secondary Schools*.[15] The amorphous conception of the middle years does not enable disadvantaged, working-class, disruptive, or ethnic minority children to be identified. Indeed, in the most mystifying instances, the concept of 'educational disadvantage' is given a completely new meaning and is used to refer to the relative disadvantage of one generational grouping compared to another (mainly in terms of pupils aged nine to thirteen as compared to older pupils), instead of to racial, sexual, or class-based disadvantages (e.g., NUT, 1979, p.20). Drawn from social democratic ideology, the concern of middle school reform and debate with problems of generation therefore tends to reinforce the classless content of social issues which are otherwise imbued with conflict. Consequently, middle school ideology makes its own contribution, however small, to the maintenance of an overall conception of classlessness, and hence to the continued dominance of those advantaged groups whose interests that view ultimately serves.

Individualism

Throughout the ideology of the middle school there runs a thread which seemingly runs counter to the general emphasis on uniqueness and identity. This stresses (i) the *individuality* of the middle school's pupils as well as (ii) the necessity to build an *individual* institutional ethos in each school depending on the needs and constraints particular to that school and its locality, which can only be perceived and resolved pragmatically as they arise. The first element, *pedagogical individualism*, does not have such a specific reference to middle school ideology as the other elements mentioned, and for that reason I shall not discuss it here. It is the second element that I now want to consider. In this view, the identities of particular middle schools are seen to depend on the needs and constraints particular to each school. These local factors are not conceived of as part of any structurally coherent whole, rather they are seen as freely variant, accidental contingencies. The consequences of this conception are twofold. Firstly, it protects practitioners and administrators from the notion that the middle school is systematically determined by a wider set of structural forces of an economic, political, and administrative kind. Secondly, it preserves an image of autonomy in decision making so that the character of each middle school can be seen as the outcome of a unique set of locally patterned needs, constraints, and professional judgements, though within the broad limits set by the concern for a more general middle school identity.

In the most optimistic representations of this process, middle schools, like other schools, are seen to serve local needs, even at the expense of a coordinated national system (e.g., Burrows, 1978, p.18). Now whilst it is true that in a relatively decentralized education system such as the British one, the local circumstances in which schools operate are highly variable, to construe such circumstances as needs rather than constraints is to impute a benevolence to the process of educational decision making which may be less than fully justified. The limitations imposed upon the possibilities for middle school teaching by many such schools being housed in old secondary modern school premises, and the origin of such a situation in the fact that middle schools arose as a way of implementing comprehensive schooling whilst minimizing the expenditure on new buildings, are hardly an example of a form of schooling developing in response to educational need.

Local circumstances are not always discussed in terms of need, however. But even where the existence of constraints is admitted or even directly addressed, as in circular 10/65, the discussion still seems significantly flawed. This mode of explanation is readily apparent in Working Paper No. 42 where it is asserted that:

> The decision taken for each school will be unique to that institution in detail and will reflect the judgements of the professional people concerned. (p.21)

Later the authors refer to 'factors which taken together create in a school an atmosphere or ethos that belongs to that school alone' (p.60). They then itemize a formidable list of factors which include school buildings, environments, types of child, skills, enthusiasms and philosophies of the teachers, local traditions, the influence of parents, inspectors, architects, administrators, education committees, advisers, providers of in-service training, etc. My contention is not that these factors are irrelevant. On the contrary, my own investigations suggest that school buildings for example (e.g., purpose-built open-plan versus inherited secondary modern school premises) can have a significant effect on the way a middle school is organized (Hargreaves, 1978). Rather, I wish to point out that the treatment of these factors as independent variables deflects attention away from the structured relations within which such constraints are organized.

This penchant for conceptualizing problems atomistically (as small, discrete particles) has its roots in the wider political and social sphere where policies are conceived and implemented in piecemeal fashion according to pragmatic necessity (Robinson, 1977). However, as long as the problems of liaison, of the coexistence of two teaching traditions under one roof, of the effects of setting on the distribution of life chances, of the inheritance of unsuitable buildings, and of administrative convenience to name but a few, remain as separate, 'accidental' difficulties to be overcome as individual problems in individual schools, then the prospect for a relatively optimistic future for the middle school looks dim. No rhetoric about the identity of the middle school and no concessions to headteachers' autonomy in a decentralized educational system by way of exhorting them to develop their own institutional ethos, will remove the problems which headteachers and teachers confront daily, nor combat the political and economic assaults with all *their* attendant problems, which they are increasingly having to face.[16] If the middle school is to remain as a significant part of the education system in British society, then its personnel will need a much more powerful conceptual armoury than social democratic ideology can provide.

Whose ideology?

I have argued that middle school ideology misrepresents the workings of the educational system just as social democratic ideology misrepresents the organization of the society as a whole. In closing this chapter I want to point out that while, as I have repeatedly implied, various distortions are contained in middle school ideology, those distortions are only rarely the outcome of plots, conspiracies, or insincere statements on the part of headteachers, administrators, and so on.

Of course, most headteachers and deputy heads of middle schools are able to articulate and reiterate certain aspects of the ideology in a fairly coherent and systematic fashion. The reason for this is one of social position. Given their seniority within the school, they are at all times in a position of accountability. That is, they are frequently called upon to provide accounts of the nature and purpose of their institution and of the broader category of the middle school, of which their institution is an instance, for interested parties such as parents, teachers, advisers, inspectors, and researchers. In this respect they hold much in common with administrators and advisers who also find themselves engaged in legitimat-ing the middle school to public and professional audiences. The very credibility of heads and deputy heads therefore depends on their ability to rationalize their own middle school as well as middle schools in general. Headteachers, many of whom have been actively involved in the establish-ment of middle schools and the construction of the ideology which sur-rounds them,[17] are therefore able to draw on this systematic, albeit distorted expression of the middle school's function and purposes, in accounting for the nature and practices of their own institution.

The position of other teachers is rather different. Their professional, classroom autonomy insulates them from the critical gaze of outside bodies and, as a result, they are rarely placed in a position of having to publicly demonstrate their accountability. Their conceptions are organized much more closely around the principle of making actions meaningful to them-selves and rendering them accountable to staffroom colleagues, who are less interested in rationalizations of high generality.

The knowledge of teachers is much more fragmented in character. It is constructed out of diverse elements filtered through from middle school ideology and from impressions arising out of their own experience.[18] In consequence, middle school teachers talk much less about the general nature and purpose of middle schools and do not espouse middle school ideology in any clear, systematic form. Their social position seldom requires them to do this. Instead they speak much more of specific prob-lems such as the merits of generalist versus specialist teaching, which have more immediate practical relevance.[19]

In communicating the purposes and possibilities of middle schooling to different outside audiences, headteachers may believe sincerely, even passionately, in the views they put forward. Indeed, it would be grossly unfair to regard the distortive character of middle school ideology as the outcome of any wilful deception on the part of individual headteachers and administrators. The source of the distortions is to be found rather, at a higher level; that of social democratic ideology from which middle school ideology is one particular selection. The complex process of selection does not end there, however, for it would be equally unfair to suggest that there was tight agreement amongst senior educational personnel as to what middle schools should be doing or even be said to be doing. Each individual, through oral or written statement, makes his/her own personal selection from the range of explanations available in middle school ideology. The product, as expounded on any one occasion, is what might be called an item of *rhetoric*. These personal selections or rhetorics are remarkably varied though they do tend to fall within certain limits, given that all are constructed in the main from the range of conceptual materials at hand in the ideology of the middle school and beyond it of social democracy. To close, I want to give some indication of this variation by quoting two pieces of rhetoric, as spoken by the headteachers of two middle schools where I carried out some case-study research.[20]

The first, Mr. Kitchen, is head of a small, purpose-built, open-plan, nine–thirteen middle school. His characterization of the middle school is a mixture of the extension and invention types. Given the age-range of the school, perhaps the most surprising feature of this particular piece of rhetoric is the strength of the extension element within it.

> It should be an environment for learning, I think. I think it should be a happy place. It should be a place of opportunity as far as children are concerned. In terms of how I saw the middle school, I've often argued at the time . . . um . . . that change was *how much secondary, how much primary*. I think that *having its own identity* is concerned at this point. But if my back was against the wall, I would say I would have a primary-middle and *extend* the . . . the primary influence as opposed to a secondary set up. And so perhaps my idea of a middle school is my idea of *a good primary school extended* to meet the needs of children who are a little older and slightly more complex in their make-up. (my emphases)

Mr. Butcher, the head of a ten–thirteen middle school in converted secondary modern school premises advances viewpoints which seem to fall much more clearly into the invention type, though even here not all the elements (as I have outlined them in this chapter) are present.

> Well . . . um . . . a middle school should be *an entity in itself*. Initially it depends, I suppose, what the background of the . . . uh . . . each member of staff as to what . . . how it functions initially. But its got to have *its own identity*. It's not *just a transit camp* between the primary school on the one hand and the secondary school on the other . . . uh . . . but nevertheless it's got to take account, I think, of the *best practices of primary education* and also the *desirable practices for the lower end of the secondary school* which secondary schools were not always able to implement, because of all sorts of other factors. And they should be . . . it should be an amalgam of these two things . . . but it's got to have *its own ethos* and it's got to have *its own objectives*. (my emphases)

Such rhetoric stands at the interface of passionate sincerity and unintended distortion. It refracts rather than reflects the actuality of middle school practice. For that reason, it merits very close scrutiny.

Notes

1. See Hargreaves (1978) for evidence on this point.
2. Such critics include Edwards (1972), Marsh (1973), and Bryan and Hardcastle (1976, 1978).
3. My emphasis.
4. The relevant extract is well known.

   There is a tide which begins to rise in the veins of youth at the age of eleven or twelve. It is called by the name of adolescence. If that tide can be taken at the flood, and a new voyage begun in the strength and along the flow of its current, we think that it will 'move on to fortune'. We therefore propose that all children should be transferred at the age of eleven or twelve from the junior, or primary school.

5. In the quotation which follows, the emphases are my own.
6. Such phrases are especially prevalent in Schools Council Working Paper No. 42 and in Gannon and Whalley (1975).
7. Schools Council Working Paper No. 42, 1972, p.7.
8. This is not meant to imply that such preparation is uniformly effective or that it meets with no resistance.
9. Attachment to primary or secondary approaches does not *necessarily* mean that the person concerned has either trained or been employed in the primary or secondary school sector respectively, though this is more usually the case. For illustration of this point, see Hargreaves (1978).
10. For a more detailed analysis of the transitional model of middle schooling see Chapter 9 by Meyenn and Tickle (in this volume).
11. Some substantiation of this point through case-study work can be found in Hargreaves (1978).
12. See, for example, the account in Schools Council Working Paper No. 55 (1975) of the brief that was given to teacher working parties who were involved in its compilation.
13. For an extended discussion of these various points see Clarke et al. (1976).
14. Two examples of a classless analysis of youth are those of Musgrove (1964) and Wardle (1974).
15. The title of another Schools Council working paper.
16. For an indication of these political and economic constraints and their effects upon the problems of middle schooling, see Chapter 7 by Lynch (in this volume).
17. Two headmasters interviewed as part of my own case-study of middle schools had both been closely involved in the early establishment of middle schools and in associated programmes of curriculum development. The head of one school, for example, before his appointment had been headteacher of another school which served as a pilot for 'Science 5–13'. The headteacher of the other school had previously worked as an advisory teacher within the LEA, where his work

was particularly concerned with middle schools. Before this he had taught within a Leicestershire plan scheme in the Midlands where he was 'converted' to three-tier education. For more details see Hargreaves (forthcoming).

18. For empirical illustration of this point see the study by Ginsburg et al. (1979) on teachers' reactions to the Great Debate.

19. Of course, headteachers also engage in practical, specific discussions about the problems of specialism versus generalism and so on. What separates them from teachers is that it is they who are at present the ones who repeatedly confront outside audiences and who therefore have access to a wider range of contexts than teachers, where different kinds of discourse are used. We should note, however, on the basis of the chapter by Warwick, that if the base for genuine participation in the organization and control of middle schools were broadened to include greater involvement on the part of teachers, then the differences between teachers' and headteachers' speech would diminish accordingly.

20. There is nothing special about this example. Others could just as easily have been used. A piece of local authority rather than headteacher rhetoric would illustrate the point just as well. For an analysis of such rhetoric see Hargreaves and Warwick (1978).

CHAPTER SEVEN

LEGITIMATION CRISIS FOR THE ENGLISH MIDDLE SCHOOL[1]

J. Lynch

Ideologies are important operants for legitimation. They are like the weather; fronts take a while to build up and often appear in families, their impact can be forecast but not predicted, they are subject to ebb and flow, sometimes to relative stability, often followed by unsettled periods. In some ways they have a similar impact too, with men setting their sails and trimming to make the best of what is available, to use either the weather or the ideological winds of change to navigate to particular goals. And, just as weather is part of climate, ideologies, both progressive and reactionary, make up a network which we call the political orientation of a particular society or part of the world.

Previously, I have argued that the advent of the English middle school must be seen in the context of the overall ideological climate of Western society in the post-war era and its pursuit of the ideal of democratization (Lynch, 1975). More narrowly and explicitly, the working out of that ideal into the English educational system, its structure, content, pedagogy, and interpersonal relations, led to the much described reform of primary education and, supported by administrative convenience, to the establishment of middle schools in specific response to one aspect of educational democratization, namely the movement to comprehensive education. The commitment to the value of open education which is inherent in the middle school development, reflected a similar commitment in the wider society.

It is against this ideological background that the initial success in launching English middle schools has to be seen and identified in major part as the source of the effective legitimation of the new organizational form. Without the grass-roots infusion of new technology (i.e., ways of thinking and working by teachers), without additional inputs of finance from state sources, it is true, the achievement would not have been so smooth, so rapid, and so convincing.

The major resource was the good will, commitment, application, and creativity of the teachers involved, who were guided and sustained by their ideological commitment to democratization. That the teachers were and continue to be the major 'providers' of the resources for the launching is supported in general by the more recent DES (1979(a)) survey of teacher in-service provision on which I have commented elsewhere (Lynch, 1980).

Any major new innovation needs its greatest resource input at, and immediately after, launching. Like an aircraft, should its 'fuel' fail at that time, it is likely to fall. It is the crisis of the English middle school that, so shortly after take-off, the economic and ideological weather in Britain began to change so rapidly and to starve the fledgling of its essential nourishment.

The year 1974 in particular was a disastrous year for English education, and the identifiable beginning of the legitimation crisis for English middle schools. Significantly it was also the year in which the building of open-plan schools peaked. In that year, local government reorganization changed the boundaries (and control) of many local education authorities, some of which, such as Southampton, had played a pioneer role in the introduction of middle schools. Bureaucracy proliferated, chains of command distended, and a cold wind attacked the warmth of close relations between teacher and administrator which had sustained so much of the early work. Worse still, levelling began in pupil-teacher ratios, in capitation allowances, part-time staffing and, especially in combined first and middle schools, in the provision of peripatetic and advisory staff and crucial ancilliary staff such as nursery nurses. The number of advisers per head of school population declined by 10% between 1974 and 1977.[2]

The birth rate continued its downward trend from 863,000 live births in England and Wales in 1965 to 602,000 a decade later. The consequent worsening of teacher-pupil ratios in many local authorities combined with falling rolls in middle schools to make such ratios even more crucial than had previously been the case. As schools became smaller, their entitlement to part-time assistance was reduced. Such factors militated against those specialist teaching commitments which had begun to be a distinctive feature of the middle school, and led to it becoming little more than a glorified primary school, half of which was secondary chronologically but not financially speaking. Formulae for pupil-teacher ratios magically produced a 'welcome' fall in the money set aside for teachers' salaries, and schools found themselves falling beyond that limit below which a reduction in the number of staff jeopardized the maintenance of the recognized curriculum. At a time of standstill budgets, essential subjects could not be covered when a crucial member of staff left.

Three or four years later sporadic findings revealed, with the advantage of hindsight, the extent of deterioration in the education service caused by three years of cuts in educational spending. The 1979 Scarborough conference of the NUT was faced by an action report on educational standards and the need to represent a different meaning for the word 'standards' to that used by politicians so extensively over the previous several years.[3] In actual costings there was a drop in educational spending in the five years 1974–75 to 1978–79, due particularly to underspending. The Government allowed only for sufficient extra teachers to maintain existing standards and, in the same period, in spite of a DES survey of school buildings revealing bad conditions in many old schools, including no doubt many middle schools, capital spending on schools began to fall sharply.

Comments by the Director of the Oxford University Department of Educational Studies may help to locate these technical and structural problems within a wider ideological and structural framework, and particularly in relationship to the social democratic values of openness and diversity which were at the heart of the middle school movement. 'Democracy is much better adapted to dealing with expansion than with contraction or redistribution. . . . Power will therefore need to pass from the periphery to the centre.'[4] The force of these remarks is that they link the crisis in education, and for our purposes here in the middle school system, to the broader society-wide issues which are raised by Habermas, such as economic recession, the structural failings of capitalism, and the bankruptcy of social democracy.

Perhaps equally crushing was the gradual dénouement of the myth of the trendy revolution of English primary education. Evidence challenged the very existence of such a revolution of progressive methods and indicated that, where it had existed, it had reached its peak around 1969; paradoxically the year the first black papers appeared and the first year of appearance of middle schools in *Statistics of Education*, produced by the Department of Education and Science.

The Great Debate itself, initiated by the Prime Minister's Ruskin College speech, was set in motion by concern at falling standards, which nowhere seems to have had greater substance than a man of straw. A second major theme of importance to our analysis was concern with the inadequate reproduction of the social relations of production by schools or, as the preparatory papers for the regional meetings put it, of 'school and working life' (DES, 1977(c)).

In addition, survey after survey indicated the orthodoxy of English primary educational practice. A survey conducted by the Schools Council in the early 1970s, work by Professor Neville Bennett in 1972–73, evidence provided by the Bullock Report in 1975, research findings from 1976–77, by Michael Bassey of Trent Polytechnic, and most recently the survey of primary education conducted by HMIs from 1975 to 1978 indicated the continuing directedness and latent authoritarianism of English primary methods, notwithstanding the wider use of group methods, etc. In the Nottinghamshire research, in particular, the indications were that well over a third of teachers never had the children working on self-organized individual assignments, that it was rare for the ones who did have the children doing so to allow it to exceed four hours per week, and that barely a third allowed children to choose where they sat in class (Bassey, 1978). Moreover, even where teachers did not use traditional, commercially available syllabuses, they relied on such material to devise their own syllabuses.

Perhaps the *coup de grâce* in 'tilting' at the man of straw was, however, the still secret 'yellow book' prepared by HMIs to brief the Prime Minister for his critical speech at Ruskin. Giving credence to the by now widespread attacks on the vicissitudes of progressive primary teaching, the report, contrary to evidence already accruing from the work of other HMIs, proposed that the time was ripe for a corrective shift of emphasis. The primary survey published in 1978 gave the lie to that interpretation by finding that approximately three-quarters of teachers in the survey classes used a mainly didactic as opposed to an exploratory approach (DES, 1978).

But the confidence of the gradual bootstrap operation by teachers, which had sustained the broadening of the curriculum in middle schools, was further challenged by doubts expressed from elite quarters concerning the quality of three-year B.Ed. graduates, many of whom were now providing the specialist teaching dimension of the middle school curriculum. This is a curious but significant critical generalization, in view of the arguably more professional orientation of such courses since the publication of the James Report of 1972, and the certainly more diverse and sophisticated approach to professional studies in the B.Ed degree by the late 1970s.[5]

As if endorsing such concern, an article by an adviser and a college teacher, in addition to identifying the 'many things to many people' phenomenon of the middle school – always a major inhibition of successful legitimation – indicated what it termed persistent and specific curricular problems (Bryan and Hardcastle, 1978). Amongst these were the teaching of French, with several authorities considering omitting it from the middle school curriculum altogether, the effectiveness of mathematics and science teaching caused by the inability of many middle schools to recruit specialized staff in these areas, and the problem of appropriate provision for gifted children, were again the absence of staff with curricular specialisms prejudiced development.[6]

To these problems of the curriculum were added organizational and administrative ones which struck at the heart of the middle school and the reasons for its initial establishment. Middle schools tended to be larger than many had wished, and this meant a wider catchment area with consequent difficulties in the philosophy of maximum parental involvement. This particular contradiction was compounded in general by the need for many children to travel some distance to school and in particular by bussing policies adopted by certain local authorities, ostensibly in order to overcome English-language learning and attendant educational problems of immigrant minorities, but in fact as much in order to avoid a major change in the cultural characteristics of inner-city schools.

Then, too, the issue of organizing curricular continuity to project into upper schools which had only a further three years after transfer to prepare pupils for external examinations such as GCE, came to the fore. Again, the middle school had been born in response to grwoing concern about selection for secondary education in the 1960s, but by 1979 most authorities had in any case abolished selection and the remaining twenty or so apparently had few designs on middle schools. Further, the pressure on primary school curricula to conform to the needs of secondary education was less than that on middle schools, in some cases two years less! Already in 1974 a survey of middle schools by the Assistant Masters' Association (1976) included the above criticisms, and added others such as the relative lack of maturity of children who had attended middle schools until thirteen plus, liaison problems associated with the process of multiple feeding of many middle school children into a number of high schools, inadequate records transferred to upper schools, and not just the curricular ground to be covered but also the style of subject and teaching, traditional or modern.

Many middle schools, too, were not party to the innovatory zeal of the first births. Some derived from run-down secondary modern schools with falling rolls situated in inner-city areas, and they faced half a decade or more of boundary protection, conflict, tension, and a marked absence of innovation.[7] In some local authorities, members of the teachers' grouping, Rank and File, found themselves in explicit disagreement with the trend of development, and in some cases with both the school philosophy and the LEA policy on middle schools; a phenomenon which, to the great discomfort of many headteachers, sharpened in the period 1976–79. But these schools too were part, if not of the ideology, then certainly of the overall practice which had somehow to be legitimated. The highroad of educational progressivism on which the new middle school had ridden was gradually revealed to have its backstreets too, and the contradictions inherent were beautifully epitomized by the title of a book published by a former HMI who had been deeply involved in the development of the middle schools: *The Middle School: High road or dead end?* (Burrows, 1978).

The illustrative power of headlines to capture a mood, a crisis, a problem, or a difficulty, and convey it concisely and graphically, is apparent. Such a one was the headline that appeared in *The Times Educational Supplement* in late 1976: 'The End of the Middle?' (Doe, 1976). In addition to repeating the common criticisms of middle schools listed above, the article raised a number of other issues with deeper implications, such as, for example, that in numbers alone the middle schools were never likely to cater for more than 25% of children. It pinpointed the problem of lack of harmonization with what comes before and after the middle school and – again crucial in its legitimation function – stated that only a minority of middle schools set out to provide something distinctively different from primary or secondary schools, and that there were, in any case, two main types of middle school each claiming superiority: the eight-twelve and the nine-thirteen middle school. Finally, the article raised the question of the demands for greater coordination and control, the rationalization of curricula, and accountability on standards. These same demands had risen to a crescendo by the time they became enshrined in the Queen's speech at the beginning of the first session of Parliament after the return of the new Conservative Goverment in May 1979. The implications seemed clear. If school children were to be expected to reach common standards, this could only be irrespective of school type. Where, then, was the justification for a separate organizational pattern which complicated and confused a society increasingly susceptible to geographical mobility and desperately seeking the reality of an illusory stability?

As Education Pamphlet No. 57 states, forms of educational organization are not absolute but pragmatic responses to current problems made within a historical context (DES, 1970(b)). By the late 1970s not only was the overall ideological climate militating against the middle school, not only were economic and financial circumstances stifling its aspirations to organizational and curricular distinctiveness (and perhaps to educational independence), not only were falling rolls causing massive logistical problems, but the arguments of its own advocates were being turned and used against it; and this in spite of the establishment by this time of extensive social and academic systems to support it, such as publications, extensive research projects and conferences.

Take the argument concerning the most appropriate age of transfer which had figured so large in Plowden's deliberations. If eleven plus was not correct, thirteen plus could not be argued to be more correct; there just is no right age. Nor was the middle school pupil entity more identifiable than previous primary or secondary ones. Some argued that, had the same amount of resources, publicity, research, and writing been dedicated to the existing system in the same condensed period of time, the effect would have been educationally more advantageous.

Moreover, as the novelty began to wear thin, the compelling logic of certain developmental facts came to be tested against the reasons for introducing middle schools. Surely the progressively lowering age of puberty is a case for lowering not raising the age of entry to secondary school? Could not the apparent juvenility of middle schools for some senior pupils compound already increasing behaviour problems? Does the division into three tiers not introduce a further division into an already socially divided occupational group, particularly in view of continuing and differing patterns of professional preparation? (There are few PGCEs in first schools and few B.Eds in grammar schools.)

But perhaps the very efforts of the advocates of the middle schools themselves helped to cast the greatest doubt through the coining of the phrase 'the middle years of schooling', a new stage in childhood which clearly was not intended to include only those children in the middle years of schooling who were in middle schools. Once again, the myth of a distinctive structural entity based on a unitary or at least coherent ideology was exposed, for the logic of the term was that the middle years of schooling need not take place in middle schools.

The very openness of its ideological framework gradually came to be a major crisis in legitimating the middle school, even before the trend towards economic efficiency in education had received structural expression in the establishment in 1975 of the Assessment of Performance Unit (APU) within the Department of Education and Science. The individualistic, almost charismatic ambience of so many of the early middle schools clearly found the ethos of evaluation inimical. It offered no base-line for the evaluation of what could be measured, and little room for compromise on the importance of the educationally immeasurable. In a brief initial comment on this problem, Professor Alan Blyth (1978) foresaw the possibility of decreasing the attention to personal/social, aesthetic, physical, and even scientific curricular areas; those very areas which were seen by many to comprise the major curricular innovation of the middle school. Indeed, the writing on the wall for middle schools appeared in the 1977 Green Paper (DES, 1977(b)) and was quoted a year later in the comments of the Director of the APU when he stated: 'This undoubtedly entails for 9–13 middle schools a serious obligation to give the greatest care possible to assessment and record keeping' (Marjoram, 1978). Seen as a reassertion by central authority of its control over a divergent and potentially inadequately bridled sector of the education system, the comment is perfectly congruent with the growing pressure to social conformity and conservation in the broader society in the mid- and late seventies. It may also be seen as part of the process of dealing with what has been described as the problem of authority in English primary education.

As if sharpening the Occam's razor on which the English middle school appeared to be poised, in early 1979 the largest teachers' association, the National Union of Teachers, published the results of the deliberations and fears of its Middle Schools Advisory Committee. Fearing that such schools might become neglected and isolated, the report castigated the Department of Education and Science on account of its lack of enthusiasm for middle schools, and local authorities for their unwillingness to provide the necessary resources to develop the new image. Pointing out the extent to which middle schools had been accommodated by building adaptations rather than purpose-built schools, the report argued that adapted buildings often shaped and limited educational practice. The report was entitled *Middle Schools: Deemed or doomed?*

Before the strands of the analysis are tied into the wider ideological weft of English society in the late 1970s as a whole, there is one further institutional dimension which must be added, that of community involvement. In spite of a large number of cosmetic alterations in the composition of governing bodies, and notwithstanding the publication of the Taylor Report (DES and Welsh Office, 1977) and the issue of a DES circular (1977(e)) on the provision of information to parents in particular, parental choice and involvement had not advanced in essence and in their specific functions by the mid-1970s. True, the moves and documents above had begun to generate the components of an ideological dimension fully in line with the ideology of openness to which the middle schools owed so much. But the wind of ideological change was already turning by the time they appeared, and the momentum generated was insufficient to survive the major and broader social changes.

A survey published in late 1978, for instance, correctly located the time when most of the changes towards an increase in the number of participatory governors took place, as being in the early to mid-1970s, at precisely that time when middle schools were being launched with such enthusiasm, riding high on the ideological streams generated in particular in the 1960s (Sallis, 1978). The survey found that in spite of major changes in the composition of governing bodies, their role in finance was passive, and that there was little change from the situation of half a decade previously (Baron and Howell, 1974). The article makes reference to the ritual posturings which greeted and, seen in historical perspective, stifled the Taylor recommendations for revolutionary changes in composition, power, and control in the government and management of schools. Coincidentally, but not insignificantly, the same issue of the journal which reported the survey had two further contributions on 'the secret service' that is called the education system. The 'new partnership' envisaged for schools by the Taylor Report was clearly not to be a partnership of equals, either in power or in that prerequisite to the effective achievement and use of power, knowledge.

If any clearer indication had been needed of the change of ideological orientation in English society by the late 1970s, that indication was given by the change of political control in May 1979, by which date the middle school was firmly locked into the organizational structure of newly created comprehensive systems and increasingly subject to immense pressures of harmonization. Certainly by that date it did not seem possible to unscramble middle school systems, although it was reported at the North of England conference that year that some local authorities were looking at ways of tackling the problems of middle schools by a return to the traditional break at eleven. The only alternative seemed to be to change the nature and function of the schools. The pinpointing of this date is important for future analyses, because it may be mistakenly interpreted in future as the cause rather than also as the product. The Queen's speech to the new Parliament effectively identified the priorities of social control within the educational system, but those within the broader society had already been clearly enunciated in the form of huge pay awards for the police and armed forces at the same time as disruption was widespread in the education service over teachers' pay. All of these are now matters of historical report and interpretation.

Ideologies, transient and changing as they are, nonetheless provide a climate which serves an important legitimating function in modern society. They provide a spectrum of explanations for justifying different approaches to and measures for social control and integration, and particularly for reproducing the social relations of production. Schools have an important conserving and integrating function, directly related to the effectiveness of that social control and are, therefore, the institutions that are most likely first prone to feel the effect of a build-up towards a change of ideology, and first prone to suffer criticism when it is felt that the social relations of production are being inadequately reproduced.

Changes in ideology inevitably lead to legitimation crises in institutions still committed for their justification to previous ideological orientations, and trapped within broader structures already committed to that changed orientation. It is a measure of the robustness of the middle school, caught in the interstices of economic recession, rapid contraction, and ideological change, that it has thus far survived the buffetting of the ideological tremor which English society is experiencing, and which is the major reason for the current legitimation crisis of the institution. The precise 'dramatic significance' of that crisis is a legitimate theme of contemporary educational discourse and social perception, and an important dimension of the social conditions which gave rise to it (Freire, 1976).

Notes

1. The phrase 'legitimation crisis' is taken from the work of the German sociologist Jürgen Habermas and, in particular, his book of that title (1976). Whilst I am much indebted to his work for the general concept, it should, however, be pointed out that as used here the phenomenon is seen as much more ideologically

derivative than is the case in Habermas' work. That such ideologies are economically, socially, and politically located is not in question since, to apply the analogy of the essay, changes in weather (ideologies) cannot be entirely divorced from geophysical considerations, and the higher order concept of (ideological) climate is interdependent with issues at the levels of ecosystem (social democracy) and ecosphere (world order). The intended effect of this 'shift' in meaning is to heighten the importance of ideological change in the legitimation process, whilst at the same time endorsing the need for far-reaching structural changes in social democratic society, of which middle school change is one thread in one subsystem. The policy implications of the crisis certainly reach far beyond the middle school itself, or even the educational system.

2. Survey reported in *The Times Educational Supplement*, 3rd November, 1978.
3. For example, see Cohen (1978) and 'Educational Standards – Action Report 1979', *The Teacher*, 1979, vol.34, no.4, p.2.
4. 'Education: A new frontier', *The Times*, 18th October, 1978.
5. For further details, see Alexander and Wormald (1980).
6. This latter point is also raised in a DES discussion document, prepared by a working party of HM Inspectorate (DES, 1977(d)).
7. See, for example, an insightful and compassionate article by the Head of Clarendon School (1977–78).

Acknowledgement
I am grateful to Andy Hargreaves for his comments on the first version of this chapter.

Part III

CURRICULUM AND ORGANIZATION

INTRODUCTION

The curricula and modes of organization in middle schools are issues about which there is no shortage of writing at a generalized, prescriptive level or in documents produced in local areas in preparation for, and hence in ignorance of, middle schools. In the first decade of their existence, the attention given to rhetoric and to establishing procedures for organization failed to extend fully to the problems involved in the implementation and innovation of curricula. Inadequate consideration was given to the problems of policy making on curricular issues at school level. This section on curriculum and organization raises questions relating to the practical problems of implementation. Notions of uniqueness and identity are here related to the question of whether middle schools are different in only limited and superficial respects. The uneasy relationship between ideas and practice in middle schools' curricula is a theme which recurs in this section of the book. Each contributor takes a critical look at particular aspects of attempts to implement ideas drawn from the central features of middle school ideology. In turn, the writers relate the rhetoric and practical moves towards implementation to the constraints impinging on particular schools. Contributions consider the nature of and problems in curriculum management arising from architecture, staffing, attempts to implement particular ideas and modes of organization, and there is a deeper consideration of some key concepts which have been part of the growth of middle schools' curricula.

Wallace critically considers the relationships between the different perspectives which are applied to school building design – by the planners on the one hand and by teachers and headteachers on the other – with particular reference to the development of middle schools. The study focuses on two aspects of school buildings. The first is concerned with the characteristics of space provided for the activities of overt curricular aims, defined in terms of the middle school. The second and unusual aspect considers theories of the relationships between people and space, and the problems of accommodating and moving personnel within middle schools. An historical analysis sets the context of reducing cost limits and the provision of minimum spaces and facilities which corresponded with the rise of 'progressive' middle schools. The implications are viewed in the specific context of one local education authority which was a forerunner in the development of middle schools. Wallace's research provides evidence from a study of five middle schools within that LEA, demonstrating the effects of architectural constraints imposed upon the aims and practices of the schools, particularly as seen by the headteachers. She suggests that lip-service to progressive educational ideas justified economy rather than supported innovation, especially in relation to the introduction of open-plan school design. Identifying an uneasy conflict of interests, the study offers some explanation for the failure of innovation to take root in schools which were deemed to be progressive.

Various models have arisen providing principles around which the internal organization of middle schools might be developed. Meyenn and Tickle consider one of these, the *smooth transition* model. Officially it was claimed that this form of internal organization would gradually lead pupils within the middle school from the conventional 'primary' arrangements of the first school to the 'secondary' modes of organization of the upper school. The writers discuss the origins of this model and show the contradictions to be found in proposals to produce something unique whilst maintaining and combining existing traditions. They suggest that the implementation of transitional arrangements in middle schools is highly problematic and limited in extent. This argument is followed by two case-studies providing data from nine–thirteen middle schools in which attempts have been made to operate a transition model. The degree of achievement of the organizational aims in the two schools is shown to be limited. Discrepancies between intentions and practices are identified in features which show that the organizational patterns do *not* meet a desired gradual transition, but that abrupt changes occur at different levels in each of the two schools.

The ways in which salary-related points and scaled posts are awarded and distributed is a contentious problem for teachers. In middle schools the conflicts are paramount, not just in terms of personal remuneration and career potential, but because staffing arrangements both determine and reflect the influences which affect the curriculum of a school and the way in which knowledge is selected and organized. In the chapter on staffing structures in middle schools, Bornett considers how these are defined in the hierarchies of salary scales and authority positions. He discusses the implications of middle school staffing arrangements for the stratification of school knowledge, and considers particularly the relationships between year tutor and subject coordinator, two key positions in middle schools which reflect horizontal and vertical curriculum control. Bornett shows that this relationship continues to prove problematic in curriculum organization. Data from twelve middle schools are compared, showing how external factors affected internal school arrangements through a comparison of pre-Houghton and post-Houghton distributions of scaled posts. Studies of two schools, one traditional and the other comparatively progressive, show the ways in which the details of curriculum organization were negotiated by individuals within schools. It is suggested that the earlier impact of external factors on individuals within schools will be followed by a further disruption of staffing patterns through economic cuts, falling rolls, and demands for core curricula which will have important consequences especially for year tutors and subject coordinators in middle schools.

Derricott and Richards place middle schools in the context of the Great Debate, the Green Paper, and the work of the Assessment of Performance Unit. Current inspections by HM Inspectorate of primary, secondary, and middle schools in their turn, and the rapid pace of the accountability ideology in English education are seen as events which are likely to leave middle schools in a very vulnerable minority position. Through a well-documented review of curriculum theory, Derricott and Richards give meaning and form to some of the key notions of middle school curricular policies, particularly structure, integration, continuity, and progression. The 'unpacking' of these concepts is discussed in relation to the problem of categorizing diverse types of middle school curricula. These are identified in practice according to a typology of modes of organization and curricular decision making. Clarification of the meaning of the key concepts is stressed as vital in the role of working out curriculum policy at school level. This, they claim, is necessary not only for the individual school but in order to bring about a more adequate charting of middle school territory in general, in order that its assets might be more fully realized and made public.

CHAPTER EIGHT

THE CONSTRAINTS OF ARCHITECTURE ON AIMS AND ORGANIZATION IN FIVE MIDDLE SCHOOLS

G. Wallace

Introduction

There is a considerable amount of literature which bears out the assumption that any relationships which exist between the principles upon which school buildings have been, and are being, constructed and modernized, and the purposes to which these buildings are put, are confusing and contradictory (Pearson, 1975; Ader, 1975).[1] Furthermore, it can readily be observed that school buildings vary widely.

This chapter begins by noting key aspects of the different perspectives which are brought to bear on the problem of school design, by the planners on the one hand and by teachers and headteachers on the other, as revealed particularly in literature relevant to middle schools. The historical record then provides a background to school building development and suggests that space is an important factor in organization.

Finally, five case-studies of middle schools provide empirical evidence of the architectural constraints imposed upon aims and practices in middle schools. The constraints are viewed as they are reflected in the organization of the schools and as they are seen by the headteachers, the key figures in the implementation of school organization.

This study focuses upon two aspects of school buildings. The first aspect is concerned with the characteristics of the spaces provided for specific activities related to the overt curriculum, as it may be defined in terms appropriate to the middle school, and looks at the way in which these spaces may be seen to constitute resources for achieving declared curricular aims. The second aspect develops from theories of the relationships between people and spaces, and is concerned with the way in which the organization of pupils is related to the actual problem of accommodating and moving personnel within the middle school buildings studied. The latter process may be seen as significant in terms of the 'hidden' curriculum.[2]

Two perspectives

If the dilemma facing the planners is considered first, it may be noted that the problem of accommodating children in school buildings, interrelated as it is with the problem of cost, has a long history which is well documented by Seaborne (1971) and Seaborne and Lowe (1977). In post-war Britain, the economic problem was made explicit in government policy when the need to provide 'roofs over heads' for a rising and mobile school population, concentrating itself in new estates and new towns, was recognized as the only reason for new school building.[3] However, there was also a need to make the best use of existing buildings in declining inner-city and rural areas, and each local authority had its own unique problems to solve in the context of a national economic and social climate which will be situated later in its historical setting. Suffice it to say here that, whilst gaining DES approval for building projects was itself a complex and hazardous process,[4] actually building a school at a time when the real value of government-imposed cost limits was being eroded by inflation (to the point of their abandonment in 1974), tended to become an exercise in cost cutting.[5] Such an exercise has demanded a constant and progressive erosion of overall space (Baron, 1974), and the extensive use of industrialized building systems.[6]

In terms of the teachers' perspective, however, the problems presented by school structures need to be seen in relation to the functions which teachers are expected to achieve. Following Spady (1974), these may be defined as the custodial and controlling functions, which arguably require coercive power for their achievement, as well as the evaluative, socializing, and instructive functions, which arguably demand normative power (Etzioni, 1961). Furthermore, the literature produced by the Schools Council and by working parties of local teachers in the area of the five schools, leaves little doubt that the progressive philosophy of the Plowden Report (1967), which advocated an extension of primary, child-centred schooling into 'the middle years', had a significant effect upon the way in which teachers destined for the new middle schools were planning for them. This is a philosophy moreover that emphasizes desirable educational ends and tends to assume that pupils are motivated to achieve educationally desirable goals. It stresses normative rather than coercive control.

Hence it was reasonable for planners of middle school buildings to assume that flexible open-plan designs, which allow children to work in small groups or individually, involving themselves in many sources of information (Medd, 1976), might not only cut costs, but would also be aids to curriculum innovation in middle schools seeking to extend progressive, primary school practices.

Yet there is evidence that teachers have been slow to innovate along progressive lines (Pearson, 1975), while the Great Debate launched by the Prime Minister, James Callaghan, in October 1976, was symptomatic of a shift away from progressive attitudes and towards a concern for basic standards, a core curriculum, and a more authoritarian attitude to pupil discipline. The indication then is of structural pressures working in contradiction to child-centred theories of learning. Furthermore, it seems that manifestations of such pressures will be apparent in the physical structure of the middle school building itself (Foucault, 1977, pp. 202–228), while buildings, it can be argued, convey their own messages to those who use them. What those messages may be will need interpretation in terms of environmental theories.

Some spatial perception theories applicable to middle school design and teacher-pupil interaction.

It is the contention of this author that the human perception of the physical environment, which inevitably enshrines social processes, is able to affect those processes by feeding the individuals concerned with two types of data with which they will interact. The first type I will call *physical sense data*, and by this I mean data which relate to such things as temperature, lighting, smell, hardness and softness, and associated factors such as noise and general comfort levels. I suggest that, given the opportunity, individuals respond to such factors in order to achieve a balance which suits their own particular, personal tastes.[7] Opening a window, adjusting heating and noise levels are obvious examples. Furthermore, if the opportunity to respond to physical sense data is denied to people, to the point where they are aware of discomfort, then it seems likely that the social processes operating within the uncomfortable environment will be viewed with distaste.

The second type of data, *physical-environmental data*, relate to the human awareness of space, spatial relationships, and boundaries, which may be related to aesthetic considerations, but which also relate to the learned, symbolic boundaries observed in interpersonal contact. These are relationships and boundaries which have been explored in environmental psychology in terms of the concepts of privacy, personal space, and territoriality.[8]

From the evidence available, the indications are that human perception of both physical and social environments and the interrelationship of these perceptions, affect the way in which experience is evaluated. As new experiences are judged on the basis of perceptions affected by an accumulation of perceptions over time, and as it is generally accepted that experience is an effective means of learning, then it must be accepted that human preference for comfortable and attractive environments, human need for periodic escape into privacy, human reactions to the violation of their personal space, and human tendencies to 'mark' the territories they occupy with personal possessions in a claim to temporary ownership will, consciously or unconsciously, affect the way in which teachers and pupils in middle schools perceive and react to their environment. It is possible to argue then that a teacher in a classroom of his own is in a position to lay claim to it as *his* territory. This act allows him to make it attractive to himself, to use it to gain privacy from other teachers, and to arrange its furnishings to indicate to others how they are expected to behave. Furthermore, it puts him in a position of status, endowed by ownership which enables him to exercise surveillance and dictate to those who enter his territory how they must behave (Lee, 1976, pp. 70–75). Conversely, teachers who share rooms or spaces are likely to find the building less supportive of individual teacher status and authority. Hence they will need to develop alternative forms of pedagogical control. This idea is supported by Bernstein's concept of invisible pedagogy (Bernstein, 1975, p.116).

Yet perhaps the most crucial observation for teachers is one which can be drawn from the literature on personal space, and derives from the evidence that violation of personal space, without an accompanying desire for intimate exchange, amounts to being, or treating others as being, 'nonpersons'. 'Being a non-person or treating others as such, means simply refusing to recognize interchanges (for example tactile contact), that in other circumstances would be highly charged.' (Mercer, 1975, p.142.) Pupils who are free to move around at will in a classroom, or who are walking en masse about a school, must continually tolerate the violation of their personal space. As the adoption of non-person strategies is hardly compatible with teaching strategies, movement and interaction according to specific school rules (Hargreaves, 1975), together with the traditional pattern of forward-facing desks, to which pupils may be confined for much of the day, may be seen as serving to limit interactions between pupils and thus to limit the level to which tension is allowed to rise. For, thus seated, pupils see themselves interacting with the teacher, who addresses them from an impersonal distance. Conversely, it might be expected that allowing movement and interaction between pupils who are confined in a limited space will lead to tension and disorder (Stebbins, 1976), unless such movements and interaction can be effectively formalized.

The problem of providing an organization in schools which ensures a corporate order interrelated with the wider economic order, and yet promotes the essential love of learning which a humane society desires for each individual child, has been recognized for centuries. With the post-war acceptance of the desirability of making schooling interesting and attractive, the trend in school building has been towards open-plan design, on the assumption that it is supportive of progressive methods. However, the record of development of mass schooling is also the record of spending priorities. A brief survey of the relationship between building provision and spending by governments this century provides the background of economic constraint which places progressive middle school rhetoric in a more realistic context.

Some historical evidence

The 1902 Education Act legitimated vastly different spending priorities for secondary, as opposed to elementary schools. In the former there was provision for specialist teaching and classes of twenty-five scholars with a statutory eighteen square feet of space each. In the latter, there were still shared classrooms or, for the fortunate, classrooms built for sixty, with allocations of ten square feet per pupil (Seaborne and Lowe, 1977). However, the radical ideas of Pestalozzi, Froebel, Dewey, and Montessori were slowly infiltrating educational thinking as the century progressed, although the good intentions of the rhetoric which the new philosophies generated were never matched by the means to achieve them. Nevertheless, progressive idealism pervaded the Hadow Report (1926) and pressaged a spate of provision for elementary pupils over eleven years old. Where new schools were built, they contained laboratories, gymnasia and workshops, administrative blocks, wash basins, and indoor lavatories (Seaborne and Lowe, 1977, p.114). In Middlesex, somewhat ominously, an architect saved money by incorporating a considerable amount of glass into school design.[9] It is likely, moreover, that space provision varied widely. A 1924 report found that allowances in elementary schools ranged from fourteen square feet per pupil in Durham to thirty-three square feet in Derbyshire.[10] The report suggested that 'as a measure of economy', ten square feet for seniors and nine square feet for juniors were sufficient. No doubt some of these buildings now accommodate middle schools.

In the course of the war from 1939–45, some five thousand schools were destroyed or damaged by air raids and well over a decade later, in 1962, it was reckoned that half the thirty thousand schools in existence had been built mainly in the nineteenth century, with only six thousand built in the post-war period (DES, 1962). Post-war building regulations, which were born of idealism and which required that a school of 480 pupils provide twenty-two square feet of space for each junior, or fifty square feet if built for seniors, rapidly succumbed to economic reality. Cost reductions to the order of 25% were called for in 1949, and by 1951 architects were given freedom to experiment in order to cut costs (Godfrey and Cleary, 1953). In 1954, the statutory requirements were reduced to eighteen square feet and forty-four square feet respectively. Experiments in Hertfordshire reduced traffic routes but allowed classroom size to increase from five hundred to seven hundred and eight hundred square feet, while costs dropped from £200 to £140 per place (Pearson, 1972, p.24).

The overriding problem for planners had become explicitly economic once again, yet the educational principles to which new school buildings were to subscribe were found in the rising tide of progressive rhetoric, with its expensive implications in terms of space and resources. In practice, the deplored shared rooms of the 1920s now became legitimated as new open-plan designs for innovative team teaching.[11] Comprehensive reorganization became economically attractive, because of the desperate need to provide 'roofs over heads' for the rising numbers of secondary school-age pupils, without indulging in prestige grammar schools. Comprehensive reorganization, using middle schools, allowed twelve- and thirteen-years-olds to be accommodated in one-third less space than was required in a secondary school (Bryan and Hardcastle, 1977), and existing buildings were readily utilized in new schemes. Throughout the nation, the effort to provide schools within the cost limits imposed by government meant that where new middle schools were erected, there was a persistent decline in the overall space provided; circulation space was reduced and absorbed into teaching space, walls were omitted or replaced with flexible partitions, and prefabricated systems replaced traditional building methods (Smith, 1973; Baron, 1974). The traditional school hall was seen as an uneconomic use of school space and was deemed capable, in some schools, of serving as a dining area and perhaps also as a gymnasium.

If it is now recalled that middle schools were born to the accompaniment of progressive, child-centred ideals which were interpreted in terms of resource-based or experiential learning, mixed-ability groups of flexible size, team teaching, the integration of traditional subject matter in the cause of relevance, and a general belief that order could be maintained through dispersed patterns of authority, rather than by authoritarian control (Schools Council, 1972), it might be argued that open-plan classrooms, flexible barriers, and shared work areas are well-designed aids to progress-ive teaching. However, in spite of considerable enthusiasm in some of the literature and calls for, for example, 'an enthusiastic belief in the work being done' (Nicholson, 1970), or 'a new breed of teachers' (Pearson, 1972), the evidence was that structural pressures for formal, selective schooling remained (embodied, for example, in the examination system), that teach-ing was not perceived by many in progressive terms, and that many teachers found open-plan designs so uncongenial that they would go to considerable lengths to acquire classrooms of their own (Building Performance Research Unit, 1972). It is also perhaps significant that high-status teaching may still command specialist equipment in specialist rooms, while the Great Debate called into question the effectiveness of methods based on progressive ideology.

Field-studies

At the time of the field-studies which follow, the Great Debate was in progress. The county from which the five schools were drawn had decided, in 1963, to establish its first middle schools in association with a planned fourfold expansion of a designated area. The effect of inflation on national trends in school design may be gauged from the fact that in 1974, when the Government itself suspended cost limits, the Local Authority was planning its middle schools and adapting its existing buildings to meet the minimum standards of the DES in terms of space.[12] Table 8.1 was taken from this LEA's notes of guidance for planners.

It is worth recalling, at this point, that while the more generous post-war regulations concerning space in schools had suffered from economic cut-

Table 8.1   *Copy of planning document circulated to architects by LEA*

Middle School Buildings

In planning all new schools the central problem is one of deploying the available space so that the building will support a variety of forms of organisation, accept alternative uses of the individual spaces as effectively as possible and ensure that specialist facilities meet the specialist requirements as far as these can be accommodated in the overall 'balance' of space.

Currently all schools are being planned as closely as possible to minimum teaching areas and it is interesting to note the amount of space per child that the regulation requires.

Number of pupils aged under 16 for which the school is designed	*Appropriate teaching area per pupil according to the ages of pupils for whom the school is designed (metres)*	
	Aged under 11	*Aged 11 and 12*
Not more than 150		3.72
151–300	2.14 ⎫	
301–450	2.01 ⎬	
451–520	1.95 ⎭	3.62
521–700	1.86	3.53

These regulation requirements can be assembled in minimum areas for typical sizes of middle school.

8–12 Size	*m²*	*9–13 Size*	*m²*
240	602		
280	703	280	806
360	877	360	1019
420	1023	420	1189
480	1136	480	1337
		560	1511
		700	1887

Typical allocations of space according to use in several recent middle schools illustrate the deployment of space in more detail.

| | 8–12 | | 9–13 | | |
	A	A	B	C	D
Hall/Gymnasium	159				140
Hall	89	179	200	175	55
Gymnasium		(178)	198	173	
Year centres or groups of general teaching spaces	747	1320	1075	1185	814
Science	74	92	85	82	65
Craft	111	150	212	146	126
TOTALS	1180	1919	1770	1761	1200

Note
The schools used as illustration in this document should not be confused with the case-study schools in this chapter.

backs in 1951 and 1954, LEAs generally appear to have regarded them as the lowest possible minimum, rather than the norm. Hence the need to draw attention to current planning policy in Table 8.1. Historically, LEAs appear to have slowly, but steadily, cut overall space provision to a minimum which, on the basis of previous practices, they had tended to regard as inadequate (see also Baron (1974) and note 5). Furthermore, following the advice of the DES (Building Bulletin No. 35 on middle schools) of the 3.5 square metres (approximately) of teaching space per child, this authority aimed to provide about 2 square metres per child in any new classroom. (0.65 square metres is commonly reckoned as desk space (Oddie, 1964).) The other stated aim was to make 60% of the building count as teaching space. From Table 8.1 it may be seen that corridors and cupboards do not count as teaching space, but year centres, including overspill or work areas, do. Hence the planning of year areas in middle schools has followed the logic of economy in cutting out wasteful circulation space. A similar logic accounts for shrinking cloakrooms and the near disappearance of built-in cupboards. A study of Table 8.2 (below) shows how far the logic of economy had affected both new buildings and the conversion of the old. The widening of the corridors in school E, for example, and their redesignation in terms of overspill or work areas, was one of the adaptations to an old school which allowed DES teaching space requirements to be met.[15]

Table 8.2 *Characteristics of the five middle schools*

Characteristic	School				
	A	B	C	D	E
Age-range	9–13	9–13	9–13	9–13	9–13
Year became middle school	1972	1972	1970	1971	1970
Type of building	Built as primary 1969. 1973 extension of systems-built, two-storey block; three classrooms and work area on each floor. Primary classrooms converted for craft and science. Not all year groups based together.	Purpose-built, open-plan. Space described as generous by LEA. Distinct year areas opening on to shared work areas which also housed coats on open racks. Open-plan library and 'dirty' craft area.	1939-built senior elementary/ secondary modern. Quadrangle design. Original open corridors now enclosed but not heated. 1971 addition of four classes, open block, with shared work area: first years (6 FE) based in turn.	Built in 1971. Designated infant and junior school on plan; separate gymnasium provided additional space. Systems-built with four year areas, classrooms opening on to work areas which also house coats, on open racks.	Built 1929 as infant school. Converted 1940s for secondary. Closed for a year for extensive work before opening as middle school. Old kitchen/dining area converted to classrooms. New dining area, indoor toilets and sinks in widened corridors, these designated work areas by LEA.
Catchment area/ population	Predominant middle-class village	Predominantly working-class	Mixed working- and middle-class	Predominatly working-class, new estate	Mixed working- and middle-class
No. of pupils	396	465	629	530	587
No. of staff inc. head	17	23	29	25	26
Pupil-staff ratio	22.7	20.2	21.7	21.2	22.6

The five nine–thirteen middle schools

The schools for the study were selected because they varied widely along social dimensions as well as in size, age, and design, since the study of buildings was only one aspect of a number of researches undertaken.[14] However, given the history of English education and the course of middle school development, variation rather than conformity in design is likely to be the norm for middle school building. The research represented an attempt to discover to what extent the heads of the schools found their buildings appropriate to their aims and organization, in the light of the theories and literary evidence outlined so far. Information was collected in the summer of 1977. Interviews with the heads of the schools and walking tours were made possible, and the data presented here represent selected aspects of a larger study.[15] A local authority official was also interviewed and gave significant help in understanding the issues from the planning point of view. Table 8.2 sets out the basic facts about the five schools and sketches in some background detail about the buildings.

Data summary

The assumption that progressive rhetoric represented a consensus of the early aims and intentions of teachers was qualified by each of the heads in terms of the need to prepare pupils for the high schools, and hence ulti-mately for their leaving examinations and career directions. In spite of acknowledging these structural pressures, heads claimed that they aimed at a balance in their planning between the satisfaction of the needs of the individual and the needs of society. Personal philosophies appeared to vary along a continuum from traditional to a more progressive approach, and aspects of this will emerge later. For the present it must suffice to note that the problems of organization, for all the heads, were essentially practical ones, with progressive heads more likely to lament the difficulties of implementing more progressive methods, while traditional heads claimed the fact that their methods 'worked' to be the best criteria in judging them.

With the exception of school A, it can be broadly claimed that the more traditional heads of schools C and E occupied the more traditional build-ings, and that for these heads the major disadvantage was that they had no year areas which would allow year identities to be associated with distinct territories, and provide space for year assemblies. Nevertheless, the domi-nant factor in time-tabling in each of the schools was considered to be the provision of sufficient bases for teachers to work with groups of thirty to thirty-five pupils. Exceptions to this were, notably, slightly smaller groups for 'setted' subjects such as mathematics, English, and French after the second year, and for science in the laboratory (this was also predominantly reserved for third and fourth years). Apart from remedial work, time-tabling for smaller groups applied only to the half-classes long deemed necessary for craft work. Environmental studies, a designation covering a variety of work ranging from history and geography (in school C) to nature in the classroom (in school B), had not proved to be the progressive area envisaged in early planning documents. In all the schools, year staff cooperated on planning but did not venture into team teaching. However, 'lead lessons' in school B for a social studies course did involve cooperation over audio-visual methods. Music, religious education, and PE complete the basic curricular framework for these schools, although rural science complemented science, and art lessons, consisting of drawing, painting, and other activities possible for a whole class group, supplemented craft.

Leaving the specialist provision aside for the moment then, the practical outcome of the pupil-teacher ratio and the accepted purposes of the middle school[16] meant that, at least for the first two years, pupils spent much of their time in class groups with their own class teacher. The last two years saw the break-up of this pattern, but most groups remained large and everywhere classrooms were in demand. Many of the problems perceived by heads followed from this.

'Open plan is imposed from above. . . . The first thing that teachers ask for is something to close themselves in', declared the head of school A, while the head of school D regretted that his rural science room was too small to accommodate a class. In school C, the new extension had had its missing walls symbolically replaced with boundaries of cupboards, while in schools A, B, and D tables and chairs had been arranged into symbolic class patterns in overspill areas. French specialists (schools A and B) and re-medial classes (schools A and D) were candidates for these territories. The more progressive heads were conscious of the difficulties of using overspill areas in anything but a formal way. The head of school D declared that the opening of dividers had been tried but 'is used less and less as the super-vision of children is more difficult and these children seem to need the security of four walls'. The head of school B pointed out that she had negotiated for the coat racks to be put on castors, which allowed more flexibility than the fixed racks in school D's overspill areas, but that pupils moving out of class bounds had to take chairs and tables with them (there was no carpeting to sit on as an alternative), and that teachers tended to find the effort involved in supervising movement less than worthwhile. They did use one dark corner, where a single window was covered with black plastic, for their audio-visual 'lead' lessons.

The head of school D, however, was planning to divide up the small collection of books which constituted the school library and put them into year areas in an effort to make better use of the space. The corner designated 'library' could then be used for additional remedial teaching, an activity which up to then had taken place in the medical room cum deputy head's office.

Indeed, given the emphasis on resource-based learning in the progressive literature that heralded middle schools, it might be considered surprising that by far the most adequate library appeared to be that in school C, and had been inherited from its secondary modern days. School B's library was open-plan and sited in front of a main entrance, a fact which raised problems of disturbance and security. School E's collection of books was in a small room which had once held coats, while school A's headteacher had built up a collection in an area open to the hall cum gymnasium cum dining hall, again an area too noisy for working in.

The dual or even multi-use of halls also gave heads cause for complaint. School B was equipped with a single communal hall space, as was A, and both heads pointed out the difficulties of not being able to time-table PE in periods directly before and after lunch. In school A, pupils also had to circulate through this space when the weather was too wet for them to move outside the building between the staffroom and administration block and classrooms. School D's separate gymnasium compensated for the lack of space elsewhere but, as the numbers in the school were growing, that was already being adapted with hatches in preparation for its use as dining space. Again, the older buildings, schools C and E, were better equipped, with separate gymnasia. School E even had a separate dining space.[17]

Furthermore, the size of halls in relation to numbers of pupils had led to a decline in the practice of school assembly. Only the head of school A persisted with a daily service in cramped conditions. The head of school B held a packed assembly once a week 'for a sense of community', but school D never assembled as a whole. In school E the head felt he could manage an occasional full assembly when he needed to address the school, 'two or three times a term', but the head of school C only brought the school together for an end-of-year ceremony in the open air. Alternative forms of assembly were held by year groups or, in the hall, by dividing the school into upper and lower years. This practice added to the sense of division in schools, brought about by the move from primary-orientated to secondary-orientated curricula at the start of the third year. This change in orientation, which derived from the structural pressures to equip pupils for the high school, led to a variety of setting policies, all of which served the purpose of selection, and which tended to harden in the last two years of the middle school. In terms of building provision, the setting policy led to more movement around the schools, as top groups went to specialist teachers and also moved to the single science laboratory. Every head however considered that keeping movement to a minimum was desirable.

All but the head of school A were avowedly proud of the science laboratory and its equipment. It was obviously an area of special status. The head of school A, however, was endowed with a primary-size classroom which had been enlarged by incorporating a circulation route. Unlike the other schools, it was impossible to black it out for film projection and there were problems of security and disturbance.

One other form of specialist provision was for craft, but here schools varied widely. It was general practice for middle schools to have 'clean' and 'dirty' craft areas, with scope for a variety of activities in each, on the grounds that pupils might be engaged in a variety of activities at the same time. However, space available varied widely and school E's second craftroom was still in process of conversion. Again, the head of school C, with two rooms converted from secondary modern, woodwork and metalwork rooms, was in a favourable position,[18] compared with the primary-sized rooms in school A, rooms which were still equipped with primary-size furniture. School B's 'dirty' craftroom offered a particular problem in that it was open-plan and situated opposite a main entrance. The head had erected a boundary of cupboards for safety and security, and parents were raising money for a more permanent barrier.

The variety of craft provision and the fact that half-classes are common practice for craft activities, ought to have made the craft areas the most progressive within the schools. In practice, heads adopted a variety of time-tabling tactics in order to give pupils a taste of different crafts, but pointed out the difficulties for staff working in areas where the way in which equipment was provided assumed that they could supervise a range of craftwork simultaneously.

The final major area of difficulty which may be dealt with here concerns the problem of noise. Flexible barriers were not effective sound barriers and no subject was more difficult to accommodate, in this respect, than music. Planners generally associated music teaching with the hall space and in schools D and E, areas of the hall had been designated for music provision. In school B this concept had led to the siting of a music room at one end of the hall beyond a flexible screen. Given that the hall was also used continuously as a gymnasium, music teachers were difficult to retain. The head of school C was again the most satisfied as he had moved music into an old HORSA hut.

As far as resource provision for particular curricular activities is concerned, it can be seen that heads were constrained by the facilities at their disposal when time-tabling, and that economic and other structural pressures affected the notion of achieving a balance between the needs of the individual and the needs of society. However, the contention of the theories of space outlined earlier is particularly concerned with the effect of space constraints in terms of interaction with the environment, and with the relationship between the amount of space available and the problems of sharing it harmoniously. The generally inflexible use of space in the schools studied and the emphasis on class territory and organization may be seen as resulting in part from the expressed need of heads that movement must be restricted and controlled in order that discipline may be maintained. The general exclusion of pupils from the school building at lunch-time, unless they were engaged in formal activities under staff supervision, together with the 'traffic' rules and systems of control used in corridors during mass movements, may be seen as additional evidence that under 'crowd' conditions in schools, freedom to interact results in rising tension and disorder. Indeed pupils may be in a state of permanent competition for space unless they are 'in their place'. It is also worth noting that none of the schools was free of problems associated with temperature and that, for a significant part of their school day, many pupils would be either uncomfortably cold in winter, or uncomfortably hot in summer.

Conclusions

The most controversial aspect of modern school building has derived from the introduction of open-plan design. This chapter has contended that the introduction of open-plan designs to new middle schools has been accompanied by the progressive erosion of both the overall space and the facilities that might have made such designs operable.[19] Given that the statutory requirements of the Department of Education and Science are still those of 1954, and that these refer to teaching space only, thus allowing a considerable loss of nonstatutory areas, the effect has been to eliminate circulation space as far as possible and to create compact school designs. From the point of view of the users of such space, class methods of teaching which, even in open-plan areas, are organized to formalize and reduce interaction, are attractive to teachers because they aid the maintenance of order, while for pupils they reduce the tension associated with crowd conditions. Peter Newsom has observed that declining numbers in inner-city schools has resulted in decreased tension (Field, 1977).

In the case of middle schools then, it appears that lip-service to progressive educational ideas has justified economy rather than supported innovation, although it may be that where middle schools have been generously built, equipped, and staffed, the ideological justifications have been vindicated in practice. Nonetheless, there is surely a case for giving much closer attention to the relationship between educational theory, resource provision, and practice, with school buildings seen as basic tools for a task which extends well beyond the single, statutory space criterion for 'roofs over heads'. Given that the present decline in numbers allows something of a breathing space, the time seems right to consider the nature and the effects of the 'hidden curriculum' on children, confined as they are, in the mass with their own age-group, in their formative years.

Notes

1. This literature is fully reviewed in Wallace (1977).
2. 'This curriculum is an aspect of the teacher's real power and reality defining functions.' (Sharp and Green, 1975, p.218.) See also Bruner (1966).
3. Eighth Report of the Select Committee of the House of Commons on Estimates, 1953, Annex 5, referenced in Vaizey and Sheehan (1968, p.18).
4. For an account of this process see Griffith (1966). After abandoning cost limits in 1974 because of inflation, the DES moved away from approving expenditure for individual projects, to approving a maximum expenditure figure for each LEA. See also Dennison (1979).
5. In 1974, Donald Baron complained of newly built, 'mean, cramped schools (which) make life harder for teachers, restrict many desirable educational activities and totally inhibit others' (Baron, 1974).
6. See, for example, Oddie (1975), Seaborne and Lowe (1977). The LEA whose schools form the subject of the field-studies is a member of the Second Consortium of Local Authorities (SCOLA) and uses the latter's prefabricated industrialized systems in its new buildings. (See also Table 8.2.)
7. This idea has affinity with the concept of 'homeostasis', the motivating drive which activates a person to seek food when hungry and to sleep when tired.
8. Full reviews of this literature may be found in Lee (1976) and Mercer (1975).
9. See *Journal of the RIBA*, 1933–34, vol. XLI, pp.918–924.

10. Unpublished report in the Public Records Office, Ed. 11/173. Quoted in Seaborne and Lowe (1977, p.117).
11. In 1921, C. S. Phillips suggested that large groups of children working together would 'both improve the children's power to work by themselves and save large sums in rates and taxes' (Seaborne and Lowe, 1977, p.114).
12. This fact was stated on memoranda issued to architects.
13. Figures regarding the space available in the particular schools in the study were not made available, but these (Table 8.1) figures were provided as an indication of likely space. School B in the study, however, was described by an LEA official as being 'generously built'. Schools A and D suffered from basic plans designed to primary specifications, while school E's widened corridors counted as overspill areas. (See also note 19 below and Table 8.2 and also DES (1966).)
14. For a more extensive study of other aspects of these five schools, see Ginsburg et al. (1977).
15. See note 1.
16. See above p.123, 128 and 132.
17. The 1951 Building Regulations declared that separate dining accommodation was no longer a requirement.
18. The former domestic science room and 'flat' had been converted to two middle school classrooms and a store.
19. A favourable pupil-teacher ratio is also a factor here.

CHAPTER NINE

THE TRANSITION MODEL OF MIDDLE SCHOOLS: TWO CASE-STUDIES

R. J. Meyenn and L. Tickle

Within the formulation and development of a middle school rationale, a move towards what we will call the *transition model* of the middle school can be clearly identified. The Staffordshire County Council (1974, p.138) made the transition model explicit:

> The middle school will at the outset provide a transition from the junior school atmosphere to a more formal one which will be encountered in the upper school, and from the class teacher system to the specialist teacher system.

More recently Razzell (1976), speaking of the early development of middle schools, said:

> John Burrows, then chief inspector for primary education, summed up the mood of the period when he envisaged these new middle schools as embracing the best of primary and secondary practice.

It was from the *way* in which these were to be combined that the transition model grew, often supported by ideas derived from child development studies.

The foundations of the transition model

In the early discussions from which middle schools emerged and developed, one of the foremost characteristics of the middle years age-range was seen as being a period of transition during which, it was claimed, pupils could be characterized by a number of identifiable features. For example, characteristics noted by the writers of Education Pamphlet No. 57 (DES, 1970) were:

> The range and relative unpredictability of individual abilities; the powerful

effects of the expectation of parents, teachers and the children's own contemporaries; the general trend for all save the exceptionally able or mature to learn most effectively from the concrete; . . . and their tendency to congregate and work in groups.

During discussions concerned with three-tier comprehensive reorganization in Staffordshire, some stress was laid upon the 'unity in transition' of the eight–thirteen years period with regard to physical, intellectual, social, and emotional characteristics of the children in this age-range. Similar considerations were identified in Hereford and Worcestershire by Comber et al. (1977). The search for identity and uniqueness associated with 'middle years' pupils, and the development of a corresponding middle school rationale where attempts were made at 'cementing the diverse elements which make up the middle school (in) an attempt to substitute unity for contradiction' have been discussed at length by Hargreaves (1977(b) and in this volume).

Even before the advent of middle schools, and in areas of two-tier modes of organization, there was and still is a recognition of the desirability of the upward extension into the secondary schools of practices and developments in terms of the organization, teaching and learning methods, and curriculum content which are characteristic of primary schools.[1] These may be characterized by:

1 Concern for systematic instruction in basic skills and understanding, particularly in language development and mathematical concepts.
2 Flexibility in accounting for and the accommodation of individual children's needs, interests, and abilities.
3 Contact with fewer individual teachers for greater periods of time, providing the teacher and parents with a more accessible, intimate knowledge of all aspects of a child's development and achievement.
4 Greater opportunities for the integration of subject matter with accompanying ease of organization of experiences, with the implications that the teacher's interest and subject expertise must be wide-ranging rather than specialized.

An equally powerful downward influence of organization and approaches characteristic of the secondary school was also seen as desirable.[2] Such characteristics are identifiable as:

1 A mainly specialist, subject-based time-table with the provision of

specialist staff and facilities.

2 Departmental organizational hierarchy largely subject-based with often separate pastoral provision.

3 A structured, continuous curriculum content determined mainly by examination systems.

4 The movement of pupils between teaching spaces with associated interruption of learning and sharing of rooms by staff and pupils.

These notions were, and in some cases still are, symptomatic of desires to overcome the problems of abrupt change and meet the needs of a meaningful continuum across the age of transfer at eleven plus.

With the growth of the idea that an alternative age of transfer might be desirable, educational policy and rhetoric concentrated upon the central issue of the provision of schooling which would cater for all the recognized needs of children of the middle years age-range. In particular, ways were sought which would overcome the problems of abrupt change at eleven, providing instead a transitional period of education, drawing upon the advantages of both primary and secondary organization which were deemed most appropriate to children of this age-range.[3] The Scottish Council, for example, made positive recommendations that the transition from primary to secondary education should extend over the whole period from age ten to age thirteen. These years, it was said, should be regarded as a transitional period, during which there is a gradual change in curriculum and style of teaching (Nisbet and Entwistle, 1966).

Middle schools came to be seen as potentially achieving such an aim within one institution. The DES (1970(a)) recognized that in organizational terms the characteristics of the primary school ought to combine with those of the secondary school to provide a gradual transition within the middle schools.

> For the youngest children there is certainly much to be said for the flexibility towards which primary schools are moving. At this stage there are some ndoubted advantages in the class teacher having responsibility for most of the curriculum. . . . As children become older, a greater measure of differentiation in the curriculum becomes suitable. . . . By the time the children near the end of the middle school, some will certainly be ready for a more elaborate framework round which to organise their knowledge. (Education Pamphlet No. 57, pp.15–16)

The Schools Council (1972) project *Education in the Middle Years* admitted in its first pages that the creation of middle schools was especially significant for views about curricula related to the middle years in *all* types of schools. The project recognized the pressures of primary and secondary school traditions upon those views, but determined that:

> It would seem desirable for this new departure in our educational organisation to be marked by an attempt to produce a curriculum based not on an amalgam of existing traditions for younger and for older children but on fresh thinking about how children of this age range might best be educated. (p.7)

In the following paragraph, the extent and limitations of the 'fresh thinking' on the part of the project team were defined as the transition model, which took on further momentum and justification.

> The task of working out a curriculum for the middle years must be done bearing in mind the single sweep of a total education bringing a child from infancy through childhood and adolescence to adulthood. It is to be hoped that attention now being given to the middle years will result not in the introduction of further unnecessary breaks in the child's education but in the creation of a *transition* period that will *smooth* rather than interrupt the change from work that is distinctively 'primary' to work that is distinctively 'secondary'. (p.8, our emphases)

At this relatively early stage in the development of both rhetoric and practice relating to middle schools, the foundations for a model of a *transitional* institution in which *smoothness* of change would be possible, were clearly established. The model became a part of the rationale of middle school development and can be identified widely in literature relating to middle schools.

The transition model – a reality?

The introduction and development of middle schools in the late 1960s and early 1970s as part of comprehensive reorganization was accompanied by a number of characteristics which have come under scrutiny. Edwards (1972, p.27), for instance, pointed to the overstated ideological justifications used by LEAs for the introduction of a form of school organization that had not been tried or validated. More recently, one of the widely recognized outcomes of the problems faced by those involved in the introduction of middle schools has been a diversity of types of middle school organization, even within a small area. Doe (1976), in an article entitled 'The End of the Middle', reflected this graphically.

> Within a single authority it is possible to have ex-secondary modern-turned-middle schools which launch 9 year olds straight into a secondary school style

timetable of specialist teachers; middle schools owing more to the mother hen approach of primary schools; and those which are trying to forge a weaning link between the two styles, as well as opening up new areas of education such as interdisciplinary work. . . .

The Schools Council (1972) also recognized that some middle schools were more like primary schools, others like secondary schools, some offering two years of each approach, with a minority attempting to provide a distinctively different approach and organization.

Some of the reasons for this variety of types have been discussed by recent commentators on middle school development. In a number of cases the writers identified some of the problems of the intermediate position of middle schools in a three-tier system of school organization. In particular discussion has been concerned with recognized difficulties in overcoming the sharp division between the patterns of organization, and conflicting views of the curriculum associated with primary and secondary schools. Griffin-Beale (1977), suggesting that there was little evidence that middle schools operate curricula which are 'genuinely new' in overcoming the primary-secondary split at eleven plus, described them as being 'not so much virgin soil as no-man's land with both primary and secondary approaches vying for influence'. Doe (1976) recognized the same situation when he described middle schools as catering for 'an awkward age group on the plateau between the need for basic skills teaching in the primary school and the pressures of examinations in the secondary school'. The traditional division between primary and secondary orientations has continued as a pervasive difficulty for middle schools, although the location of the split in relation to the age of the pupils varies.[4] The conflict is a theme of concern at levels of local government, administration, advisory service, headteachers, teachers, and pupils.[5] This conflict underlies much of the development of the rationale of middle schools and has also acted as an underlying feature of middle school practice.

Blyth and Derricott (1977, p.96) propose a model of the middle school curriculum in terms of 'areas of potential conflict between primary and secondary traditions'. These conflicts have been accompanied by more general innovatory problems in some schools. Edwards (1972, p.49) drew attention to proposals for the introduction of 'sophisticated teaching methods' such as team teaching, the integrated day, and interdisciplinary studies into middle schools which, he said, were ignored in early discussions about middle schools. If it had been ignored in 1972, it would appear to have gained currency in discussion more recently. Ginsburg et al. (1977) found that mixed-ability arrangements seemed to be 'losing favour' in the schools they studied. Some of the reasons which they identified were the call for 'standards' and 'accountability' resulting from the Great Debate,[6] the demands of mixed-ability organization on the teachers (without corresponding reduction in class sizes), the lower effectiveness (as seen by teachers) of traditional didactic roles with heterogeneous school classes, and increasing pressure on the curriculum from high schools.

In a summary of the 'unique features' of the role of middle school teachers in their study, Ginsburg et al. identified a number of constraints impinging upon teachers in middle schools. They say that these teachers:

1 have been charged with the responsibility of achieving a smooth transition from a primary to a secondary type instructional approach within one institution.
2 must work with and meet the pressures of colleagues from both the first and high schools.
3 face built-in assumptions of extensive relations with colleagues.
4 in the aura of innovation are subject to considerable ambiguity and confusion as to the most appropriate way to perform their role.

It was in this kind of light that Doe (1976) wrote:

> There are those who hope the minority of middle schools will have a creative influence on the education of 8–13's wherever they go to school. But the minority within this minority which has tried to do anything different has to grapple with serious questions about how and what should be taught, and middle school teachers are left wondering whether a different approach does their pupils or themselves any good.

To the extent that a different approach entails, or is seen to entail, the bringing together of conflicting elements into a smooth transition, a specific form of provision has been sought. Attempts to embrace both primary and secondary school approaches have continued in some middle schools in response to the adoption of the *transition model*. Ginsburg et al. (1977, p.17), reporting their research in five middle schools, say that the resolution of this conflict is a continuing process, 'an attempt to define the middle schools' instructional model'.

The requirement for the type of provision which might provide this resolution, as we have already discussed, was and is seen as the development of a new form of organizational structure *within* the middle school. We hope to show that with the commitment and endeavour in two particular nine–thirteen middle schools, patterns of organization have been devised in an *attempt* to provide for the requirements of gradual development and smooth transition. By documenting three selected organizational factors, an attempt has been made to assess the degree to which this has been realized.

Two case-studies[7]

School A is a former girls' secondary modern school, built in 1959, which became a middle school as the result of reorganization to comprehensive education, the implementation of which began in September 1974, and was phased over a two-year period. The headteacher was appointed in 1970 in the knowledge that reorganization was impending, and with a strong commitment towards the idea of middle schools. There was intensive preparation over two years involving all teachers in the area to try to ensure a continuum in the curriculum from five–sixteen or eighteen years. The buildings are essentially unchanged from the original secondary provision, with the exception of provision for boys' showers and toilets, and the conversion of existing craftrooms to accommodate technical studies. Teaching spaces are at a premium with 'temporary' accommodation widely used. In 1977 there were approximately 540 pupils and 24 teachers. On reorganization, the school was left with most of the existing, mainly female, specialist staff intact. The normal processes of change – retirements, transfers, and pregnancies – have led to the present staff mixture of ex-secondary, ex-primary, and a few initial appointees. The school has seven feeder schools, all except one in rural villages, and is itself one of three middle schools (all ex-secondary) serving the area and feeding the same upper (ex-grammar) school.

School B is a purpose-built middle school which was opened in 1970–71. The original head had been involved in the earlier working parties that set up the three-tier system in the county, and was (and still is, as is the present head) very committed to making middle schools 'work'. The school serves a new town estate and when it opened had children from eighty-five different schools. Now the area has settled down there are two main feeder schools and one other middle school in the pyramid. There are 530 pupils and a staff of 25 (including the head). Fifteen out of 22 teachers (i.e., excluding the head, deputy head, and senior mistress) were appointed direct from college.

Table 9.1 *Pupil time allocation – Teacher contact*
School A

	A % Time with form teacher	B Subjects or curriculum areas with form teacher	C Number of other teachers met	D For which subjects or curriculum areas	E % Time with other teachers
1st year (4 forms)	75%	All except those in section D	4	Music.........................7.5 French ....7.5 PE.............................7.5 Library.......................2.5	25%
2nd year (4 forms)	67.5%	All except those in section D	5	Music.........................7.5 French ....7.5 PE/games ....10 Library.......................2.5 Science 5	32.5%
3rd year (5 forms)	20%	Humanities and science Some in maths and English sets Humanities, science Some in maths and English sets Humanities Some in English sets Humanities Some in maths and games Humanities and RE Some in maths and English sets	10	Music.........................5 French ....10 PE/games....................7.5 Library.......................2.5 Science......................10 English ....12.5 Maths ....15 Art ....5 Technical studies ....5 Home economics..........5 RE 2.5	80%
4th year (5 forms)	5%	Maths French PE/games Some technical studies Some English	13	Music.........................7.5 French .... 10 PE/games....................7.5 Library.......................2.5 Science ....7.5 English .... 12.5 Maths ....15.0 Art ....5 Technical studies ....5 Home economics..........5 RE ....2.5 Geography.................7.5 History......................7.5	

Table 9.1 *Pupil time allocation – Teacher contact*

School B

| | A
% Time with form teacher | B
Subject or curriculum areas with form teacher | C
Number of other teachers met | D
For which subjects or curriculum areas | E
% Time with other teachers within year | | |
					year	others	
1st year (4 class groups)	67½%	All except those in section D Maths except express and remedial	5	French – year team plus specialist Maths – year team plus specialist Music – year team plus specialist Design – year team plus specialist PE – year team	2½% 7½% 2½% 2½% 5%	5% 2½% 2½% 2½% —	32½%
		withdrawal Some in French Some in music Some in design Some in PE					
2nd year (4 class groups)	55%	All except those in section D Some in Maths sets Some in French Some in design Some in PE/games	6	French – year team Maths – year team plus two specialists Music – year team Design – year team plus specialist PE/games/swimming	5% 9% 5% 2½% 15%	— 6% — 2½% —	45%
3rd year (4 class groups)	30%	English Integrated studies Some in design Some in PE/games Some in maths sets Some in French sets	9	English – year team Integrated studies – year team French – year team plus specialist Maths – year team plus specialist Science – year team plus specialist Music – specialist Design – year team plus specialist PE/games/swimming – team plus specialist	5% 7½% 5% 10% 5% — 2½% 10%	— — 5% 5% 5% 5% 2½% 2½%	70%
4th year (4 class groups)	20%	Integrated studies Some in English sets Some in French sets Some in maths sets Some in design Some in PE/games PE/games	10	English – year team plus specialist Integrated studies – year team RE – year team plus specialist French – year team plus specialist Maths – year team plus two specialist Science – year team plus specialists Music – specialist Design – year team plus specialist PE/games/swimming – team plus specialist	12% 5% 1% 7% 10% 5% — 5% 5%	3% — 1½% 3% 5% 5% 2½% 5%	80%

Table 9.2   *Pupil time allocation – Teaching spaces and resources*

School A

	A % Time spent in home base or classroom	B Subjects or curriculum areas in home base or classroom	C % Time out of home classroom in other nonspecialist teaching areas	D For which subjects or curriculum areas	E % Time in specialist areas	F Subjects studied in specialist areas
1st year	87.5%	All except those in section F	—	—	12.5%	Music .... 5% PE/games .... 5% Library 2½%
2nd year	82.5%	All except those in section F	2.5%	TV broadcasts (humanities)	15%	Music .... 5% PE/games .... 5% Library .... 2½% Science 2½%
3rd year	20%	Humanities	40%	Maths .... 15% English .... 12½% French .... 10% RE 2½%	40%	Music .... 5% PE/games .... 7½% Library .... 2½% Science .... 10% Art .... 5% Tech. studies ..... 5% HE/nwk 5%
4th year	2.5%		55%	Maths .... 15% English .... 12½% French/German ... 10% Geography/History ... 15% RE 2½%	42.5%	Maths .... 7½% PE/games .... 10% Library .... 2½% Science .... 7½% Art .... 5% Tech. studies ..... 5% HE/nwk 5%

	A % Time spent in home base or classroom	B Subjects or curriculum areas in home base or classroom	C % Time out of home classroom in other non-specialist teaching areas	D For which subject or curriculum areas	E % Time in specialist areas	F Subjects studied in specialist areas
1st year	70%	English Integrated studies French Science Some music Some design Some maths	10%	Maths 10%	20%	Some music ....2½% Some design ....2½% PE/games/ swimming 15%
2nd year Some music2½%	55%	English Integrated studies French Some design Some maths Som	22½%	Maths ....15% Science............................5% Some music 2½%	22½%	Some design ....5% Some music..............2½% PE/games/ swimming 15%
3rd year	32½%	Some English Integrated studies Some in French sets Some in maths sets	32½%	French ....10% Maths ....15% Some music ....2½% Some English 5%	35%	Science...........................10% Design ....10% Some music ....2½% PE/games/ swimming 12½%
4th year	20%	Some integrated studies Some in English sets Some in French sets Some in Maths sets	47½%	English ....15% Some integrated studies...........................5% French...........................10% Maths ....15% RE 2.5%	32½%	Science...........................10% Music...........................2½% Design ....10% PE/games 10%

Table 9.3: *Pupil ability and social groupings*

School A

	Mixed-Ability Grouping				Other Grouping				
	Individual learning	Grouping within a class	Class teaching as one group	Divided or re-grouped classes	Remedial withdrawal	Express group withdrawal	Setting	Streaming	Different sex groups
1st year	English Maths French Humanities Music Science PE/games Art/crafts				Language (reading) Maths (number)				Games
2nd year	English Maths French Humanities Music Science PE/games Art/crafts				Language (reading) Maths (number)				Games
3rd year	Art/HE/Tech. studies Humanities Science Music PE/games/swimming				Language (reading)		English French Maths		PE Games Swimming
4th year	Art/HE/Tech. studies Humanities Science Music PE/games/swimming				Language (reading)		English French Maths		PE Games Swimming

Table 9.3: *Pupil ability and social groupings*

School B

	Mixed-Ability Grouping				Other Grouping				
	Individual learning	Grouping within a class	Class teaching as one group	Divided or re-grouped class	Remedial with-drawal	Express group with-drawal	Setting	Streaming	Different sex groups
1st year	English, Integrated studies, French, Science, Music, PE/games/swimming, Design				English, Integrated studies, Maths, Science	Maths			Games
2nd year	English, Integrated studies, French, Science, Music, PE/games/swimming, Design				English		Maths		Games
3rd year	Some English, Integrated Studies, Science, PE/games/swimming, Design			French	English		Some English, Maths, French		Games
4th year	Integrated studies, Music, PE/games/swimming, Design			Some science, French	English		English, French, Maths, Some science		PE, Games

The preceding tables present an analysis of three specific organizational factors which reflect the attempt to meet the requirements of gradual development. These are:

Table 9.1   Pupil time allocation and teacher contact.
Table 9.2   Pupil time allocation to teaching spaces and resources.
Table 9.3   Pupil ability and social grouping.

This information is examined for the four years of each of these nine–thirteen years middle schools, and shows some aspects of the change in organizational patterns within each, as well as the differences between the two schools. Table 9.1 looks at the amount of time pupils spend with their own teacher, and for which curriculum areas. It also identifies the number of other teachers with whom pupils have contact and the relative time and curriculum areas involved. Table 9.2 looks at the amount of time pupils spend in their 'home' room, other rooms, and specialist areas, and for which parts of the curriculum. Table 9.3 looks at the forms of grouping – mixed ability, setting, express group, and remedial withdrawal – being employed in both schools. It is recognized by those involved in organizational decision making within the two schools, and will be clearly seen from the tables, that there are problems yet to be overcome.

There are some conditional factors which we would point out before analysing the tables.

1 We recognize that certain other identifiable variables portraying similar transitional characteristics could also be selected for analysis.
2 Structure of curriculum content has not been analysed as it forms another dimension worthy of study in itself (see Comber, Foster, and Whitfield, 1977).
3 While patterns recorded here are not stable in detail, they do reflect the overall organizational patterns present in both schools.
4 There are difficulties of separating subject disciplines in the allocation of time and teacher expertise, etc., especially where languages and humanities are concerned, and particularly where topic-centred learning occurs.
5 Additional time spent, e.g., sports teams, music practices, rural studies, etc., is not accounted for in the time analyses.
6 Remedial and express group provision forms complex patterns superimposed upon the outlined analyses.
7 Analysis of information does not take account of *desirability* of recorded or alternative patterns of organization, the constraints

which impinge upon school administration, or the perception of existing patterns as necessarily satisfactory.

8 In school B (purpose-built) each year group occupies their own area (four classrooms plus activity area), so that when there is class division, regrouping or setting, most children will in effect be either in their own classroom or another classroom in the same year area.

9 Additionally, in school B, with the policy of year-group teams, most of the other teachers encountered by the pupils will be members of the year-group team. This is especially so in the earlier years with extra staff coming in to supplement the class teachers.

10 Finally, in school B, many specialists are year-group team members with few specialists teaching only their specialist subject.

It can be seen that in the earlier years of these middle schools, attempts to combine what could broadly be described as a primary school pattern or organization, with elements of specialist provision which may otherwise only have been present in the largest primary schools or after age eleven, may have resulted in some discontinuity[8] between the first school and the middle school at nine plus. This appears more obvious in the data for school B. Children in the first year spend 75%/76% of their time with their form teachers (Table 9.1 (A)) and 87.5%/70% of their time in their 'home' room (Table 9.2 (A)). They spend 25%/32.5% of time with other teachers (Table 9.1 (C and E)) for a number of specialist subjects (Table 9.1 (D)) in areas other than their home room (Table 9.2 (F)).

In the case of both schools this provision of specialist expertise, coupled with the related amount of movement to other resource areas, and with other teacher contact kept as far as possible within the year group, reflects a move towards the achievement of the promotion of secondary school advantages into the lower year group. It may well be, with the development of a distinctly middle school form of organization, placing emphasis upon a year-group/team teaching approach, that such potential discontinuity of this nature may become a feature of the transfer between first and middle schools.

By the fourth year pupils spend only 5%/20% of their time with their form teacher in a form group (with additional contact for some children in some subject groupings) (Table 9.1(A)) and only 2.5%/20% in the 'home' room (Table 9.2(A)). They in turn spend 95%/80% of time (Table 9.1 (E)) in specialist subjects with as many as thirteen/ten different teachers (Table 9.1 (C)) in a variety of specialist and other areas (Table 9.2(F)). This reflects the attempts to prepare pupils for a totally specialist, subject-based curriculum which is encountered in the upper school, and affords the provision of contact with teachers of deeper subject expertise which is felt desirable for pupils at this age. It also demonstrates clearly that the full impact of such provision, which is often encountered in the first year of secondary schools, takes place more gradually. In practice this means that adjustment is made in a known, stable situation, with peer groups established, with educational records more readily transferred within the middle school, and with the children knowing the staff and the physical provision of the school. The relative age differentials and maturity of the pupils may also be important, possibly, with the other factors granting greater social and emotional stability for that period. (It also reduced the difficulties of provision in eleven–eighteen secondary schools for both child and adult populations.)

It might be remembered too that adjustment in terms of size of school population can be of overall importance throughout the period. Whilst school size and its effects is a 'hot' issue, from the small rural schools facing closure through to the largest comprehensives facing criticisms, it is a factor worth noting in relation to these two schools. The variation in a three-tier transition might be from a first school of, say, 50 or 100 pupils to a middle school of, say, 500, to an upper school of, say, 1200. The alternative two-tier system might take children direct from a school of as small as 50 direct to one of 1200.

Table 9.3 reflects the provision made to accommodate the developing nature of the intellectual, physical, and social characteristics of middle school children. From the first-year pattern of mixed-ability form groups, with remedial and some express set withdrawal, and the accompanying implications for organization within each group, pupils proceed to a fourth-year pattern of organization involving regrouping within the year group on a basis of setting in some subjects, sex differentiation for physical activities, mixed-ability forms for integrated studies/humanities, smaller reallocated mixed-ability groups for practical subjects, and remedial provision.

The critical issue of this study is to explore whether the organizational pattern from the first to fourth years meets the desired aim of *gradual transition*. Whilst some differences are evident between the two schools, first- and second-year patterns within each school show similarity. Differences of only a slight change in time or teacher contact and related curriculum areas occur between the two year groups in both schools (Tables 9.1

and 9.2). Parallel similarities between the two year groups can be seen in Table 9.3. Thus the pattern established for pupils entering the school continues in general terms for the duration of the first two years.

On transfer to the third year, pupils in school A experience considerable change in all the factors which are the focus of this study. For example, from 67.5% of their time being spent with their form teachers in the second year, form teacher contact is reduced to 20% in the third year, with corresponding changes in the other aspects (Tables 9.1 and 9.2). Grouping patterns also show considerable change on transfer from the second to third years (Table 9.3). The tables would suggest that pupils of school B also experience a greater change on moving from the second to third year than is experienced between the first and second years or, later, between the third and fourth years, though this is less abrupt than in school A. Transition from the third to fourth years reflects a smaller degree of change than that between the second and third years.

Summary

The full implications of the similarities and differences need to be extracted carefully by the reader from these tables. However, several points seem worthy of further discussion and elaboration, bearing in mind that certain features are seen as *not* entirely meeting a desired gradual transition. We have already referred to the disjunction which appears to occur in transfer from first school to middle school. (Just how great this disjunction is would require information concerning organizational patterns in the first, feeder schools.) Should it prove to be an abrupt change, then its inevitability and the underlying reasons are subject to question.

The apparent similarity between the first two years within the middle school, where a greater degree of transition might have been expected, raises the questions of whether the smallness in the degree of change is inevitable, and if it is inevitable, what are the underlying reasons and constraints which produce the situation? If it is not inevitable, how can the situation be remedied?

Similar questions might be asked regarding the disjunction between the second- and third-year patterns described earlier. Clearly these questions, in practice within the school, cannot be separated from those affecting the earlier years. Nor can they be unrelated to questions about the inevitability/desirability of a fourth-year organization based largely on subject/teacher specialization.[9]

For example (see Tables 9.1 and 9.2), what is the relationship between the relatively small disjunction on transfer *between* schools into and out of school A, and the abrupt change within the school between the second and third years? Is the relationship similar between the relatively abrupt change on transfer *between* schools into and out of school B, and the less abrupt change within that school between the second and third years.

Some of the factors influencing these relationships may be seen as *constraints* which prevent the realization of the ideal, and these are a matter for empirical investigation. Several investigators recently (Hargreaves, 1977 (a), 1977(b); Blyth and Derricott, 1977; Ginsburg et al., 1977) have pointed towards some of these problems, and our involvement in the two schools would support their assertions, namely that provision reflects influences such as:

1 Headteachers' and teachers' training and previous experience, which affect their role perceptions and interests.
2 Demands for accountability and ensuring that standards are *seen* to be maintained.
3 Upper-school pressures, especially upon the curriculum of the third and fourth years (our experience suggests little interest in or pressure upon the earlier middle years).
4 Staffing ratios, and the provision of salary-related 'points' which limits staff expertise/distribution.
5 Architectural constraints, especially the provision and location of teaching spaces which limit flexibility in the curriculum.

Each of these and other possible constraints may interact, forming cumulative constraints in a complex situation, resulting (in both schools) in concern that the disparity between first and second and third and fourth years is greater than is desirable.

Clearly the kind of organization outlined in the three tables has direct implications for teachers, in terms of the nature of their time allocation and involvement with teaching groups, and the range of subjects covered. These implications are a new-found characteristic of the requirement for the staffing of middle schools, raising questions about role perceptions and expectations which warrant further investigation.[10]

Given that time and resources might allow these constraints to be minimized, there is no doubt that within the middle school, the pattern already identified and seen to be developing could manifest itself in more clearly meeting the ideals on a formal, organizational basis. It should also be noted that even though there appears to be a 'less than ideal' transition at a number of points, there is a considerable amount of incidental contact which may minimize in some degree the failure to meet the 'ideal'.[11] For example, contact between pupils in the earlier years and teachers within their year group other than their form teacher, between these pupils and specialist teachers other than those identified in the tables, between the pupils and other specialist teaching areas and facilities, and extracurricular activities. In addition, teachers within the first- and second-year groups have the support of and professional contact with subject specialists, who can be seen as providing expertise for pupils and acting in an advisory capacity for staff. It will be appreciated that this type of contact and its effects are very difficult to quantify, but are none the less significant.

Whilst demonstrating that individual differences in the detail of the patterns of organization occur between the two schools under discussion, reflecting particular contexts, both schools illustrate the organizational attempts made to interpret and implement a distinctively middle school form of organization involving pupils in a gradual transition between different types of organization. We would hope that this study may provide the basis for analysis of organizational patterns in other nine–thirteen middle schools. An attempt might be made to assess whether the features of transition in other schools reflect similar patterns of development to those portrayed in these case-studies. They might also show whether any of the problems discussed here can be characterized as more general features of middle school development with the possibility of identifying and locating the constraints which impinge upon, and to some extent determine, the characteristics and practices encountered in middle schools.

Notes

1. This impression is supported by the views of many teachers known to one of the authors and appears to have some correspondence to courses for 'junior-secondary' teaching. Empirical evidence from within secondary and primary schools would be valuable to quantify or substantiate the impression.
2. In particular, the influence of 'specialist' teaching in primary schools has received attention.
3. The debate about the age of transfer is a complex and long-standing one which cannot be adequately dealt with here.
4. Examples are known to the authors where 'splits' occur at nine plus, at ten plus, at eleven plus, *and* at twelve plus in different three-tier systems or different middle schools.

5. We have not had the opportunity of assessing the views of parents on this matter.

6. Launched by the then Prime Minister, James Callaghan, in his famous Oxford speech of 1976.

7. We would like to thank the headteachers and staff of school A and school B for their help and cooperation in making the publication of this chapter possible.

8. The extent of this discontinuity is of course dependent on the organizational patterns of the feeder first schools.

9. Additional factors, focusing on *different* elements in a *different* sample of schools, have been noted by Comber, Foster, and Whitfield (1977), who found *no* support for 'the view that there is a marked change between the second and third years'. The factors which they studied were the years of teaching experience and the sex of the teachers. However, we would contend that a different interpretation of some of the data which they present would support the view of a marked change at this point in the middle schools.

10. Some of these related questions have been discussed at length by Blyth and Derricott (1977). A related topic is considered in this book by Bornett. The issue of staff mobility and motivation in middle schools appears to be a growing one.

11. Such incidental contact is relevant mainly to the first dimension – pupil time allocation and teacher contact. We recognize of course that this 'ideal' is an unknown quantity which implies that a gradual transition is possible/desirable. The 'ideal' may well be different according to different interpretations in different situations.

CHAPTER TEN

STAFFING IN MIDDLE SCHOOLS: THE ROOTS AND ROUTES OF HIERARCHY

C. Bornett

Sociologists have drawn our attention to the importance of viewing the school curriculum as a consequence of social relationships and social activities. The task of a 'sociology of the curriculum' is to relate social structures to particular arrangements of knowledge which are represented and experienced through the curriculum.[1] In this way, staffing structures in schools, typified by the hierarchy of salary scales and authority positions, can be seen to have implications for the stratification of school knowledge. This chapter attempts to approach this area of sociological interest by looking at the ways in which teachers are deployed within middle schools, and focuses in particular on the roles of year tutor and subject coordinator. An exploration of these two roles as they are developed within the system of salary scales, and within actual and perceived career structures, provides some useful illustration of the complex correspondence between staffing arrangements and the ways in which the curriculum is organized in middle schools.

The bulk of the empirical data[2] on which this account is based was collected during the summer term of 1975 from twelve nine–thirteen middle schools in a rural area, through the use of observation and question-naire. (This will be referred to as Survey A.) In two of these twelve schools, chosen as case-studies, more detailed information was gathered by inter-viewing teachers in both structured and more informal situations. Sup-plementary data were obtained through a second questionnaire to the schools in the summer term of 1978, and were useful in assessing the extent of changes during the intervening three years. (This will be referred to as Survey B.)

The two case-study schools, which I shall call Highlands and Saltmarsh, both opened in 1972 and send children to the same upper school. Highlands is larger, and is a relatively traditional school using the premises of an ex-secondary modern school, while Saltmarsh is a purpose-built school, with some open-plan features and could be classified as comparatively progressive. In 1975 both schools contained fairly equal proportions of ex-secondary school teachers, and of teachers from primary schools or direct from college. Initially though, Highlands was completely staffed by teachers from the reorganized secondary modern school except for one from outside. The choice of these contrasting schools is important in so far as they highlight how the structural features we will be discussing are subject to modification by the particular circumstances of individual schools.

The timing of the main research during the summer term of 1975 is also important for the subsequent discussion, as this was the time when head-teachers were having to review their staffing policies and arrangements in the light of the Houghton Report (1974) proposals for the restructuring of salary scales, and in particular the merger of Scales 2 and 3 to form a new 'Houghton Scale 2'. The situation was complicated by the fact that the Houghton Committee apparently failed to take account of middle school circumstances. Their proposal, based on the finding that 'the job-level differences between teachers on the two scales are minimal' (section 87), did not adequately reflect the half-primary, half-secondary circumstances of the nine–thirteen middle schools, many of which were also comparatively small. Thus, although this was a time of particular upheaval and readjust-ment for middle school teachers, it did provide a useful opportunity to study the ramifications of the restructuring of the middle management posts and the corresponding changes in teachers' career perspectives.

One of the more obvious features of newly formed middle schools was the way in which secondary teachers and primary teachers were frequently rerouted into the same institution. This led many observers to comment upon the differences in curriculum organization resulting from the way in which teachers with contrasting professional backgrounds and expertise were deployed within the schools. For many of the teachers themselves, reorganization was accompanied by a radical reappraisal of entrenched occupational identities. Certainly, the possibility of new career routes in middle schools was an objective fact, but the subjective perceptions of individual teachers were very mixed.

Many of the teachers in the case-study schools of Highlands and Saltmarsh entered middle schools because they had 'nowhere else to go'. Others felt that they had more of a choice, and the reasons given for applying to middle schools varied widely. As may be expected, career advancement was the main reason given, especially for men. Some secondary modern teachers, who did not possess a degree, felt that they would be at a disadvantage in an upper school and saw the middle school as a 'more likely bet'. Some of the few secondary teachers with degrees who are now in middle schools felt a disillusionment with the 'secondary set-up', and were relieved to have escaped from the 'strait jacket of examinations'.

The middle schools under discussion are now well established and the unsettling period of reorganization is fast becoming history, while the original distinctions between secondary- and primary-orientated teachers have become increasingly blurred. Even so, the distinction has left a residual impression on the overall framework of many middle schools.

All teachers entering middle schools are faced with the typical school bureaucracy of hierarchical staffing arrangements, represented by salary scales and positions of responsibility. The number of teachers on each scale in the samples from the twelve research schools for both 1975 and 1978 is shown in Table 10.1. This is compared with the national picture of middle school teachers in 1976. The major difference to be noted is that there are proportionally more teachers in the research schools on Scale 3 and correspondingly fewer on Scale 2, than in middle schools nationally.[4]

It is the balance between Scales 2, 3, and 4 which is particularly interesting. In middle schools these positions are held by either year tutors, or by teachers with subject responsibilities, or by teachers combining the two. Year tutors are generally, though not always, on a higher scale than teachers with subject responsibilities. Year tutors are variously described as year leaders, year consultants, year-group coordinators, and so on, while accounts of their job specification, where they exist, are equally various and differ in particulars from school to school. Even so, the following account of year tutor responsibilities extracted from a staff manual in one of the research middle schools is fairly typical.

The role of the year tutor
To be responsible for:
1 The organizational control of year-group staff team and children in collaborative teaching situations.
2 The pastoral care of children in the year group and to know each child as intimately as possible.

3 The establishing of parental links and the organization of parent visits.
4 The overall supervision and recording of individuals progress within the year group.
5 The briefing of the staff year team and the organization of planning discussions.
6 The supervision of resources for year base.
7 The particular supervision of probationary teachers who are allocated to the year team.
8 To liaise with colleagues in other age-groups and, for first- and fourth-year tutors, to liaise with first and upper schools respectively.

Teachers with subject responsibilities are variously described as subject coordinators, subject area consultants, or by the more traditional nomenclature of heads of department. The name itself sometimes *does* represent a real

Table 10.1   *Numbers and proportions of middle school teachers on each salary grade*

(a) The number of full-time teachers in middle schools deemed secondary in England and Wales on each salary grade in March 1976.[3]

Grade	Number
Headteachers	502
Deputy headteachers	520
Second masters/mistresses	170
Senior teachers	2
Scale 4	100
Scale 3	1599
Scale 2	3903
Scale 1	3545
TOTAL	10,341

(b) A comparison between the number of teachers on Scales 2, 3, and 4 nationally in 1976, and in the twelve research schools in 1975 and 1978.

Scale	National (see (a))		Local (June 1975)		Local (June 1978)	
	No.	%	No.	%	No.	%
4	100	1.8	—	—	1	2
3	1599	28.5	29	41	20	38
2	3903	69.7	43	59	32	60
TOTAL	5602	100	72	100	53	100

difference of function. At Saltmarsh, the subject coordinators were seen to be primarily advisory and consultative rather than directive. In many subjects, especially 'integrated' humanities, they were seen to be merely coordinating the activities of year tutors. This is suggested by the following representative comments:

Second-year tutor:
> 'At Saltmarsh we emphasize the year group and the team work behind it.'

PE coordinator:
> 'Subject coordinators do not have enough say. It appears to me that things are run on the pastoral side than otherwise. . . . The year tutors steer the ship.'

At Highlands the function of subject coordinators is more directive:

Fourth-year tutor/science coordinator:
> 'Although my official title is as a coordinator, I see myself as a specialist being involved in more than just merely as an adviser. I have structured, as I said earlier, the whole of the third- and fourth-year science. People who come to teach in this school, teach my particular worksheet system.'

Despite these differences, the brief for subject coordinators to be found in the same staff manual mentioned above, indicates their general scope.

Some subject coordinator responsibilities
1 To advise other staff within particular subject.
2 To provide teaching resources.
3 To provide core schemes of work for the four age-groups in consultation with year tutors.
4 To collaborate with year tutors in liaising with colleagues in first and upper schools.

From these accounts it can be seen that year tutors have primarily administrative and pastoral duties together with responsibility for coordinating work in the age-group 'across the board'. This primarily 'horizontal' pattern of control and responsibility is in contrast with the way in which subject coordinators have responsibilities across age-groups and exercise 'vertical' patterns of control.

Fig. 10.1

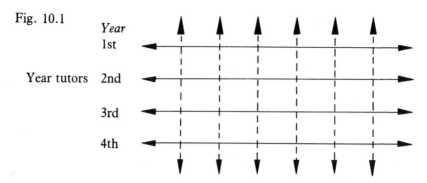

Subject coordinators and their subjects

A year tutor can frequently have more influence on the selection and organization of the curriculum within his or her year group than the subject coordinators, though, as will be seen, the extent of this influence varies from subject to subject and from age-group to age-group. Thus, the general emphasis on the autonomy of the year group in most middle schools has made the year tutor a key figure in subject matters as well as in strictly pastoral or administrative ones. In Figure 10.1 this is indicated by the unbroken lines of year tutor influence.

Headteachers and deputy headteachers possess most control over details of curriculum organization,[5] but as we have seen, year tutors and subject coordinators sometimes possess considerable delegated powers. In this context, it should be noted that these roles are frequently embodied in one person, a year tutor/subject coordinator, while deputy heads and senior masters or mistresses can also adopt one or other of these two roles as part of their overall responsibilities. These combinations of roles will necessarily affect the equation of control over curriculum matters and the ways in which these are negotiated. But the general implication of the two roles outlined above is that there is a problematic middle ground of overlapping influence which has to be negotiated by year tutors and subject coordinators.

That the overlapping functions of year tutors and subject coordinators could give rise to conflicts of interest, is a situation of which many teachers in the schools were well aware. One year tutor had prepared a discussion document for a local middle school conference. It contained the following:

The question of subordinacy is a thorny one. The year leader is appointed for

his expertise with his age group; the subject leader for his specialist knowledge throughout the school. Conflict is conceivable if not inevitable. . . .
With duplicity or even multiplicity of aims must come confusion unless the
year leaders and specialists can agree on aims and objectives.

The problematic relationship between year tutors and subject coordinators
was also recognized at administrator and adviser level. A local curriculum
development officer who was interviewed found it surprising how much
power the heads of middle schools delegated to year tutors, considering the
traditionally 'autocratic' nature of the primary school head with regard to
syllabus and time-table construction, etc. He referred to year tutors as 'mini
heads', and felt that the considerable autonomy of year groups was leading
to a lack of continuity through the school, and that subject coordinators
were frequently ineffective. Similarly, at a locally organized week-end
conference for year tutors, the printed guidelines for a discussion on the
duties and responsibilities of tutors and coordinators contained the following questions:

1 Consider the possibilities of conflict between year tutors and subject
   coordinators. Is there a 'pecking order'? Who has the 'last word'? How
   may harmony be maintained?
2 Is the 'wearing of two hats' as year tutor and subject coordinator
   feasible? Is this dual role more acceptable with some subjects/years
   than others?
3 Does the role of year tutor change significantly through first to fourth
   year?

There is, then, considerable awareness at classroom level and at school
adviser level of the potential for conflict arising from the overlapping roles
of year tutor and subject coordinator.

We have already seen how the role of subject coordinator contains both
advising and directing functions, and that the extent to which one or other
of these functions is emphasized varies between schools and between year
groups. Similarly, the way in which aspects of the year tutor role varied
according to context could be seen in the two case-study schools. Analysis of
the way in which the year tutor's role changed from year group to year group
is best related to the fact that teachers perceived their schools as dividing
into 'lower' and 'upper' segments. A teacher at Highlands put it like this:

I feel that there is a lot of almost tension between the lower end of the school

and the upper end . . . perhaps being crystallized as between general education and specialist education; whether you're teaching children or teaching
subjects.

This tendency of middle schools to 'dichotomize', particularly in their
initial stages of development, is a feature noted by a number of commentators (e.g., Schools Council, 1972; Blyth and Derricott, 1977). In the
case-study schools, Saltmarsh retained mostly class teacher-based learning,
typical of primary schools, up to the orthodox line of demarcation between
primary and secondary at age eleven; Highlands school, on the other hand,
introduced some fragmentation of the time-table at the age of ten, if not
before. Year tutors of the perceived 'lower' school tended to have more
control over curriculum details as individuals, than their counterparts in the
perceived 'upper' school. That there were differences, for example, over
time-table construction, is clear from an interview at Saltmarsh, from which
the following extract is taken:

C.B.:

'Have you made any changes in the time-table for your year group
next year?'

Fourth-year tutor:

'I didn't have a say in the time-table. The only people who have a say
in the time-table are the first- and second-year tutors, because the
third and fourth years are just like a secondary school – the time-table
is made up by the deputy head.'

We have now seen that both subject coordinator and year tutor roles are
subject to variation according to context. These variations are important
because they are instrumental for how the problematic middle ground of
overlapping functions is negotiated. In any particular situation they can
influence the way in which one or other of the groups emerges to dominate
such matters as time-tabling, the distribution of resources, or syllabus
construction. Other variables can also be important, such as the role of the
innovatory teacher. The second-year tutor plus humanities/English coordinator at Highlands, who enjoyed considerable support from the headteacher in his innovatory role, had this to say:

I think I have more authority in the school than any other year tutor, possibly
. . . certainly more freedom to do things within my year group than any other
one.

So far, for the purposes of the argument, I have been assuming that year tutors and subject coordinators were separate people, but, of course, in many cases year tutors also coordinate subjects. This situation is clarified in Table 10.2 (a) where it will be noticed that two-thirds of all year tutors in the sample were also subject coordinators (i.e., twenty-one out of thirty-two).[6] The combining of posts in this way was largely the result of the need to attract well-qualified specialist teachers into middle schools, with a salary comparable to that found elsewhere. In fact seventeen out of a total of twenty-one year tutor/subject coordinators were recruited from secondary schools. Table 10.2 also indicates that this dual-role post predominates in the upper end of the middle school, which is no doubt related to the relative dominance of specialist teaching in the upper years.

Another interesting feature of the survey results presented in Table 10.2 is the way in which some subjects rather than others are selected for coordination by year tutor/subject coordinators. Humanities, maths, English, and science are strongly represented, while subjects such as French, music, PE, and drama are completely unrepresented, for these subjects are the complete preserve of subject coordinators. How typical this pattern is of all nine–thirteen middle schools is debatable in the absence of a more thoroughgoing survey of middle school teachers, but it does raise some interesting questions. A survey of advertised posts in *The Times Educational Supplement* and *The Teacher* reveals that middle school year tutor posts are seldom combined with 'practical' or nonacademic subjects. It could be that this tendency to combine year tutor posts with academic subjects is a reflection of the perceived demand of upper schools that, since year tutors are often influential in curriculum matters, they should be associated with traditionally high-status areas of school knowledge. It is certainly useful for fourth-year tutors with upper school liaison responsibilities to be knowledgeable in academic subjects, as these are frequently used by upper school teachers for grouping children by ability on transfer from middle schools. However, this tendency could also be explained in terms of administrative convenience. Some subjects may not be so consistent as others with the duties of year tutor; they may, for example, take the year tutor away from his or her year base through the exigencies of specialization across the years. Examination of underlying causes, however, can only remain speculative in the absence of evidence about LEA and headteacher appointment policies, though there are indications that similar trends can be found in both eight–twelve middle schools and secondary schools.[7] The tendency for year tutor/subject coordinators, who hold senior positions in middle schools, to be associated with high-status academic subjects can have interesting con-

Table 10.2   *Year tutors, subject coordinators, and year tutor/subject coordinators analysed according to year group and subject responsibility* (Survey A)
(a)   Year tutor/subject coordinators
(b)   Subject coordinators

Year group	Subjects					
	Remedial	Design	English	Humanities /Social studies	Science	Maths
(a)						
1st	1					
2nd			$\frac{1}{2}$[1]	$2\frac{1}{2}$[1]		1
3rd			2	3		1
4th		1	1	1	3	4
Total no.	1	1	$3\frac{1}{2}$	$6\frac{1}{2}$	3	6
Total %	5	5	16	31	14	29
(b)						
1st	1					
2nd	1	1				
3rd		3		1		
4th	1	1		1	3	
unattached	1	4				
Total no.	4	9		2	3	
Total %	10	22		5	8	

Notes
1. $\frac{1}{2}$ represents a double subject responsibility. In this case humanities/English.
2. Music/resources coordinator.

sequences for the stratification of knowledge, and for the way in which the curriculum is balanced between academic and nonacademic subjects. There may be pressure, for example, for more time or more staff to be allocated for the teaching of academic subjects.

Analysis by graduate status provides another interesting perspective on the relationship between year tutors and subject coordinators. Warwick (1974) has noted the somewhat caste-like distinction between graduates and nongraduates that can be found in secondary schools, with graduates having a better chance of promotion than nongraduates.

French	Music	PE	Drama	Resources/Library	TOTAL	All year tutors Total
					1	7
					4	8
					6	7
					10	10
					21	32
					100	
					1	
	$1\frac{1}{2}^2$			$1\frac{1}{2}^2$	5	
4	1	1			10	
4	3	2	1	2	18	
1					6	
9	$5\frac{1}{2}$	3	1	$3\frac{1}{2}$	40	
22	14	8	2	9	100	

For middle schools the evidence is sparse, but an analysis of the survey results did pinpoint some differences (see Table 10.3).

There are no overwhelming differences, but fewer graduates are to be found in year tutor-only posts than in the other two groups. Again, this has implications for how seniority is developed, particularly where, as sometimes happens (see Table 10.8), year tutors and subject coordinators are on the same salary scale.

The problematic nature of this segment of the middle school staffing

Table 10.3   *The graduate status of subject coordinators, year tutors, and year tutor/subject coordinators* (Survey A)

	Graduates	Total	% Graduates
Subject coordinators	12	40	30
Year tutors	2	11	18
Year tutor/subject coordinators	8	21	38
All groups	22	72	31

hierarchy can be further illustrated by looking at the way in which external changes in the salary structure disrupt structures of seniority and subordinacy. The impact of the Houghton Report and the resultant restructuring of the salary scales was commented upon earlier. The immediate effect of the 1975 Houghton/Burnham settlement within the middle schools surveyed, was to increase the number of points allocated but at the same time to reduce the number of differentials, through the merger of pre-Houghton Scales 2 and 3. This meant that headteachers had to review their staffing structure of posts in the middle range, and to reallocate some of their points according to their priorities and at their discretion. The results of this reallocation, in its initial stages, can be seen in Table 10.4.

Prior to Houghton, most year tutor/subject coordinators were on Scale 4 and most year tutor-only posts were designated as Scale 3. Approximately half the subject coordinators were on Scale 2 and the other half on Scale 3. The immediate post-Houghton situation 'levelled' all subject coordinators to Scale 2, whereas nearly all year tutors, regardless of whether they coordinated subjects or not, found themselves on Scale 3. This clearly reflected and accentuated the higher status of the year tutor in relation to the subject coordinator. It also reduced the difference in seniority between year tutors with subject responsibility and those without. This created some problems in the two case-study schools. There, the solution was to upgrade those who were year tutors–only by giving them extra responsibilities (see Table 10.5).

Thus, at Saltmarsh the second-year tutor was put on a par with the third- and fourth-year tutors, all on Scale 3, by being given the provisional

Table 10.4   *The position of year tutors, subject coordinators, and year tutor/subject coordinators on pre- and post-Houghton salary scales* (Survey A)

	SCALES*						TOTAL
	Immediate pre-Houghton			Immediate post-Houghton			
	2	3	4	2	3	4	
Year tutor/ subject coordinators		1	20	21			21
Year tutors	2	7	2	2	9		11
Subject coordinators	21	19		40			40
TOTAL	23	27	22	42	30		72

* Note that pre-Houghton Scales 2 and 3 became post-Houghton Scale 2, while pre-Houghton Scale 4 became post-Houghton Scale 3.

responsibility of 'stock control', a bogus coordination post. The female first-year tutors in both schools were promoted to senior mistress posts (deputy head scales) in September 1975; in Highlands on the retirement of the previous occupant, in Saltmarsh because the new points allocation after Houghton permitted the introduction of this post in Saltmarsh-sized schools.[8] The distribution of female year tutors through the schools is of interest (see Table 10.6). Most female year tutors tended to congregate in the lower half of the middle schools and were less likely to coordinate subjects.

Table 10.7 gives some indication of how the 'above Scale 1 posts' were being shared out three years after the Houghton settlement. In 1975 there were no year tutor/subject coordinators on Scale 4, while in 1978 there was a small percentage on this scale. In 1975 there were no subject coordinators on Scale 3, in 1978 there were 11% on this scale. A number of year tutors-only were still to be found on Scale 2 in 1978. There is clearly some overlap in seniority represented here, especially in larger schools where some subject coordinators are on Scale 3, and also in smaller schools where some year tutors are on Scale 2. The situation becomes clearer if we look at

Table 10.5   *Year tutors in Highlands School and Saltmarsh School and their extra responsibilities* (Survey A)

Highlands School	Saltmarsh School
Year tutors *Responsibilities*	*Year tutors* *Responsibilities*
1+ (Senior Mistress) (Sept. 1975)	1+ (Senior Mistress) (Sept. 1975)
2+ Humanities/English	2+ ('Stock control') (June 1975)
3+ Maths	3+ Maths
4+ Science	4+ Humanities

Note
Post-Houghton responsibilities are shown in brackets.

Table 10.6   *Year tutors and year tutor/subject coordinators analysed by year group and sex* (Survey A)

Year group	Year tutors		Year tutor/ subject coordinators		TOTAL
	Female	*Male*	*Female*	*Male*	
1st	6			1	7
2nd	1	3		4	8
3rd		1		6	7
4th			1	9	10
TOTAL	7	4	1	20	32

the staffing structure profiles of one relatively large and one relatively small school from among the twelve middle schools surveyed in 1978.

At the points marked * in Table 10.8, the delineation of seniority can be particularly problematic and other contingencies apart from salary position will need to be taken into account. Again, the profiles emphasize the point that the general structure of the relationships under discussion is frequently modified in relation to the particular circumstances of schools, in this case their relative size.

Another slant on the question of staffing hierarchies is revealed when we look at the differing career 'routes' of subject coordinators and year tutors (see Table 10.9). It can be seen that among those year tutors and year tutor/subject coordinators who gave a positive response, most saw deputy headships in middle schools as their first priority for promotion. It is also interesting to notice that some year tutors saw possibilities of moving into primary or secondary schools as alternatives, and this tendency was even more marked when second or third priorities were taken into account (not shown in Table 10.9). Year tutors in the first and second years perceived that headships in primary schools were open to them, while tutors in the third and fourth years perceived that pastoral or head of department posts in secondary schools were possible career openings. In contrast, subject coordinators, while also sensing the opportunities available to them in primary

Table 10.7   *The position of year tutor/subject coordinators, year tutors, and subject coordinators on the post-Houghton Scales 2, 3, and 4 in (a) June 1075 and (b) June 1978* (Surveys A and B)

Position	Scales							
	2		3		4		TOTAL	
(a) June 1975	No.	%	No.	%	No.	%	No.	%
Year tutor/subject coordinators			21	29			21	29
Year tutors	3	4	8	11			11	15
Subject coordinators	40	56					40	56
TOTAL	43	60	29	40			72	100
(b) June 1978								
Year tutor/subject coordinators			8	15	1	2	9	17
Year tutors	3	6	6	11			9	17
Subject coordinators	29	55	6	11			35	66
TOTAL	32	61	20	37	1	2	53	100

Note
Survey B, June 1978, also contained two deputy headteachers with year tutor responsibilities and three deputy headteachers with subject responsibilities.

Table 10.8   *Staff structure profiles of two middle schools*

School 1: Twenty-six staff		School 2: Sixteen staff	
Positions	No. of staff	Positions	No. of staff
Headteacher	1	Headteacher	1
Deputy headteacher	1	Deputy headteacher	1
Senior mistress/ year tutor	1		
Scale 4	1[1]		
* Scale 3	2[2]	Scale 3	2[1]
* Scale 3	5[3]	{ * Scale 2	2[2]
Scale 2	4[3]	{ * Scale 2	6[3]
Scale 1	11	Scale 1	4
TOTAL	26		16

Notes
1. year tutors/subject coordinators
2. year tutors
3. subject coordinators

and secondary schools, tended to realize that promotion to a deputy head-ship necessitated becoming a year tutor first. However, this was not clear cut; some subject coordinators on Scale 2 aspired to coordinator positions on Scale 3, and some subject coordinators on Scale 3 saw deputy headships as being within their grasp without an intervening stage as year tutor.

Clearly we can only hint at some of the contingencies which middle school teachers have to take account of when planning their career routes. However, support for the suggested ambivalence of the career contingencies facing subject coordinators can be found in Ginsburg et al.'s (1977) study of five nine–thirteen middle schools in Herefordshire and Worcestershire. In discussing the unclear promotion route for subject coordinators, they point out that specialists in middle schools sense that their promotional path involves assuming or retaining generalist, class teacher responsibilities, which will better qualify them for year tutor posts. The remedial coordinator at Saltmarsh School explained this dilemma, as it applied to her, like this:

Ideally, I would like to be Head of Remedial and Senior Mistress. I think the two go well together – they are both pastoral. And it seems wrong that I should have to change my job, lose the remedial work, and become a team leader, which is something on a different line, in order to become a Senior Mistress. Obviously, if that is the only way to become a Senior Mistress, and the right job seems to be there, then I would be willing to think about it.

The varied career routes through and within middle schools create a need to diversify and keep as many options open as possible. A semi-specialist, Scale 1 teacher at Saltmarsh said: 'I think it is worth keeping up the specialist line as well, as a two-pronged attack for promotion.' Not all teachers saw the 'number of subjects taught' as an important, or the only factor for future promotion. Some of the year tutors interviewed felt that the need to 'experience different age-groups' was a more important factor. The ex-secondary school fourth-year tutor at Saltmarsh felt it necessary to have experience of other years:

> What I asked for in fact was could I do a couple of periods a week with the first year and a couple of periods a week with the second year, as well as with the third and fourth years.

At Highlands, such a wish to extend age-group experience could be accommodated to a certain extent, but at Saltmarsh it was 'subject diversification' within the year group that was encouraged and 'year-group diversification' that was discouraged. So this year tutor's request to take other years was turned down.

Year tutors, then, and other teachers as well, may find that they need to extend subject experience or age-group experience as a requirement for later successful promotion. This will clearly vary according to previous experience and subject career orientation. Thus, some teachers may perceive the need to extend subject experience, and will resist demands to specialize and the possibly concomitant requirement to take other year groups. Some other teachers, or the same teachers at a later date, may perceive the need to extend age-group experience and will resist demands to make them take more subjects which may tie them to one year group only. In this way, conflicting career orientations and strategies, operating within a particular school, may well have an impact on the organization of the curriculum, particularly as it varies between year groups.

In this chapter I have attempted to show in some detail how the hierarchical structure of staffing arrangements in middle schools has a basis not only in the way salaried posts are allocated, but also in the way teachers are 'routed' through the schools in relation to actual and perceived career

Table 10.9   *Promotion and future career orientations of (a) subject coordinators analysed by salary scale, and (b) year tutors and year tutor/subject coordinators analysed by year group (Survey B)*

Respondents were asked: Do you intend taking any of the following courses of action within the next five years? Yes/No.

If yes, please indicate in order of likelihood against the relevant statements. Thus, a 1 against a statement denotes that you are more likely to take that course of action than any other.

Apply for a post in a primary/first/junior school as:
   1.1   Subject coordinator or equivalent
   1.2   Deputy head
   1.3   Head

Apply for a post in a middle school as:
   2.1   Subject coordinator
   2.2   Year tutor
   2.3   Deputy head
   2.4   Head

Apply for a post in a secondary/upper school as:
   3.1   Head of department
   3.2   Pastoral post (e.g., head of lower school)
   3.3   Senior teacher/deputy head
   3.4   Head

   4   Leave teaching

   5   Go abroad to teach

   6   Other teaching or administration post (please specify)

contingencies. It was suggested that the structure of relationships represented by the school hierarchy had implications for the way in which the detailed organization of the curriculum was negotiated. These implications were explored through an analysis of the division of labour between year tutors and subject coordinators. It was suggested that the relationship between year tutors and subject coordinators can become problematic for the participants, particularly where status differences are blurred and where responsibilities overlap. Stress was laid on the way in which this

Course of action	(a) Subject coordinators			(b) Year tutors and year tutor/subject coordinators					Total (a) and (b)
	Scale 2	Scale 3	Total	Year 1	Year 2	Year 3	Year 4	Total	
1.1									
1.2	1	¹/₃	1¹/₃	1	1½			2½	
1.3				1				1	
2.1	1 11/22		2						
2.2	5 11/22	3¹/₃	9¹/₃						
2.3	1 11/22	3	5		2½	3½	1 11/22	8	
2.4									
3.1	1½		1½				½	½	
3.2		¹/₃	¹/₃			½	½	1	
3.3									
3.4									
4	3	1	4						
5	1½		1½						
6	1	1	2						
No response or uncertain	8		8	2	2	1		5	
Total	26	9	35	4	6	5	3	18	53

Notes
1. Scale 3 includes Scale 2 post plus special class allowance.
2. ½ or ¹/₃ indicates equal first priority. That is: (a) Scale 2: (2.1 = 2.2) (5.0 = 2.1) (2.2 = 2.3) (2.3 = 3.1); (b) Year 4: (2.3 = 3.1) (2.3 = 3.2).

relationship varied according to the contextual circumstances of the year group and school. In most situations it was seen that the year tutor, especially when combining subject responsibilities, was able to dominate the proceedings, and this in turn was related to the general emphasis on the year group as an organizational feature of middle schools. This emphasis on the year group, and the horizontal pattern of control by year tutors over curriculum matters, can be seen as part of an *integrationist ideology* where subject barriers are crossed. It could also be seen as a convenient way of breaking down the school into workable administrative units whereby heads can more easily delegate their authority.

Discussion of the Houghton Report's impact on the staffing arrangements of middle schools highlighted the way in which broader structural relationships, embedded in institutions external to the school, influence the interactional setting within the school. It will be interesting to see how this interactional setting will be affected by a more recent external contingency – the contraction in pupil numbers. The response of administrators and headteachers to falling rolls may well have important consequences for the relationship between year tutors and subject coordinators, and for their position in the staff hierarchy. Which of the two posts will be most vulnerable if scale posts are to be lost? How will the career prospects of the two groups be affected? What will be the consequences for curriculum control?

The disruption of dominant patterns of staffing relationships within schools does help to identify those contingencies which underlie these hierarchical structures. This study has only been able to hint at some of the contingencies involved. An important area of future investigation would be the staff appointment and allocation policies and practices of LEA officials and headteachers. But the difficulties facing an investigator, in this sensitive and frequently covert area of decision making, should not be underestimated.

Notes

1. A sociological approach demands that the school curriculum be viewed as a social system, i.e., as the product of certain social arrangements or relations. Every curriculum presupposes a set of meanings which are embedded in social structures. People within a social structure *produce* a curriculum.

   The curriculum can be viewed as a particular selection and organization of knowledge. Young argues that the central task of the sociology of education is to 'relate these principles of selection and organisation that underly curricula to their institutional and interactional setting in schools and classrooms and to the wider social structure'. See 'An Approach to the Study of Curricula as Socially Organised Knowledge' in Young (1971).
2. See C. R. Bornett (1975).
3. DES (1976). The data are based on Table 22, pp.38–39. It should be noted that 'middle schools deemed secondary' was the category of schools chosen for comparison as this contains a high proportion of nine–thirteen middle schools.
4. This is possibly due to the discretion of the LEA in controlling the number of promoted posts in schools through the use of the points system.

   Comparison of the samples from Survey A and Survey B as shown in Table

10.1 (b), with figures available from the Area Education Office for the area in which the surveyed schools are situated, revealed that the samples were representative for the area as a whole.

5. It should be noted in this context that the scope of headteacher autonomy in curriculum matters is closely circumscribed. The extent of the control that heads and deputy heads possess over curriculum details is subject to constraints emanating from broader social structures, which define what is acceptable and what is unacceptable.

6. Comparison with Survey B figures shows that in 1978 this proportion was approximately half-and-half (see Table 10.7).

7. See NUT (1979). The example of an eight–twelve middle school given in this booklet shows that year tutors and subject coordinators in English, humanities, maths, and science are regarded (and rewarded) as the most senior posts below deputy head level. See Warwick (1974), who suggests that secondary teachers whose subject is more literary-theoretical will always consider their chances of career mobility greater than those whose subject is more practical-expressive.

8. Locally, at least, this new provision was a boost to the career prospects of female teachers in middle schools. It perhaps went some way in alleviating the well-known imbalance between the promotion possibilities of female teachers and those for men.

CHAPTER ELEVEN

THE MIDDLE SCHOOL CURRICULUM: SOME UNCHARTED TERRITORY

R. Derricott and C. Richards

It is the contention of this chapter that in the first decade of existence of English middle schools, inadequate consideration has been given to policy making on curricular issues at school level. Middle schools are, and are likely to remain, minority institutions. Much of the energy that is usually expended in establishing an innovation has, in the case of middle schools, been concentrated on the rhetoric of justification and on establishing the mechanisms and procedures of organization. Both are necessary features but have received undue attention compared with working out the details of curricular policy at school level.

The ideology which is at the basis of the justification of middle schools is explored elsewhere in this book, so that here it is sufficient for us to mention some of its more salient features. The smallness of middle schools has been seen to be intrinsically desirable as providing a secure alternative environment to the large all-through comprehensive school. Middle schools have been portrayed as caring institutions, concentrating on providing tutoring systems and pastoral care so that children and teachers can really get to know one other. They have been justified as transitional institutions with the task of easing the social, emotional, and intellectual passage from childhood to adolescence. Middle schools have been described as places where children 'learn how to learn' and where 'options are kept open' against the dangers of early specialization. Much of what has been written in justification of middle schools can be characterized as defensive, in that it is either ultra-cautious in tone in anticipation of professional, parental, and community criticism, or that it has been aggressively assertive and perhaps overstated in order to browbeat any opposition.

In this debate the middle school curriculum has been discussed, but it has been approached in very much the same way that nineteenth-century explorers must have approached an unknown land mass. The charting of this land mass has begun but, we contend, it has got little further than beginning to sketch in its outline and to make assumptions based on experience of other areas (primary and secondary curricula) about what will be found in the unmapped interior. There has been no shortage of general advice and suggestions. Working Papers Nos. 42 and 55 (Schools Council, 1972, 1975) and publications from the Department of Education and Science (DES, 1970(a), (b)) have made suggestions about what might be called the 'grand design' and have mapped out possible broad areas into which middle school curricula might be divided. The writings of the early proponents of middle schools (Gannon and Whalley, 1975; Charles, 1974) have provided examples of how curricula based on broad areas have been used in individual (and often purpose-built) schools. Unpublished documents representing thousands of hours of teacher effort have been prepared by local education authorities as part of their plans to implement middle school systems.[1]

The vast majority of these writings have been supportive of middle schools as innovatory institutions. Until recently, the most critical comment about middle schools had come from Edwards (1972) and the AMA (1976), which is a professional association representing, in the main, viewpoints from the secondary tradition. However, the Great Debate of 1976–77 focused attention on standards in schools and the need for accountability. The Green Paper, *Education in Schools: A Consultative Document*, saw the challenge to teachers in primary schools as one of restoring 'the rigour without damaging the real benefits of the child-centred developments' (HMSO, 1977). This was to be done by laying stress on progression in learning and striving for continuity of experience. Echoing the slogan 'back to the basics', the skills of literacy and numeracy were seen in the consultative document as 'part of the core of learning, the protected area of the curriculum'.

This then was the message from the Department of Education and Science to those concerned with the curricula of primary schools. By strong implication the message could also be seen to have some relevance to middle schools. The consultative document comments only briefly on middle schools:

For the most part middle schools do not present unique curricular issues, though their size and organisation highlight certain problems, particularly those connected with continuity. . . . A middle school system with careful co-ordination between the phases of schooling can work well. . . . It can, however, cause some difficulty for pupils who transfer into or out of the area. Since middle schools are in a minority, transition is a matter to which the local education authorities and teachers in such areas need to give special consideration. (HMSO, 1977, para. 2.4, p.9)

There follows a warning that the smallness of middle schools, seen by some as a favourable feature, may lead to insufficient depth of specialist treatment in some areas of the curriculum such as science, modern languages, and handicrafts.

The assertion in the consultative document that middle schools do not present unique curricular issues will have to be weighed against the evidence of the Keele survey of middle schools[2] and the forthcoming survey of HMI which is to be a middle school counterpart of the primary school survey (DES, 1978). If the issues are to be defined in terms of how the middle schools have catered for progression in learning and continuity of experience, both within and between stages (i.e., within middle schools themselves and between first and middle and middle and third-tier schools), then we will certainly find ourselves in uncharted territory. In just over a decade, almost 1500 middle schools have been established in England.[3] The innovative community of people concerned with middle schools was, in the early days of their development, closely knit. The ideas of some of the early pioneering authorities such as the West Riding of Yorkshire, Hertfordshire, the Isle of Wight, and Worcestershire formed the agenda of many conferences and were taken by enthusiastic proponents to other local education authorities. This diffusion of activity showed evidence of more consensus over middle school pastoral and organizational matters than has been achieved over curricular matters. Perhaps the consensus over pastoral matters arose because ideas about counselling and tutorial schemes were part of the general currency of management courses developed in the first place to support the establishment of large traditional (eleven–eighteen) comprehensive schools. Ideas about pastoral systems and tutor groups were found to translate directly to the middle school situation. On the other hand, any general agreement about curricular issues was more difficult to achieve because of the firmly held beliefs in the autonomy of individual schools over decisions about 'what', 'when', and 'how' things are taught. As we have seen, advice about broad areas of curricular design was abundant, but the translation and adaptation of these general statements on middle schools to the point where they provide the basis for school curricular policy is where, to us, the problems lie.

The translation and adaptation of general statements about the design of curricula from broad areas and the macro level of planning[4] to the curricular policy of a school, the micro level of planning, involves a careful examination of what is meant by *continuity* of curricular experience.

We shall consider the notion of continuity in relation to two concepts, both often used and less frequently questioned. These concepts are *structure* and *integration*.

Structure

It is possible to collect together many different uses of the word 'structure'. Courses, learning experiences, classrooms, learning environments, planning, teaching, and resources have all been described as structured.[5] The word has come to be used as a synonym for organized, systematic, or controlled. We wish to distinguish three uses of the word in our discussion of middle school curricula. We distinguish between:

(a) logistical structure
(b) logical structure
(c) psychological structure

Logistical structure

When used in this sense, structure refers to organizational and managerial aspects of teaching. It is concerned with how the use of a classroom, a work area, or a shared space is planned as an environment in which teaching and learning are expected to take place. The logistical structure of the work area will allow for noisy or messy activities to be separated from quiet activities, it will separate paint and glue from library books and worksheets, it will allow for individual study, small-group cooperation, or large-group activities. Location of resources will be planned to take into account their predicted frequency of use to avoid log-jams of children in any particular space.

Logical structure

We use this term to refer to the attention paid to the structure of knowledge that makes up the curriculum. Structure in this sense is concerned with attempts to provide children with experiences of different ways of knowing (Hirst, 1975). Some middle school curricula based upon broad areas have been claimed to be derived from a philosophical analysis of forms of knowledge (Gannon and Whalley, 1975). In this way, distinctions have been made between the symbolic aspects of learning language and mathematics, the empirical aspects of finding out in science and in environmental studies, the aesthetic and expressive aspects of art, drama, and movement, the ethical aspects of moral education, and the practical aspects of 'knowing how' that are the essence of involvement in craftwork. Logical structure used in this way refers to the conscious efforts of the designers of middle school curricula to provide essential experiences of different ways of knowing for the children they teach. The labels used to describe the components of this logical structure are, to us, immaterial. A consciously planned structure of this kind can take place under a time-table with traditional subject headings or it can use such labels as investigative studies, language and communication, and recreative activities.

The term logical structure has a second, important meaning. It can be used to refer to the logical structure which exists, or is believed to exist, *within* a subject area such as mathematics or history, or *within* a broad area such as humanities or environmental studies, and which provides teachers with a basis for selecting, organizing, and sequencing content. There appears to be more consensus about what constitutes a logical structure in a subject like mathematics than there is in a field such as social studies.

Psychological structure

Satterly (1970) reminds us that 'well established relationships between laboratory phenomena and out-of-laboratory phenomena do not exist in the social sciences'. Teachers can therefore only expect general guidance about the nature and quantity of learning from theories of learning and cognitive development. Middle school teachers, in planning curricula and in the act of teaching, are likely to be influenced at differing levels of conscious awareness by the following set of principles or guidelines, all taken and freely adapted from learning theory, or accounts of how cognitive development takes place.

1 Progression in learning in the middle years is likely to be related to development from concrete to formal operations.
2 Progression in the quality of thinking of children in the middle years is likely to be related to developments from what Peel (1960) has called 'describer' thinking to 'explainer' thinking.

3 In the middle years there is likely to be a wide range of individual differences in the pace of learning.

4 The ability to manipulate variables in solving problems will be limited.

5 Coping with the uncertainty of there not being a single 'correct' answer to a problem posed will prove difficult for many children of middle school age.

6 In interpersonal learning the peer group is likely to be strongly influential.

7 Children of middle school age show an interest in other people and their ideas, but the starting point for developing a view of 'the other' is likely to be egocentrism which could be said to be the antithesis of empathy.

These principles, which are in no way taken to be an exhaustive list, provide what we call a psychological structure.

The three faces of structure as presented here do not represent exclusive sets of ideas. What we have attempted to do is to make the point that the term structure is often used as a general descriptor. It needs unpacking; we have tried to begin this unpacking. In practice the elements of structure are interrelated. Bruner (1966), in searching for a theory of instruction, puts this point clearly:

> A theory of instruction must specify the ways in which a body of knowledge should be structured so that it can be most readily grasped by the learner . . . since the merit of a structure depends upon its power for simplifying information, for generating new propositions and for increasing the manipulability of a body of knowledge, structure must always be related to the status and gifts of the learner. (p.41)

To return to our theme then, in translating broad ideas about curricular design into a policy that a school can actually begin to implement, insufficient attention has been paid to the various kinds of structure in which this process of implementation is likely to operate. In particular, less attention has been paid to the interrelation of logical and psychological structures than we consider to be desirable. Searching for meaningful approaches to the sequencing of content, and relating these to what we know about how children from the ages of eight to thirteen are likely to learn is, in terms of our analogy, relatively uncharted territory.

An example of the ways in which both logical and psychological structures can be taken into account in an attempt to provide continuity of learning and teaching is included below. We must, first of all, consider the second of our concepts, *integration*, in relation to the notion of continuity.

Integration

As a concept, curriculum integration has received a great deal more attention than that given to structure. Much of what has been written has been in search of meaning, an early example of which can be found in the writing of the American, Hopkins (1937), which appeared in the late 1930s. Two decades later, the National Society for the Study of Education devoted its fifty-seventh yearbook to the integration of educational experiences, with papers on the meaning, significance, and psychological basis of integration (Dressel, 1958). British interest in the concept of integration appears to have come slightly later, perhaps stimulated by the loose and often unquestioned use of integration in official reports such as Newsom's (HMSO, 1963) and Plowden's (HMSO, 1967), and the establishment of a new wave of curriculum development projects as part of an interventionist programme to support comprehensive reorganization and the raising of the school leaving age.[6] Significant British contributions to the search for meaning in curriculum integration can be found in the general analyses of Lawton (1973) and Entwistle (1970). A sociological analysis of the concept has been provided by Bernstein (1971), and philosophical interpretations have been provided by Hirst (1975) and Pring (1976). Descriptions and analyses of integrated courses and problems that have arisen in establishing them can be found in Kirk (1973), Haigh (1975), and Warwick (1973). Unpublished theses remain a relatively untapped source of analysis and practical advice. An example of the latter is Platten (1978).

The idea of an integrated curriculum infers the existence of some kind of structure, the nature of which is often relatively unexplored. In our analysis of integration and the middle school curriculum we wish to make the same basic distinctions that we employed above. We will, in turn, consider:

(a) the logistics of curriculum integration
(b) the logic of curriculum integration
(c) the psychological bases of curriculum integration

The logistical basis of integration

As one of us has argued elsewhere (Blyth and Derricott, 1977), one of the underlying beliefs that permeates much of what has been written about and some of the practice in middle schools is the development of what has been called a *collaborative ethos*. Collaboration is seen to be the keystone of general decision making and teaching. In curricular matters, this often means that teams of teachers are given the task of planning what, when, and to a lesser extent how to teach an age-group and/or a particular section of the curriculum. Team planning, team teaching, and blocking time-tables are organizational devices which are claimed to provide the necessary openness and flexibility for the establishment of an integrated approach, but as Kirk (1973) has pointed out, organizational (or in our terms logistical) factors are logically independent of a teacher's view of knowledge and of teaching method. In other words, the logistical framework provided by team planning, collaborative teaching, and block time-tabling can be used to teach history by a number of different approaches, just in the same way as it can be used to teach thematic studies, humanities, or social studies. A collaborative framework is not by itself a guarantee that curriculum integration will take place.

The logic of curriculum integration

Apart from the logistical arrangements that allow more flexible use of time and resources by both children and teachers, an integrated curriculum may also represent different viewpoints about knowledge. These differences are not always made explicit. Recent analysis such as that of Pring (1976) has done much to clarify thinking about curriculum integration.

In the broad area of humanities/social/environmental studies, a common response in middle schools has been to use themes as an integrating device. In this way, a theme such as 'pollution', 'exploration', or 'communication' becomes the label under which a number of activities take place. The theme can (a) provide 'a flag of convenience' under which traditional content sails, unchanged. Under 'communication', historians teach about the advent of canals and railways, and geographers teach about motorway networks. Or (b) the theme can be significantly related to one or more of the organized fields of knowledge, the connections between subjects being made clear and their separate contributions being interrelated to a common purpose. Thus, in the study of an inner-urban area, the economic and social history of the area is related to the physical and social geography of that area. Finally, (c) themes can not only provide opportunities to interrelate content but can also encourage common sets of skills valued by the contributing subjects. For example, historians, geographers, and social scientists have common interests in:

1 skills in data collection
2 skills in data representation
3 skills in data interpretation

A common framework of skills of this kind can provide a basis for integration. Another set of procedures for planning themes, (d), is the use of the *key concept* as advocated by the History, Geography, and Social Science (HGSS) Project (Blyth et al., 1976). (See p.193–197 below.) Key concepts are procedural devices designed to help teachers in the selection and organization of content and are advocated by the HGSS Project in planning a social subjects curriculum. The project suggests that key concepts such as communication, power, values and beliefs, and similarity/difference can be used in teaching the social subjects *separately* or *in combination*. A theme planned in the way that this project advocates should not lose sight of the distinct nature of the contributory disciplines. There are, however, difficulties. Key concepts that are high-level abstractions which overarch several subjects can have attributed to them an epistemological status that they do not possess. They may even impose upon children an idiosyncratic structuring of ideas about society, in place of traditional and tried disciplines that they have superseded. Those middle school teachers who are attracted to the kinds of alternative structures found in many integrated courses, should approach these alternatives with a constructive scepticism.

The psychological basis of integration

Integrated curricula are often justified in terms of their appropriateness for children. Children, it is claimed, do not see life in the differentiated way in which many schools offer it to them. At its most extreme, the subject-centred curriculum is seen as an attempt to unstitch the seamless cloak of learning (Jacks, 1976). In the middle years of schooling, 'learning how to learn' has been claimed to be of greater importance than what is being learned. Motivated by investigating a topic of interest, the child's own process of enquiry is claimed to be the basis of integration. This process of enquiry is most firmly grounded when it starts with what the child already knows, with what Pring (1976) has called *common-sense knowledge*. The challenge to the teacher is to use this common-sense knowledge as a departure point for encouraging children to question critically what they know and perhaps take for granted. As Pring puts it:

My advocacy therefore for a more integrated curriculum at the earlier stages of secondary education rests upon firstly, a respect for the varied mental activities of the pupils to be educated, secondly, a recognition of the common-sense language and understandings through which the pupils already engage in this mental life and *to which the more disciplined modes of enquiry must be related*, and thirdly, the need for a more flexible and co-operative teaching framework in which different teacher resources can be brought into contact with so many individual differences. (p.120, our emphases)

For children in the upper middle years then, Pring supports this advocacy of an integrated curriculum firmly with psychological justifications. At the same time, he is careful to point out his concern to link children's activity and knowledge to disciplined modes of enquiry; he is not advocating the kind of integrated course in which themes or topics are chosen to be the integrating element.

Continuity

Structure and integration now need to be linked to continuity of curricular experience in middle schools. As our emphases in the above quotation from Pring indicate, we would agree that any structured curriculum should have built into it continuity of experience and the potential for achieving progression in learning, linking common-sense knowledge with the disciplines of the curriculum as they are usually represented on the time-table. We have found very little convincing evidence that the detailed charting of the nature of this continuity and progression has been achieved *within* middle schools. Attempts to plot continuity in learning *between* stages (for example, between middle and third-tier schools) are also rare. In attempting this task, teachers find that it is easier to define continuity and progression in learning in some areas of the curriculum than it is in others. In some subjects there is certainly more material available from publishers and curriculum projects than there is in others. Reading schemes and supplementary reading material can provide a limited form of continuity between first and middle schools. The Schools Mathematics Project and, in some cases, Nuffield Combined Science, may provide some continuity in these curricular areas both within and between middle and third-tier schools. In the teaching of French, one of the well-known published 'direct method' schemes may provide a measure of continuity between schools. In other curricular areas, there is often a great deal more left to professional discretion in terms of the content and allocation of time. Agreements between schools in the area of social and environmental studies and/or the humanities, if they take place at all, usually amount to decisions to leave certain areas of content to a particular age or stage. There are some notable exceptions to this.[7] There is little doubt however, that as far as the middle school curriculum is concerned, continuity and progression in learning constitute some of the inaccessible parts of our uncharted territory.

Some guidelines for continuity and progression

To begin our charting, albeit on a small scale, we use as an example the social subjects area of the curriculum, an area that is usually organized under such labels as history, geography, social and environmental studies, and humanities. This is an area in which continuity and progression in learning are particularly difficult to define, and systematic planning is often lacking (Blyth et al., 1976; DES, 1978).

We do not intend to produce a detailed curriculum for teaching the social subjects in the middle school. This would be inappropriate, as each group of teachers will have to respond to a unique set of situational variables. We do, however, offer a structure for deriving such a local curriculum, this structure being based on developments of the work of the History, Geography, and Social Science (HGSS) Project, with which one of us has been associated since 1971. The structure consists of a series of guidelines for school policy making.

A   As resources, the social subjects offer an opportunity to introduce middle school children to a set of study skills and other worthwhile activities.

1 Finding information.
2 Interpreting and evaluating information.
3 Formulating and testing hypotheses.
4 Developing an understanding of human actions and motives.
5 Developing attitudes to evidence, distinguishing between fact and opinion, detecting bias and distortion.
6 Developing an embryonic system for analysing values.
7 Developing an embryonic framework for understanding social issues.
8 Acquiring specific knowledge from within the social subjects.

B   In order to relate children's common-sense language and understanding to the more disciplined modes of enquiry of the social subjects, we make the distinction between:

(a) pre-disciplinary activities

(b) disciplinary activities

Progression in learning in the social subjects curriculum of a middle school will be from pre-disciplinary to disciplinary activities.

Pre-disciplinary activities have as their basis the kind of common-sense experiences with which the children already have some familiarity. These are used as starting points upon which it is hoped to build developing understanding. For example, in introducing children to the idea of money as a means of exchange, a starting point that has been used is the collecting and swapping habits of the children themselves. Similarly, a study of conflict over the use of resources may start with an analysis of conflict over the use of domestic space within a home. (Who decides when a room is used and what it is used for?) Activities such as these cannot be classified as history, geography, or social science; they are deliberately chosen for the potential they provide for children to begin to exercise the skills valued by subject specialists.

Disciplinary activities are drawn from the traditional content of the social subjects. A progression is envisaged from pre-disciplinary to disciplinary activities which involves the use, in the early stages, of contrived experiences in which variables are deliberately controlled before actual case-study material with a disciplinary focus is used. Contrived situations in which the teacher deliberately controls the number and complexity of variables operating in any situation may mean using simulated examples rather than actual case-study material. Simulated examples have been used to encourage middle school children to begin to appreciate some of the factors involved in deciding where to locate a new factory, or where to site a new airport. It is often the political dimensions of actual case-studies that middle school children find difficulty in handling.

The suggested progression from pre-disciplinary to disciplinary activities does not preclude the use of interdisciplinary activity in the upper middle years. We prefer the description interdisciplinary to integrated here, because we see the essential feature of this work to be the interrelation of two or more disciplines in such a way that their distinct contributions, in terms of skills and the treatment of content, remain clear in the teacher's plan. Examples of interdisciplinary materials that interrelate history, geography, and social science and are intended for use with eleven- to thirteen-year-olds, have been produced by the HGSS Project.[8]

C   One of our assumptions is that the middle years of schooling may be the last opportunity that a significant number of children have of studying history and/or geography. We calculate that with the operation of an options programme beginning at the age of fourteen, up to 50% of the children will drop history, for good, from their lists. The figure may be lower for geography. But, for those teachers who value the place of the social subjects in the curriculum, the middle school years are important ones.

D   One of the findings of the HGSS Project, backed at a later date by the

Table 11.1   *The HGSS Project's suggested objectives*

Skills Intellectual	Social	Physical	Personal qualities Interests, attitudes, and values
1. The ability to find information from a variety of sources, in a variety of ways.	1. The ability to participate within small groups.	1. The ability to manipulate equipment.	1. The fostering of curiosity through the encouragement of questions.
2. The ability to communicate findings through an appropriate medium.	2. An awareness of significant groups within the community and the wider society.	2. The ability to manipulate equipment to find and communicate information.	2. The fostering of a wariness of overcommitment to one framework of explanation and the possible distortion of facts and the omission of evidence.
3. The ability to interpret pictures, charts, graphs, maps, etc.	3. A developing understanding of how individuals relate to such groups.	3. The ability to explore the expressive powers of the human body in order to communicate ideas and feelings.	
4. The ability to evaluate information.	4. A willingness to consider participating constructively in the activities associated with these groups.	4. The ability to plan and execute expressive activities to communicate ideas and feelings.	3. The fostering of a willingness to explore personal attitudes and values to relate these to other people's.
5. The ability to organize information through concepts and generalizations.			4. The encouraging of an openness to the possibility of change in values.
6. The ability to formulate and test hypotheses and generalizations.	5. The ability to exercise empathy (i.e., the capacity to imagine accurately what it might be like to be someone else).		5. The encouragement of worthwhile and developing interests in human affairs.

Table 11.2   *A suggested list of key concepts*

Similarity/Difference	
Continuity/Change	Methodological Key
Causes and Consequences	Concepts

Communication	
Power	Substantive Key
Values and Beliefs	Concepts
Conflict/Consensus	

primary school survey, was that much of the teaching of the social subjects to young children is *random* and *repetitive*. Topics or projects chosen, whether at the instigation of teacher or child, tend to be selected idiosyncratically and there is a great deal of repetition of subject matter from year to year. According to the HGSS Project, randomness and repetitiveness can be avoided by using planning guidelines. In order to plan progression in skill learning, a possible framework of objectives is recommended (Table 11.1), while to avoid repetition, the use of key concepts to select and sequence content is advocated (Table 11.2).

These objectives and key concepts provide a general framework for planning in relation to the policy guidelines A to D. It is not envisaged that in the five years from eight to thirteen these objectives will be achieved; indeed, as terminal behaviours, they are almost certainly unachievable. It is difficult to imagine, for example, a person achieving perfection in his ability to evaluate information. The objectives are meant to represent desirable skills and qualities that teachers might encourage in their pupils; they are roads to travel. However, for each of these objectives it is possible to build up increasing degrees of sophistication. Table 11.3 (Derricott and Blyth, 1979) shows how this idea relates to our notion of progression from predisciplinary to disciplinary activity in the ability to evaluate information. Table 11.4 shows a preliminary attempt by a group of teachers to develop a checklist which can be used to monitor the progress of children with this objective in mind. To keep records of this kind for each child and each objective is impossibly time consuming, therefore it is suggested that the activities of only three or four members of a group are detailed. This provides teachers both with information upon which to judge the progress of children and with valuable feedback about the emphasis of their own teaching.

Key concepts as in Table 11.2 are an attempt to provide guidelines for teachers in the task of selecting and sequencing content. The HGSS Project does not claim any epistemological status for the list of key concepts or suggest that, in any way, the list is exhaustive. The only claim that is made is that they contain ideas that are of interest to historians, geographers, and social scientists, that they can be used as a basis for interrelating the disciplines, and that they have potential in developing understanding of society and social issues. The methodological key concepts emphasize the process of enquiry. Recognizing similarity and difference is a basic categorizing activity essential in concept formation, and it has been found to be an appropriate process to emphasize in the early middle years. Continuity/change is a special case of similarity/difference of particular interest to the historian. Causes and consequences are key concepts which encourage explanation, and will therefore be appropriate for work with the older and abler children in the middle years.

The substantive key concepts suggest to teachers areas of content. The challenge is to use the key concepts to *select, organize*, and *sequence* content from the social subjects at a level thought to be appropriate for children of a given age. Table 11.5 shows the attempts of one group of teachers to sequence topics from the ages of eight to thirteen under the headings of the four substantive key concepts.

Guidelines A to D (pp.190–196) and the planning framework which we have related to these are but one attempt to give meaning to structure, assessment, progression, and continuity in the social subjects curriculum. They provide an outline map and it is for the schools to fill in the details and even to suggest a different 'projection'.

Implications

Our analysis of deficiencies in curriculum policy making and our attempt at guidelines for policy formulation have different implications for different middle schools. Of course, our criticisms may not apply to some middle schools, although we believe they apply to most.

The implications are likely to depend on a number of factors, only two of which we isolate here. Firstly there is the ideological stance adopted by the school. If the curriculum is informed by a Plowden-like ideology, the points we make about curriculum discontinuity and the consequent need for

Table 11.3

Pre-Disciplinary Activities.......................................Disciplinary Activities
Contrived Experiences
Controlled Variables

coping with uncertainty
encouraging opinion sharing
encouraging judgement making
coping with conflicting evidence
    or opinions
detecting bias

Use of Case-Study
Material from History,
Geography, or
Social Sciences

Table 11.4   *General objective: The ability to evaluate information*

Name of pupil .... age .... teacher ....

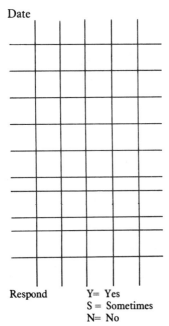

	Date				
1. Can cope with the uncertainty of there not being a correct answer					
2. Is prepared to make a judgement about a situation.					
3. Is prepared to share a judgement with others.					
4. Is prepared to comment on other people's ideas, opinions.					
5. Is prepared to have his own ideas, opinions commented on.					
6. When discussing evidence, uses words like 'probably', 'possibly', 'might'.					
7. Can distinguish between fact and opinion.					
8. Can cope with evidence from a number of sources.					
9. Can recognize conflicting evidence.					
10. Shows a wariness of possible bias or distortion in evidence.					
11. Shows a wariness of possible omission of evidence.					

Respond   Y= Yes
                 S = Sometimes
                 N= No

Table 11.5 *Sequencing of content using key concepts*

	Communication	Power	Values/ Beliefs	Conflict/ Consensus	Methodological Key Concepts
8+	Transport in a local setting. Local road patterns. Local transport services.	Preserving law and order. The Police Service past and present.	Rules: safety rules, highway code, rules in games. Belonging to groups with rules: scouts, etc.	Simulation: setting up an island society.	
					Similarity/Difference.
9+	National network of motorways. Railways. Airports. Why is the pattern as it is?	Simulation: the siting of a new airport. Who decides?	Families in different cultures. Comparison of roles of individuals in families.	Conflict over the use of domestic space, local space.	
					Continuity/Change
10+	Barriers to communication and how these are overcome. Crossing rivers, estuaries. Tunnels, the Channel Tunnel.	Floods: living with the threat of floods.	Going to school. Ways in which the young are taught in different cultures.	Providing for leisure need – conflicts of interest. Tourist versus conservationist.	
11+	Communication through the media. Newspapers, radio, TV.	Working in a factory. Trades unions. Strikes.	Victorian life.	Life during the Second World War.	
					Causes and Consequences.
12+	Advertising. Can we believe all we are told?	The oil crisis. Who has the power?	Culture clash. Aborigines of Australia.	Enclosures: simulations.	

curricular guidelines are likely to be discounted or reinterpreted. In such schools each teaching situation is regarded as unique, involving children, teachers, schools, and environments that are all different. The meaning of continuity of experience and any assessment of whether or not progression in learning is taking place can only, it is believed, be defined in terms of individual children and individualized programmes. The points we make about psychological structure, logistical integration, and psychological integration may well be taken, along with some of the comments on the logic of curriculum integration. Our suggestion of curricular guidelines involving a list of relevant skills and criteria for selecting and organizing content is not likely to appeal. However, it is our contention that the majority of primary and middle schools are not characterized by this 'romantic' ideology (Richards, 1979), and are likely in consequence to see implications in our analysis for their curriculum policy and practice.

In these schools the implications are likely to vary according to a second factor: the type of curricula in operation. Here we run into a problem of categorization; too often middle school curricula are simply characterized in very general terms. Thus curricula are said to be 'largely primary in orientation', 'largely secondary', 'part-primary, part-secondary', and just occasionally said to be 'genuinely middle'. In Table 11.6 an attempt has been made to construct a more adequate typology of middle school curricula. Such curricula are categorized in terms of three sets of distinctions. Firstly they are subdivided on the basis of whether curriculum decision-making is predominantly horizontal (i.e., taken mainly by year-group coordinators in relation to their year groups), or predominantly vertical (taken by subject consultants, heads of department, or others with a vertical responsibility throughout the school). Secondly curricula are differentiated in terms of subjects, broad areas (some which may, or may not, be integrated), and a combination of subjects and broad areas. Thirdly, curricula are categorized as to whether, in relation to the differentiated elements, there are tightly stipulated policies to which staff have to adhere, or whether there is room for considerable individual negotiation of content and time allocation. On these bases a typology of fifteen curricula has been developed covering, in our view, all the main types (others are logically possible but most unlikely in practice).

As we have stressed at various times throughout this chapter, curriculum continuity is a major issue for all types of schools but especially types 3, 4, and 5 where horizontal decision making is predominant. The necessity for

Table 11.6 *Middle school curricula: A suggested typology*

Types of middle school curricula	Predominant mode of curriculum decision making		Bases for curriculum differentiation		Predominant mode of control over content and time allocation	
	Vertical	Horizontal	Subjects	Broad areas	Stipulated	Individually negotiated
1a	X		X		X	
1b	X			X	X	
1c	X		X	X	X	
2a	X		X		X	X
2b	X			X	X	X
2c	X		X	X	X	X
3a		X	X			X
3b		X		X		X
3c		X	X	X		X
4a		X	X		X	X
4b		X		X	X	X
4c		X	X	X	X	X
5a		X	X	.	X	
5b		X		X	X	
5c		X	X	X	X	

careful sequencing of material is also common to all, but is particularly relevant to those types of school characterized by horizontal decision making and subtypes characterized by individual negotiation. Our comments about the logical basis of integration are particularly apposite in those middle schools where the curriculum is differentiated entirely in terms of broad areas or where such areas are found in the lower part of the school, with a subject-based division for older children. On the other hand, schools characterized by types 1 and 2 could profitably examine the arrangements they make for logistical integration, and could examine whether their curricula are designed in accordance with what we have termed psychological structure.

Conclusion

This chapter has stressed the importance of working out curricular policy at school level. It has tried to give some meaning and form to structure, assessment, progression, and continuity – all of which are important notions in the fast-developing debate as to how schools can be more accountable. The accountability ideology which these notions represent is now emerging as dominant. It is our contention that middle schools can give a very satisfactory account of their activities, and can provide a soundly based education for their pupils provided they attend to the details of curricular policy formulation and implementation. In our view, being accountable does not mean having to 'teach to the test' or having to resort to a restricted 'basic skills' curriculum.

The early 1980s are troubled times. Reese Edwards' comment made in 1972 was true at the time and even truer today. The middle school

> . . . was brought into existence at a time of uncertainty, launched during a time of greater uncertainty and in the years ahead faces an even greater period of uncertainty. (Edwards, 1972).

That middle school charting we mentioned at the beginning of this chapter still needs to be completed. If the middle school territory is not charted adequately and its assets not fully realized (or publicized), then there is the distinct possibility that its settlers (and map makers) may be withdrawn and the territory abandoned.

Notes

1. See, for example, Worcestershire County Council Education Committee (1968) and Rochdale Education Committee (1969).

2. This survey of middle schools is being conducted by two members of the Department of Education, University of Keele.
3. The chapter by Blyth gives the latest available middle school statistics.
4. Blyth and Derricott (1977) employ the distinctions between macro and micro levels of planning.
5. See, for example, Warwick (1975).
6. Two such projects were: Schools Council, *Keele Integrated Studies Project*, and Schools Council and the Nuffield Foundation, *Humanities Curriculum Project*.
7. For example see Oxfordshire County Council Communication Centre (1977).
8. See, for example, 'People on the Move' and 'Life in the Thirties' in *Place, Time and Society 8–13*, Pupils' Materials, 1977, Bristol, Collins, ESL.

Part IV

SOCIAL RELATIONS AND INTERACTION

INTRODUCTION

Continuity of educational experiences between first, middle, and upper schools, the formulation of common ground between middle schools, and continuity within middle schools became and remain dominant themes in the introduction, administration, and organization of three-tier systems of schooling. Blyth and Derricott's (1977) other three 'Cs', consultation, coordination, and communication have, in practice, been summarized in one word – *liaison*. The rhetoric and assumptions, expectations, constraints, and possibilities surrounding the implementation of an effective, continuous, and coordinated sequence of educational experiences through the liaison of teachers have not been fully explored. The diverse interpretations placed on the concepts, the varied enthusiasm and force with which their implementation has been attempted, and the consequences of interaction for those involved provide an intriguing phenomenon which deserves more thorough and systematic investigation.

The dynamics of a variety of three-tier and middle schools' internal arrangements cannot easily be monitored. Teachers operating in middle schools have experienced the dynamics of their particular situations. They are engaged in the interactions which are attendant features of liaison. Middle school teachers play, however, only one part in the interaction that takes place in middle schools. Questions about how pupils experience three-tier schooling are rarely asked. Similarly, while the ways in which parents view and respond to middle schools have created difficulties in local political skirmishes, little research has been done to improve our understanding of these issues. The perceptions of others who are closely connected with, but not working in middle schools, particularly teachers working in first and upper schools, are also important yet have hardly been researched. It is from the points of view of the pupils, and of teacher colleagues in first and upper schools that interaction is considered in Part IV.

The point of transfer for pupils into middle schools from first schools has been studied by Galton and Delamont. Recorded stress data elicited from pupils suggest very different patterns of stress amongst pupils transferring into each of two nine–thirteen middle schools which were part of a wider survey of pupils' classroom experiences. Whilst previous studies of transfer have tended to ignore the context of contrasting types of schools, in this study data are used to relate the experiences of the pupils to particular features of school organization and the pupils' social relationships with their peers and teachers. One school is a formal school, the other more informal. Account is taken of short-lived apprehension in pupils about treatment at the hands of older pupils or teachers, which has been cited in other studies of transfer as a stress factor. Although pupils transferring to the more formal school were initially more anxious than their peers going to the informal school, the situation was later reversed. Classroom interaction data suggest that the differences in the levels and the rate and direction of change in stress scores amongst the pupils of the two schools can be accounted for in the experience of the pupils in their relations with teachers, and the levels and pace of work. The differences are explained by the nature of the classroom regimes in each of the two schools, and the pupils' experiences of them over a period of time. The study shows that, despite superficial differences in the regimes of the two schools, the teaching-learning processes are in many respects quite similar. By the end of the first year in the middle schools, there was almost no difference in the stress scores of the two sets of pupils. Galton and Delamont suggest that changes in the anxiety levels of pupils are associated with classroom experience and schooling in general, rather than with the process of transfer as such.

Bryan, using an interactionist stance which stresses the concepts of 'career' and 'status passage', and adopting a different methodological approach, considers the question of transfer from middle to high schools as it is experienced by the pupils. The long standing age of transfer question is considered, using the pupils' own perceptions of transfer to show whether those perceptions differ with age or the types of school from and to which they move.

Data are used to compare the perceptions of pupils moving from three types of school, a five–eleven primary, an eight–twelve middle, and a ten–thirteen middle. Bryan discusses whether different types of school prepared their pupils for transfer, and whether the pupils in each type of school responded similarly or differently to their experience. In making these comparisons, the author shows clearly that the feelings, aspirations, and anxieties which pupils express are not particular to a given age, sex, or location. Bryan suggests that despite teachers' expressions of the need to foster continuity in the transition from middle to high schools, for the pupils middle schools do not present themselves as something different but are seen as schools like any other. The findings bring into question the assertion that middle schools are unique in identity, at least in the eyes of the pupils.

The importance and influence of peer relationships within the total realm of pupils' classroom and school experiences, and the interaction within and between peer groups is dealt with by Meyenn. He sees these relationships as having a crucial bearing on a pupil's adjustment and orientation to, and happiness and success in school. Yet rarely is the significance of peer relationships appreciated by teachers, and rarely is the question asked as to what effect the middle school organization is having on the pupils and their relationships with each other. It is that question which Meyenn sets out to explore. Using a variety of research techniques the author was able to explore the formation and nature of the social relationships of pupils in a nine–thirteen middle school. The character and culture of the peer networks show considerable differences between the ways in which boys and girls organize their social lives in school. Little interaction between boys and girls or between individual girls' groups was found, though for both sexes there was an increase with age in friendship choices which crossed form-group boundaries. Meyenn relates this change to an increase in setting procedures as pupils moved from a 'generalist' mixed-ability mode of organization to a 'specialist' mode with relatively homogeneous ability sets in some subjects. Not least in the findings is the point that in a school where selection procedures and differentiation processes were partly disguised, the boys in particular seemed to be unaware of the sorting and processing which was taking place. The girls on the other hand were much more aware of these subtle processes.

The perception of individuals engaged in interaction processes and the way in which those individuals define situations and relationships is important for the way they act. In this sense, the nature and extent of relationships of teachers in first and upper schools with their middle school colleagues is a significant aspect of three-tier organization which has implications for middle school teachers and for pupils' school experiences. The views of teacher colleagues 'below' and 'above' and the way they see middle school practices are the subject of the chapter by Ginsburg and Meyenn. They show that first school teachers in their study tended to see middle schools as bringing secondary practices to children younger than eleven plus, whilst upper school teachers saw middle schools as an extension of primary school methods beyond the age of eleven plus. The nature and extent of contact is shown to be subject to constraints of time and to concerns not to infringe on the autonomy of teachers in other schools, although strategies for influencing colleagues' work were identified. Adaptations and strategies in the work of the first and upper school teachers as a consequence of their contact with middle schools were also identified, with clear implications for the nature and continuity of pupils' school experience.

CHAPTER TWELVE

THE FIRST WEEKS OF MIDDLE SCHOOL

M. Galton and S. Delamont

Introduction

Children in school have to learn to change, as they move among different subjects, different teachers, different work patterns, and different classroom climates. When they transfer from one school to another all these other kinds of change coincide. In Great Britain, the advent of middle schools has meant children leaving first schools at eight, nine, ten, or eleven in different regions, and leaving the middle school at twelve, thirteen, or fourteen for an upper school of some description. Transfer therefore occurs at least twice for many pupils. In this chapter the process of transfer between first school and middle school at nine is examined by focusing on two nine–thirteen schools in an English city which we have called Ashburton.[1]

The chapter is divided into four main sections. First a brief description of the midlands city and then each transfer school is presented. Secondly the change in the anxiety levels of the pupils transferring from the feeder schools to the two transfer schools is described. Previous studies (e.g., Nisbet and Entwistle, 1966; Youngman and Lunzer, 1977) have shown that for the majority of pupils, the process of transfer is accompanied by a rise in the level of anxiety but that this increase is relatively short-lived. None of the previous studies has, however, examined their data within the context of contrasting types of school as we do here. The third and main section of the chapter presents ethnographic data on the first weeks of schooling the children experienced. These data are related to features of the schools' organization and the pupils' social relationships with peers and teachers. In the fourth and final section some explanation is offered for the changes in anxiety levels, based on the findings of the ethnographic study.

The wider research project of which this study of transfer forms a part has used a wide variety of methods: anxiety tests; formal and informal interviews with staff, pupils, and parents; tests of school achievement; sociometric questionnaires; and two kinds of observation in the classroom, one based on a schedule and the other ethnographic. In this chapter the anxiety tests, the ethnographic observation, and the informal interviews are drawn upon to present a picture of nine-year-olds entering two nine–thirteen schools. These data were collected in 1977–78 in two contrasting schools which will here be called Gryll Grange (a purpose-built, progressive school) and Guy Mannering (a traditional school in a converted secondary modern building). We collected material before the nine-year-olds made the transfer, studied the first month in the middle school intensively, and then followed the pupils through their first year in those new schools, collecting several kinds of data at all these stages.

The city and its schools

Ashburton is a city in the English midlands, in existence since Norman times, prosperous in the nineteenth century and now expanding rapidly. The old centre, built of Victorian red brick, now boasts a new glass and concrete shopping precinct, and the whole city is today ringed with new housing estates both council and private. Ashburton has grown rapidly due to 'overspill'; large numbers of people have been rehoused here from the larger midlands conurbations and from London. The education system of Ashburton and its surrounding county is a three-tier one. Children go to lower schools until they are nine, when they transfer to nine–thirteen middle schools, from which in turn they go to an upper school from the ages of thirteen to sixteen or eighteen. The upper schools are, in the main, based in the old grammar schools, while the former secondary modern schools were reincarnated as nine–thirteen middle schools. One of our two sample schools, Guy Mannering, was chosen for the research as a traditional school with a house system, uniforms, streaming, and a conventional curriculum. Gryll Grange was deliberately chosen as a contrast. It was a purpose-built show school, opened in 1972, and run on progressive lines with mixed-ability groups, an integrated day, and an individualized curriculum.

The most striking difference between the two school buildings is related to the organization of teaching, and whether this is seen as a specialist or a generalist activity. At Guy Mannering, teaching is a private activity which takes place behind closed doors. It is also a specialized activity. Each teacher has his or her own base, a subject room which the pupils visit for a specific subject and which is not legitimately visited except for that subject. At Gryll Grange teaching is less private and relatively unspecialized. A pupil stays in the form room or the year-group areas for most subjects, which are taught by the form teacher, or one of the year-group teachers. Thus new pupils entering Gryll Grange find a different world from that of Guy Mannering.

Changes in anxiety level on transfer

Anxiety data were collected through a modified form of the questionnaire used in the Lancaster study (Bennett, 1976) which was titled *WIDIS* (What I did in school). The questionnaire in its modified form consisted of twenty items which were answered either 'yes' or 'no'. Pupils completed the questionnaire on four occasions:

1 In the September of their final year in the first school (1976).
2 In June 1977 in the first school after they had visited the transfer schools.
3 In November 1977 after transferring to the middle schools.
4 In June 1978 after their first year in the middle schools.

The data are presented in Figure 12.1. The mean score for the pupils transferring to each of the middle schools is given as a percentage of the maximum possible score. When the data for each school are combined, it can be seen that the pattern conformed closely to previous findings.[2] There was a slight rise in anxiety prior to transfer which had almost disappeared by the first half-term after transfer. By the end of the year it was back to its original level of September 1976. If, however, the data for the two schools are looked at separately, there are sharp contrasts to be observed. The pupils entering Guy Mannering, the more traditional establishment, became more anxious prior to transfer, but after changing school their anxieties declined steadily. At Gryll Grange, where the first-year rooms resembled more closely the classrooms of the feeder schools, the level of anxiety reached its lowest level just prior to transfer. However, after changing school, the level rose sharply and continued to rise, albeit at a slightly slower rate, throughout the first year in the new school.

Before transfer, pupils have little first-hand knowledge of their new schools, but rely on siblings, teachers, and neighbourhood children. In our informal interviews with pupils we found that other children, especially

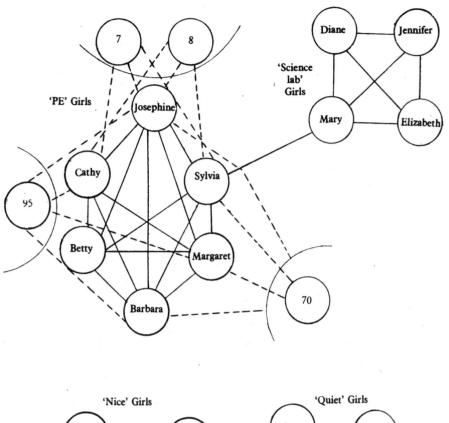

'PE' Girls

'Science lab' Girls

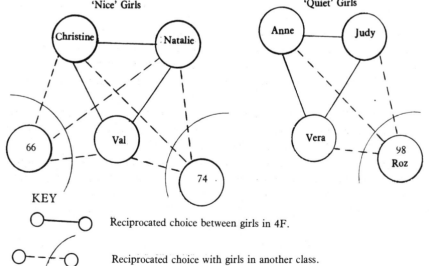

'Nice' Girls

'Quiet' Girls

KEY

Reciprocated choice between girls in 4F.

Reciprocated choice with girls in another class.

older siblings, are fond of telling their younger brothers and sisters of the horrors that await them in their new schools. Stories of heads being stuck down lavatories and of being rolled down steep, grassy banks were commonplace.[3] On the questionnaire it was the items referring to bullying by fellow pupils that were the source of the large rise in the percentage score in June 1977 before transfer, when no personal experience except a visit was available to pupils. Guy Mannering was also a strange new kind of building, and teachers of pupils transferring to Guy Mannering were fond of telling them that they would have to work much harder in the following year. In contrast, the pupils transferring to Gryll Grange could recognize much of the classroom layout in the first-year complex, and must have found some reassurance in so familiar an atmosphere. After transfer, however, the situation was reversed with Gryll Grange children becoming more anxious and those at Guy Mannering less so. This rise at Gryll Grange and the fall at Guy Mannering took place in the period between June and November. We have ethnographic data on the first weeks in the new schools. It is from these data that possible explanations for these changes should emerge. The stories about bullying were found to be nothing more than stories, and the pupils gained first-hand experience of teaching and learning in Guy Mannering and Gryll Grange. We argue that the lessening of anxiety at Guy Mannering and its rise at Gryll Grange are to be explained by differences in that first-hand experience after the myths have been exploded.

First days in the new schools

The data used to examine how the new pupils reacted to, and behaved in, their first weeks of their new middle schools are taken from notes made by the researchers during the field-work in the first weeks of the September term. These are of two kinds: field notes which were actually written inside the classroom or in the school during the school day, and a field diary, written in the evening or at week-ends, away from the schools. Extracts from field notes are indicated as *Notes* and from the field diary as *Diary*, with each extract followed by the date (e.g., 14.9.77).

The data are used to illustrate how the new school careers of our pupils began, and illuminate the anxiety scores. We begin with data on two pupils at Gryll Grange, the progressive school, a girl called Davina in Miss Tweed's class and a boy, Dudley, in Mrs. Hind's. Then similar material is presented on two children at Guy Mannering. The data begin on the first day of the new school year.

Notes (1.9.77)

The first year are let in from the playground. They find pegs in the cloakroom area and go to rooms. Much hesitation, giggling, etc. – hanging back in doorways. . . . The first thing done is dinner numbers – collected in each of the three forms and taken on scraps of paper to the office by a girl – Davina. . . . About six pupils are found in the wrong room – another three or four are missing. . . .

Early on pupils are told by Miss Tweed to get soft shoes – if they hadn't any – because of the carpet. The caretaker doesn't like mud being brought in. Miss Tweed also says they are 'lucky' not to have many carpets, so they 'can paint' in the classroom.

9.30 Davina has got safely back – bringing registers – reports to Miss Tweed and is sent to take registers into two other first-year classes.

9.35 All is peace – pupils in their classes – administration – if not work – has begun.

9.38 Three pupils receive a warning from Miss Tweed – 'for goodness sake don't leave money in pockets', followed by dire warning (of consequences – i.e., theft).

9.50 Miss Tweed sends Davina to office with dinner money. Then to check if other two first-year teachers want her to take theirs – one doesn't – the other gets her to show Candy the way. On their return Davina says to me 'We're doing nothing – it's rather boring'.

9.55 Davina leaves again with register. There is a trickle of pupils going out to the lavatory. . . .

Davina is clearly being singled out by Miss Tweed as reliable, competent, and eager to help her teacher. In the first hour of her experience in Gryll Grange she had become a 'successful pupil'. We can also see several characteristics of Gryll Grange in this extract, which are important elements in the way the school presents itself to pupils. For example, the pupils are given genuine reasons for the teacher's instructions. They are to wear indoor shoes to please the caretaker and cleaners, they must not leave money in the cloakroom in case of theft. It is also clear that the first-year teachers cooperate, for Miss Tweed sends messages offering help into the other two classes. And, we can see that pupils go out of lessons to the lavatory. More characteristics of the school will become apparent from notes taken in Mrs.

Hind's class after break on the first day.

Notes (1.9.77)

Mrs. Hind settles them – discussion of storage drawers. 'Notes into your English books.'

These are notes on the presentation of work. Dudley comes wandering out to Mrs. Hind's desk, and is sent back to his seat – then he says 'capital letters, full stops', and is ticked off. Mrs. Hind says 'I thought you were talking to yourself'. Dudley says 'I was'. They are told to put date on the top left by margin, and a heading *Presentation* underlined 'if you have a ruler'. . . .

Rule one is 'Always start your work with the date'. Dudley says he can't see. Moved nearer the board – he pushes his new pencil/geometry case onto the floor.

Rule two is 'Put the heading and underline it'.

Rule three is 'Leave a line after the heading'.

When she asks a question there are several people giving the answer. But she waits for hands to go up, chooses, and says 'Alan' or whoever. . . . Class are very quiet – noise is fidgetting not talk. . . . Mrs. Hind checks at each stage to see if the idea is familiar. . . .

11.30 To hall for Assembly.

In this extract we can see Dudley behaving in ways which are likely to annoy teachers at Gryll Grange. He leaves his desk at inappropriate moments, he talks to himself, he 'can't see' the board, and he drops things. The extract also shows one kind of experience common in new schools and with new teachers: rules for setting out work. We saw nearly every single teacher offer the pupils some guidelines of this kind, and mastering them is an important part of becoming an acceptable pupil. In addition this extract shows Mrs. Hind, like most teachers we saw, beginning to train pupils to put up their hands rather than call out. Dudley, however, learns few of these rules, as an extract from the third day of term at Gryll Grange shows.

Notes (5.9.77)

9.10 Has them copying points about sentences. Gives them ten words to make up ten sentences – not just 'I was running' but more description. Dudley's registration form looks as if it has been chewed. Mrs. Hind asked if he has been eating it – Dudley gives an explanation about plimsolls which produces a grimace. . . . Dudley gets yelled at for misspelling 'house' (on the board) and not joining up his writing – but just told to 'go away' and put it right. . . .

Here we can see Dudley behaving in two more ways guaranteed to annoy Mrs. Hind. He has mangled the form on which details of his address, parents' places of work, and so forth are recorded by carrying it from home to school in his plimsoll, and he miscopies words from the board. Pupils at Gryll Grange are expected to take messages to and from school carefully, and to copy accurately from the board. Davina, in contrast, is busy displaying characteristics which endear her to Miss Tweed, as extracts from the second week show.

Notes (6.9.77)

9.00   Miss Tweed is busy mounting the pupils' work on sugar paper. Davina is still the official runner – taking register, dinner numbers, etc. to the office. . . .

Break   Miss Tweed said in the staffroom she picked Davina for her class when making up the forms. She taught her elder brother, and likes the family. Davina is the kind of pupil she likes because she is good at work, active in games including swimming, plays an instrument, sings, and does a lot of art and craft.

1.15   Miss Tweed's class have music. Davina gives out music books.

2.00   Back in their form room, the pupils are told to: 'Finish writing about yourself. Do exercise in book. Do a pattern, based on a closed curve, and colour it.'
Miss Tweed attacks a table of boys: 'Are you having another rest? You had a long rest all morning.'
A girl takes her work to be marked: 'I like smyming. What's smyming? You've got your w the wrong way up.'

2.10   Dean has spelt rugby so it looks like rabbit. Table of boys near me are not working – their 'essays' so far consist of the name and date. . . .

2.20   Dean has been in the lavatory for ten minutes.

This extract shows that Davina has maintained her role as monitor for Miss Tweed, and reveals not only why Miss Tweed likes her, but some behaviours from other children which are in contrast to Davina's. Boys are told off for not working, for not keeping themselves busy. Busyness in the sense discussed by Jackson,[6] and Sharp and Green,[7] is a central value at Gryll Grange, and Davina's emergence as a good pupil is partly due to her ability to keep herself occupied. This value placed on busyness is one way in which Gryll Grange is very different from Guy Mannering. As we now turn to look at how the nine-year-olds faced that school, other differences will become apparent. At Guy Mannering we focus on a class in the 'A' band.

Notes (6.9.77)

9.30 First period, Mr. Legard, library and RE. Pupils are given rules on how to make library folders.

Rule three lines with pencil.

With pen write your name in capitals.

He then goes round and it is clear some of the children do not know about capitals.

'I said capitals' (to one little girl). 'Do as I say. Don't let the form down, dear.' . . . One child with the primary school still in mind tried to come out to ask a question and was sent very firmly back to her place.

Next period (RE)

Again the lesson begins by setting out the rules. . . . 'What you write down is what I write down on the board. There's your heading . . . THE BIBLE.' There then follow lots of questions: 'Do we underline?', 'Can we use a pen?', 'Do we do joined-up letters?', etc.

The teacher then goes on to tell the children that the bible is inspired by God, gives the names of the books making up the Pentateuch, and then notes on Genesis. The observer's notes are next used to show an English lesson after break.

Notes (6.9.77)

Mr. Evans begins: 'All you have got to do is to sit down quietly. It is not a club where you come in and talk. All you have got to do is sit still and listen to me.'. . . He gives them the rules for arrival.

1 Wait outside on the left-hand side of the door side by side.

2 Don't go to the other side of the door because Mrs. Y lives there and you can't steal her space.

. . . He goes over the essays they wrote for him (comments are made publicly so whole class can hear). . . . 'English has rules. If you break the rules you are in trouble. You will know if you have made a mistake, why?'

Pupils: 'Because it will have a red mark.'

Teacher: 'And what do we call that?'

Pupils: 'Corrections.'

Teacher: 'And what must you do before you go on to the next piece of work?'

Pupil: 'You correct your mistakes.'

From this extract of notes taken on the first full day, we were able to observe in Guy Mannering that several things are obvious about the school. First, like Gryll Grange, the teachers are keen to establish the rules, both for behaviour and for setting out work. However, unlike Gryll Grange, the reasons offered for the rules at Guy Mannering were frequently unrealistic or improbable. 'Stealing space' is offered rather than 'blocking the corridor', for example. Secondly, as the reader will have noticed, the pupils at Guy Mannering move from one teacher's room to the next, whereas the Gryll Grange pupils spend most of their time in their home room. In addition, Guy Mannering teachers run their lessons for the whole class, with everyone working on the same thing at the same time. Because of this, it is harder to discern children's individual responses to the school. However we have used some data on one boy, Gavin Radice, because extracts in which he features show the central points about life at Guy Mannering. Gavin wished to be called 'Radiche', but many teachers called him 'Radish' despite his attempts to correct them. He obviously felt this deeply, but his powerlessness shows the relative lack of autonomy given to pupils at Guy Mannering. In addition, Gavin is an example of a pupil who was capable of doing the work, but was frequently in trouble for carelessness, as we shall see.

Notes (9.9.77)

I go with Mrs. Forrest up to the form room. They are all present, and can leave early tonight. A class with 100% attendance all week is rewarded by leaving early on Friday.

Sonia asked if 'Gabrielle and me can swap desks'. Told they can but only after Sonia has rephrased it to 'Gabrielle and I'. . . . Maths begins. . . .

One girl confesses to not having done homework. Told gently to do it over the week-end. Here every pupil has a maths text book which they are clearly allowed to take home – indeed *have* to take home for homework.

Mrs. Forrest is moving round the room. Tells Gabrielle that because she's moved she mustn't talk – if she talks she'll be put back to her old seat. . . .

'Lawrence and Gavin you don't look as though you're working very hard. I know they're not very hard, Gavin, but you have to do them and get them all right.'

Here we can see several things about Guy Mannering which are different from Gryll Grange. The pupils have written homework with personal text books, they are supposed to work in silence, and are expected to do work which is too easy for them if their classmates are doing it. Further evidence of the problems of keeping the work rate going comes from the following:

Notes (13.9.77)

In English with Mr. Evans they are to do a comprehension exercise. He tells them about not starting till he has gone over the setting out – so does – ruling off, not wasting the space . . . stresses heading, capital letters, etc. He finds Gavin has started. Tells him he's done it wrong, rule it off and do it over again. . . . He tells them it is not a race – the first to finish may be the worst work. . . .

Gavin is obviously a very fast worker. He asked if they were to go on to question three. Told there is probably not time, except he might have time, but mustn't forget to answer the questions (i.e., not just copy incomplete ones off board).

Here we can see the English master attempting to organize the class into working in a body, and to stop the faster workers getting too far ahead. Gavin is a fast, but careless worker, and his carelessness is used to hold him back. On the 16th we saw Gavin reprimanded in maths for not listening, in English for untidy work, in science for not doing his homework, and in the last English lesson for putting his date in the wrong place. However, he was again the first person to finish his work in English, fifteen minutes before the end of the lesson, while three children had not finished when the bell went.

This emphasis on getting everything done in the lesson was common at Guy Mannering, and relates to an important difference between the schools: the issues of *busyness* and *boredom*.

Busyness and boredom

Philip Jackson (1968) suggested that busyness, an air of involved activity, was one of the things which a school child had to learn for success in the lower levels of schooling. The importance of busyness in the progressive infant school has been stressed by Sharp and Green (1975), who suggest that busyness is 'the teacher's practical solution' to the complex problem of managing a progressive classroom (p.121). At Mapledene Lane School, teachers frequently exhorted pupils to 'be busy', 'find yourself something to do', and 'get on, on your own' (p.122). Sharp and Green argue that the more seriously the children take the command, the more freedom the teacher has, and thus the more manageable her task is. Jackson and Sharp and Green argue that the good pupil in a progressive classroom learns to be busy, while the bad pupil is one who does not busy herself or himself, but does nothing, and is bored. The bad child is a bored child in such classrooms.

These two themes, of busyness and boredom, were ones in which we predicted the two schools would differ, and which had different meaning in the two schools. At Guy Mannering all work, including project work, was heavily teacher-structured. All lessons centred on the teacher, and all pupils did the same thing, at the same time, in the same way, with exhortations to the slower pupils to keep up with the pack. Copying from the board was a central feature in nearly all lessons, reading aloud round the class was common, and public question and answer sessions frequent. The pupils were often allowed to do a drawing, or to write something in their own words, but on these occasions everyone began at the same time and the teacher controlled the start and finish of the activity. Typical examples from the field notes follow.

Notes (21.9.77)

Guy Mannering – Woodwork

I walked round. Pupils are taking a piece of (graph) paper putting a 10mm margin all around, then sticking a picture made of seven types of wood – but drawing round wood pieces today – needs whole double for gluing. . . .

Mr. Bradshaw calls them to order to deliver a lecture on how to write name on work – measured guidelines – and how he likes lettering. . . ..

Notes (23.9.77)

Guy Mannering – Science

Mrs. Forrest says: 'Will you stop now please! Just stop and look at the book I've given you.' Tells them what page to put it on (in their exercise books) – what the heading is – and to do the heading first. She wants them to do the heading and then listen. There are sentences with missing words for them to do from book. Not all ready. 'Will you please be quick. I've given you long enough to write that. . . . You may underline your heading with a pencil, a felt or a coloured pencil. . . . I haven't mentioned the most important thing – a ruler. . . .'

Here we see close teaching supervision, the pressure to keep everyone working at the same pace, and the small size of each task set at any one time.

At Gryll Grange things were very different. There were some pieces of classwork set, such as sums or writing to be copied from the board, but the general pattern was for each child to work from text books of the appropriate level in maths and English, with the work set a week at a time, to be fitted in as each child chose during the week. As long as the work was marked regularly, and the child did a proper amount each week, the pacing of the work was individualized and partially controlled by the pupil. Speed was not a virtue in itself, and no emphasis was placed by the staff on keeping up with other children, only on working conscientiously. Instead the teachers stressed keeping to one's own personal time-table or schedule, and ignoring other children in the room. In other words, the Gryll Grange staff valued busyness. The children were not doing unique work, but were taking an independent path through a common set of tasks. Again extracts from the field notes illustrate the point.

Notes (30.9.77)
Gryll Grange – Miss Tweed's class
 Miss Tweed says to get on with something – *Oxford Middle Schools Maths /Reading to Some Purpose* etc. – while she talks to Mrs. Hind. Those who haven't finished their week's work have their names on the board. . . . Pupils go to trays and get their things – then large group gathers round her – she sends them away – says can sleep if they want to, or sit and look angelic for ten minutes, but go away.

Notes (16.9.77)
Gryll Grange – Mrs. Hind's class
 Mrs. Hind has put ten adding-up sums on the board. . . . Elaine has finished her sums (9.20). As she did maths yesterday she can do English. Schonell – . . . Schonell Book Two (blue) for Oliver – Louisa is on green (Book Three). . . . Louisa and Sylvia are working together – muttering all the answers aloud. . . . Charles is working through *Oxford Middle School Maths* and Oliver is working from something – Schonell plus a

dictionary. . . . Robin is on Schonell Book One. . . . This class now looks a bit like a progressive room in that pupils are spread out across two subjects (maths and English) and three kinds of work – sums on the board, *Oxford Middle School Maths*, Schonell, and *Reading to Some Purpose*, with each pupil on different levels of the book and different places through them.

Both these classroom regimes are teacher-controlled. However, the kind of control is very different, and so too are the incidences of busyness, boredom, and noninvolvement. Gryll Grange had the heavy emphasis on busyness which we had predicted. The pupil who is found doing nothing is the great sinner. The good pupil is one who does the assigned work quickly and neatly, and then reads, sews, or draws until the teacher assigns more tasks. With the weekly rhythm of work a pupil should be busy until about Thursday, and then there should always be a library book 'on the go'. Noninvolvement, if the teacher spots it, is a legitimate reason for a reprimand; but during the field-work we spotted many pupils who were not 'caught out'. The only legitimate way a pupil can be idle is to be in the queue at the teacher's desk, or trying to attract her attention by sitting with your hand up. It is possible to waste a great deal of time queuing for marking, help, or just checking that one is doing the correct thing. Going to the lavatory is also a legitimate way of avoiding work. The data collected at Gryll Grange show that some pupils wasted a great deal of time in these legitimate ways, as well as those pupils who wasted time just chatting or fighting.

Guy Mannering was very different. A pupil at that school could hardly avoid working, because each lesson began with the allocation of tasks for all pupils, and teachers checked carefully to make sure everyone was doing them. However, the whole notion of busyness was absent. Once the task was completed – the paragraph copied, the sums done, the sentences completed, the picture stuck into the book – the pupil had nothing to do but sit, be bored, and wait for the slower brethren to catch up. It was not legitimate to read, sew, draw, or even do other school work. Indeed any attempt to occupy yourself would produce a reprimand from the teacher. In many lessons no other tasks were available, for sewing, library books, and homework were kept in the form room or in the subject room. Despite the banding, the research team found that there were considerable gaps between the fastest and slowest workers, and the faster ones spent a great deal of time waiting for the others to catch up. In maths, the 'A' band teacher –

Mrs. Forrest – used a text book with parallel exercises, and the fast workers did two exercises on every topic while the slow ones did only one. However, in every other subject the fast children spent a lot of time waiting for the rest.

Two teacher strategies had been evolved to 'solve' this problem. One involved giving extra work which could be finished for homework, so that the fast workers did not have any homework because they completed the task in class while slow workers had quite a bit. The other strategy was to reject all the work done quickly, and get it redone. This meant that all the fast workers did the task twice. (The rationale offered for this was usually that the offenders had not listened to the instructions, and/or that they were careless.) Queues at the teacher's desk were discouraged, and remaining in one's place with a hand up was the preferred pattern. Most classes did not allow movement, so a seated child was clearly either working or waiting. Boredom was therefore endemic, and blamed on the slower children.

In summary, then, we would argue that at Gryll Grange busyness is valued and no one should be bored; at Guy Mannering boredom is recognized as a penalty which slow workers impose on faster coevals, and that busyness is not a valued, or even a legitimate, quality in pupils.

Such a difference between two schools might imply that they were totally different environments for children. However, we wish to argue that in one important area of school life, the curriculum, there were many similarities in what the children actually did.

Curriculum form and content

When the two schools were sampled, the research team expected to find that curriculum form and content at Gryll Grange was of the kind labelled by Bernstein (1975), as an *invisible pedagogy*, while Guy Mannering had what Bernstein terms the *visible pedagogy*.[4] Bernstein argued that where both the classification and the framing of knowledge in the school are weak, the pedagogy is invisible, that is the control is implicit, although it is still there. In the visible pedagogy, the classification and framing are strong, and the social control is explicit. In Bernstein's theory, this should mean that the subjects are rigidly separated at Guy Mannering (strong classification) and integrated at Gryll Grange (weak classification), while the teacher is in control of the pace and direction of work at Guy Mannering (strong framing) and the pupil in charge of the pace and direction at Gryll Grange (weak framing). Certainly at Guy Mannering, pupils moved from one specialist teacher to another, thus shifting visibly from a science laboratory to a geography room, while at Gryll Grange, nearly all subjects were taught by the class teacher in the same form room. (Strong versus weak classification.) The pattern of work at Guy Mannering was classwork, with all pupils doing the same task at the same time (strong framing), while at Gryll Grange the pupils were on different individual tasks at their own pace (weak framing).

However, the reality was not so simple. The field diary for the second week records:

Diary (14.9.77)

Guy Mannering has much stronger classification and framing – *but* those at Beaconsfield are not weak – maths is maths – there is not a sense of integration *across* subjects. The classifications are equally strong but the framing is weaker at Gryll Grange.

Such suspicions were increasingly confirmed as the field-work progressed.

There was a strong boundary between maths and English signalled by different text and exercise books, and exhortations to 'finish your maths', or 'get on with your English'. Then the whole class would be stopped to go to music, or games, or because the French teacher (Mr. Lyons) had arrived. Gryll Grange paid great attention to French, starting the nine-year-olds with three periods a week, which were class-taught and involved a change of teacher. Thus, the field diary for 16.9.77 records that:

Mrs. Hind said today that she thought PE and music were overemphasized and in some schools 'everything stops for music' but at Gryll Grange 'everything stops for French'.

The way in which French was clearly separated from other subjects was also clear from the field notes.

Notes (8.9.77)

As break approaches Mrs. Hind tells those who have not started their Schonell work to read their library books because Miss Tweed is coming for French. I hear groans . . .

10.55 Miss Tweed starts French.

So, we would argue, there was clear classification at Gryll Grange, even if it was not as strong or as visible to casual outsiders as that at Guy Mannering.

Regarding framing, again we would want to argue that while the system was much more visible and explicit at Guy Mannering, there was a good deal of control over pupils' pacing of their work at Gryll Grange too. The results for the slow pupil might not be so different. The reader can compare field-note extracts from the two schools.

Notes (9.9.77)
Guy Mannering – a science lesson
   Mrs. Forrest says: 'Will you finish the sentence you're writing and then close your books.' (A few seconds silence ensues.) 'Right, I think you've had time now. Stop writing. Put your pen top on and any felt-tip top you are using. . . . Close all your books please. *Essential Science* and your own books please. . . . Are they all closed at the back? No they're not. . . .'

Here we see strong framing. The class are being taught as a group, and moved forward together. But the pacing and teacher control of work is also apparent at Gryll Grange.

Notes (27.9.77)
Gryll Grange
   Miss Tweed gives back some work – marked – and says they don't read the questions. Reminds them of the rules – get each piece of work marked as they go.
   Kenneth's book is held up 'urgh – yeer – yow'. Tells whole class 'no excuse, ever, for things like this'. . . . Kenneth has miscopied from the board – eleven copying mistakes. . . . (A reprimand, given publicly for some seconds.) 'Can you imagine what it'll look like in ink?' Explains that the headmaster wants the whole first year to be writing in ink.
   Sets the whole class some work, on worksheets, which is later to go in the book. Work is on measuring. She goes over the work on the board for the whole class.

Here, we would argue, there is relatively strong framing, in which pupils are not given control over the direction and pacing of their work, but forced to listen to a general teacher instruction.

At Guy Mannering motivation was explicit, in that pupils were given letter grades or marks for their work, and credits for good work and behaviour with demerits for misbehaviour. These were credited to the pupil's house. Promises of credits, and threats for demerits were used to gain quiet, attention, cooperation, and so forth in class. This is an obviously explicit way of motivating pupils, and Gryll Grange had nothing like it. But there were extrinsic sanctions used to regulate pupil's work. A pupil who had not completed the work for the week by Friday afternoon was kept in and missed games. A pupil who had not learnt his or her tables well enough to pass the test on them would miss football or netball. One boy, Dean, was observed in tears as Friday afternoon approached because he had failed his tables test. This does not seem to us to be a very different result from the demerit awarded at Guy Mannering.

In another way too, there were similarities in the curriculum *content* between the two schools. The content of the English was very similar, and both schools demanded that the pupils learned spelling lists and then tested the pupils, both expected correct spelling and grammar, demanded that corrections were done, and wanted sentences that began with capital letters and ended with full stops. Guy Mannering children read aloud around the class more often, and copied extensively from the board, but what they read and copied was very similar. Gryll Grange did *Oxford Middle School Maths*, but also did conventional sums, and like Guy Mannering expected children to learn their tables off by heart. Perhaps the most noticeable overlap was in the area of social studies. At Guy Mannering pupils did history and geography in separate rooms with different teachers. However, the *content* of the history, the changing style of the home – from cave through Roman villa to Anglo-Saxon and hall – looked very like the topic chosen for integrated studies at Gryll Grange, which was 'shelter'. Overall the curricular differences were largely stylistic – copying from the board rather than doing worksheets – and centred on three subjects: science, French, and religion. The nine-year-old at Gryll Grange got no science, and no explicit religion in lessons, but did get French from a specialist plus *assistante*. The Guy Mannering child did not get French, but did start a general science course, and he or she did get a large amount of explicit religion in the week. Otherwise the knowledge being offered to the children was very similar.

Discussion and conclusions

In this chapter we have presented both anxiety scores of pupils, and some ethnographic data on their first weeks in their new schools. Our finding is that before transfer to middle school, pupils were more anxious about the formal school, Guy Mannering, than about the informal school, Gryll Grange, but once in the new schools, this gap began to disappear so that by the end of their first year in the middle schools there was almost no difference. Our explanation for this rests on two things. Firstly, the fears that pupils had about bullying before transfer turned out to be illusory. Secondly, the other areas of school life about which pupils had expressed anxiety – relations with teachers and the level and pace of work – turned out to be less stressful in Guy Mannering than pupils had expected, but more stressful at Gryll Grange than they had expected. In fact, as our field-note data show, the teaching-learning processes in the two schools are quite similar despite superficial differences. Indeed we found during our subsequent visits over the year 1977–78 that the similarities increased. In the first few weeks the teachers were concerned to let the children know exactly where they stand, and rule giving was the most conspicuous feature of many of the exchanges. At Gryll Grange pupils learned to be busy, while at Guy Mannering they learned to complete their work at the same time as their peers or pay the penalty of boredom or extra homework. Both schools placed considerable emphasis on the basic skills, and there were regular tests in spelling and in simple mathematical computation. In English, both schools penalized spelling and grammatical errors in almost exactly the same way. Pupils wrote out each correction a number of times before proceeding to new work. By the end of the 1977–78 school year, there seemed to be even fewer differences between the classrooms. Whereas at Guy Mannering the attitude of the teachers had become more relaxed, at Gryll Grange the pupils now seemed to be subjected to greater pressure.

We wish to relate this to the anxiety data in the following way. At Guy Mannering the rise in the level of anxiety stems initially from the treatment in the final term of the time that pupils spent in the feeder schools. During this period of research, systematic observation was carried out on a number of pupils in these classes. In the anecdotal accounts of these visits, the observers often commented on the increase in the more formal aspect of work in the summer term. Teachers were fond of warning the pupils that 'things would be different next year' and 'you will not get away with work like that with your new teachers'. Thus, prior to transfer, the pupils expectations of next year's work and the sternness of the teachers are created and this is reflected in the sharp rise in anxiety level when measured just before transfer.

In the month after transfer to Guy Mannering these expectations are only partly fulfilled. There is intense pressure on the pupils to learn rules governing the presentation of work, but after this short period, once the classes have sorted themselves out into pupils who can cope and those who cannot, pressure is gradually relaxed. All sorts of means are used to compensate and hide differences due to the effects of banding. For example, at Guy Mannering points were awarded to each house according to the number of good stars received by their members. In the 'A' band stars were usually given for good work. Within two weeks of the start of term it became abundantly clear that pupils in the 'A' band were gaining many more stars than those in the 'B' bands. Accordingly the teachers in the 'B' bands started to compensate by awarding stars for other things. For example, in one class pupils who managed to walk in a straight line to assembly were all given an award.

By the end of the year a pattern had been established where pupils with learning difficulties were left to find their own level. Once the initial period of adjustment was over, the pupils found that they were allowed to work at their own pace. Failure to succeed was inevitably put down to lack of ability and, since the rate of failure corresponded closely to the placement within the different bands, the teachers rarely criticized less able pupils for lack of effort. Thus, during the first year at Guy Mannering the children gradually became less threatened by the system, and the anxiety level dropped dramatically.

At Gryll Grange a reverse situation takes place. Gryll Grange contains all the trappings of the progressive institution. Children were allowed an element of choice in their work. There was a year teacher and, on the surface, an integrated time-table. The situation was a familiar one for both the pupils and the teachers from the feeder schools. Consequently there was less talk, prior to transfer, about the difficulties which were likely to occur in the following year. After visiting their new school the similiarities with their present classroom were so apparent, that the anxiety levels fell.

Once in the new school, however, the realities were altogether different. Although, on the surface, the school appeared to differ remarkably from its more traditional counterpart, Guy Mannering, in practice the two were very similar. Pupils in the first year at Gryll Grange were actually taught by almost as many teachers for different parts of the curriculum as those at Guy Mannering. There were almost as many rules as at the more traditional school, and far fewer concessions were made to the less able pupils. All were expected to work equally hard, even if at different levels. Thus, during the year the pressures increased on the pupils and they were expected to manage their own learning in such a way as to remain busy for large parts of the day. There were no exceptions made to these rules and lack of effort was seen as the paramount vice. Consequently the expectations of the pupils prior to transfer were not only unfulfilled but, in the event, proved misleading. The anxiety level thus gradually increased during the year.

Overall, therefore, we have argued that pupils' anxiety levels surrounding transfer to nine–thirteen middle schools are related before transfer to warnings about their new school, based on superficial features and myths, while after transfer anxiety levels are related to the pupils' own classroom experiences. The particular features of classroom processes in these two schools, which will be reported elsewhere,[5] have parallels with our data from both primary and secondary schools in cities other than Ashburton. In so far as pupils' anxiety over transfer is primarily related to these processes, we would argue, therefore, that changes in the anxiety levels of pupils appear occasioned by the problems associated with schooling in general, rather than with transfer in particular.

Notes

1. The research described here comes from a wider programme of study financed by the SSRC for whose support the authors are grateful. Further details of the project are given in Galton, Simon, and Croll, (1980).
2. For example, Nisbet and Entwistle (1966) and Youngman and Lunzer (1977).
3. Similar myths were found among pupils in Southampton and elsewhere in the midlands, by researchers using both questionnaires and interviews. See, for example, Piggot (1979).
4. Bernstein differentiates between schools where the regime, in terms of both discipline and curriculum, has clearly defined, explicit, rigid rules (visible), and those where there is apparently no structure (invisible) but which, he argues, actually have just as much control over the minds and bodies of pupils. Different sectors of the middle class are believed to favour the two types of schooling for their children because of different positions in the occupational system which they and their children occupy.
5. Five volumes of material from the ORACLE project are in press or in preparation. See Galton, Simon, and Croll, (1980) for further details.

CHAPTER THIRTEEN

PUPIL PERCEPTIONS OF TRANSFER BETWEEN MIDDLE AND HIGH SCHOOLS

K. A. Bryan

Introduction

The purpose of this chapter is to ascertain whether pupils' perception of transfer between schools varies with the age of transfer and the types of school from and to which they move. The long standing age of transfer question is identified in the context of the development of middle schools, and the significance of pupils' perceptions is assessed with reference to the sociological concepts of status passage, career, and school structure. Finally, the question is raised, in the light of the data, whether for pupils middle schools have a particular identity or whether they are just schools like any other.

The extent to which English middle schools have taken their form from economic and ideological considerations is still a matter of some contention (Bryan and Hardcastle, 1977; Hargreaves, 1977(b)). Whatever variant has been adopted in particular locations, with the exception of the five–twelve middle schools, the interface between the first and middle, and middle and high school has become formalized as part of three-tier organization, and transfer between three types of school has become a necessity. In the middle school literature of the late 1960s and early seventies (University of Exeter, 1968; Edwards, 1972; Gannon and Whalley, 1975), the strengths and weaknesses of the three-tier systems as compared with the more traditional, primary all-through comprehensives were discussed. These developments concerning the emergence of middle schools as educational institutions with a specific administrative status stimulated thought and action in the areas of curriculum, school organization, and the social processes, which previously were either taken for granted, or where they were recognized as problematic in some way, were not investigated systematically. The transfer of pupils from one type of school to another, particularly at a stated age, is an example of one such social process.

Long before the disappearance of the last all-age school, most pupils had to transfer from one kind of school to another during their educational career. For the majority transfer occurred at the age of eleven plus, when they moved from the elementary or primary level to some form of post-elementary or secondary school. With the Education Act of 1944, elementary schools ceased to exist and section 8 of that act expressly stated that transfer between schools must occur between the ages of ten years, six months and twelve. Because the various types of secondary school which had emerged at this time had different outlets for their pupils, in a climate of equality of opportunity this change point at the age of eleven plus soon acquired educational and social significance for teachers, pupils, and parents. It was not until twenty years after the 1944 Act, with the Education Act, 1964, that experimental schemes with wider ages of transfer were legally sanctioned. It was these initial schemes, often justified only in terms of educational rhetoric rather than on the basis of systematic experiment, which focused attention on *continuity* in its various aspects. By the mid-1960s, the term 'middle schools' was already part of the vocabulary of forward-looking educationalists in the state system (Blyth and Derricott, 1977), although it is interesting to speculate why such pace-setters did not call upon the experience of the independent sector, where middle schools already had a tradition, to support their cause.

The main focus of research in the twenty years between these two education acts was the cognitive and political issues appropriate to the junior-secondary interface. These included questions of whether particular tests measured fairly given definitions of ability, the predictive value of tests to secondary school performance, and whether access to secondary schooling was equally provided for the nation's children. These concerns reflected the importance of the eleven-plus examination both to the individual's perception of self and to society's requirement for a differentiated, stratified, and suitably qualified potential work-force at the age of fifteen or sixteen plus. The psychological and sociological research evidence of the late fifties and early sixties (e.g., Halsey, Floud, and Martin, 1958; Jackson and Marsden, 1963; Douglas et al., 1964) persuaded most educationalists and the three major political parties that the assumptions which had underpinned the eleven-plus examination were suspect. By 1965 there was a growing consensus that the time was now ripe for the reorganization of secondary schooling along comprehensive lines. Circulars 10/65 and 10/66 embodied both the political will of that rapidly growing consensus and the administrative recognition that its implementation would have to occur essentially within the existing school buildings, which themselves largely reflected the selective tradition (Humphrey, 1968).

A recognition of the importance of these historical, political, and educational perspectives is essential if we are to understand adequately the social significance of transfer between schools. The feelings and attitudes of teachers, pupils, and parents are the product of these considerations. We need to identify accurately what these feelings and attitudes are, and to attempt, at least, an explanation of why the various interest groups come to hold the views which they do.

For some time now, sociologists of education have been interested in the association between the wider social structure and particular forms of schooling, and whether features of this association are reflected within the organization and culture of schools (Husen, 1974; Bowles and Gintis, 1976; Willis, 1976). The extent to which organizational arrangements influence any variation in the cognitive and affective aspects of schooling remains a live issue (Rutter et al., 1979). Even a cursory review of the literature shows that when sociologists come to study schools as organizations in a theoretical manner, the different approaches and methods which contend for authoritative status in the parent discipline are again predominant.[1] This division is important; for any researcher the theoretical position which he adopts has implications for the method of enquiry and for what counts as 'fact' within that study. More specifically for the sociologist, the adoption of either an essentially structuralist or interactional perspective reflects a particular view of the status of individuals or groups under scrutiny. Whether the organizational patterns of schools or schooling impose a particular definition of the situation on teachers or pupils, or whether these participants negotiate, in this case the reality of transfer, is a crucial question in deciding how to approach pupils' perception of transfer between schools.

The theoretical position adopted here is that group perspectives are shaped at least as much by the institution[2] in which individuals work, as by wider cultural processes. By using the concepts of *career* and *status passage*[3] which are central to the interactionist position, this chapter sets out to explore how pupils perceive their transfer from a primary to an all-through secondary comprehensive school, and from an eight–twelve middle and a ten–thirteen middle to corresponding high schools. The question is raised as to whether different types of feeder schools, i.e., primary and the two types of middle school, actually prepared their pupils for the scheduled transition to the high schools, and in either event whether the pupils responded similarly or differently to their experience.

The data are derived from a content analysis of pupil essays before and after transfer. Throughout, the categories which pupils themselves have generated are accepted. The analysis attempts to show whether the pupils' declared responses to the experience of changing schools vary systematically between those who are moving through a two-tier and those who are

Fig. 13.1

Two-Tier System

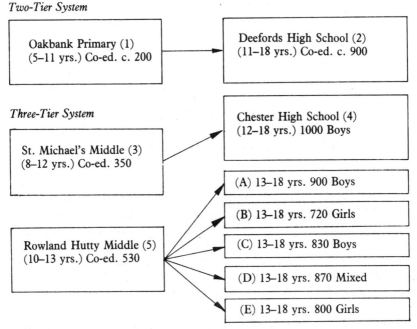

(In each case, data used below are located by use of the bracketed numbers 1–5.)

moving through a three-tier system. In this survey, then, a final-year pupil could be eleven, twelve, or thirteen years of age, and in the corresponding receiving school he would reach twelve, thirteen, or fourteen years of age during his first year. The schools used for this exercise are shown in Figure 13.1.

Because the pupils in the Rowland Hutty Middle School moved to five different high schools within the LEA, it was decided that it was impracticable to follow them through to their respective third-tier schools. Approximately four weeks before the end of the summer term in the primary and middle schools, each pupil was asked to write an essay on 'My thoughts on changing schools'. The essays were written during a scheduled English lesson and the exercise was supervised by their usual teacher. In practice, this essay ranged from a few lines to several pages. Just before Christmas in the secondary and third-tier schools, the same pupils were asked to write a second essay entitled 'My thoughts on my new school'. Similar supervision arrangements were made. In each exercise pupils were given no guidelines, cues, or structure, but were told to write freely, frankly, and anonymously, and that the essays would not be read by any of the teachers within the respective schools. The only identification to each essay was the pupil's register number which enabled their ideas before and after transfer to be compared.[4] Altogether 310 pupils were involved. The number of quotations cited for each school reflects approximately the relative incidence of the comments made, and throughout the pupils' spelling of words is given.

Age of transfer

Although no ideas were suggested to pupils when writing these essays, the content provides overwhelming evidence that 'age identity' is central to pupils' thinking. Most essays from the primary and middle schools provided an opinion as to the most appropriate age of transfer between schools.

I think leaving school at the age of 11 is right because you ought to learn foreign languages because you are getting to the age when you are likely to go abroad. (1)

I think it is a good idea to leave here at 11. (1)

The age that I think children should leave primary school is 11 or 12 years old. (1)

In September I am going to Chester High School, and think 12 is about the right age. (3)

I am sad to leave because I have got used to the people at St. Michael's. But I know why we have to change because we need more knowledge. 12 is the right age. (3)

In both the primary and eight–twelve middle schools no contrary opinions are expressed as to the appropriateness of eleven or twelve years being the 'right' age of transfer; the pupils appear to accept this stage of their schooling as natural. Within the ten–thirteen school, however, pupil opinion is divided.

I think 13 is a sensible age to leave your middle school. (5)

13 is a good age (to change school) because you're not too young or old. (5)

I think leaving to go to a new school at 13 is a good idea because the schools are evenly spaced out, about three years in each. Leaving at eleven is not a good idea because you would have too long in the next school. (5)

Although these quotations reflect approval for the ten–thirteen system, an equal number are critical of the three-tier system.

I think that we should only go to two schools . . . (one) . . . from 6–11, then 11 to 16, 17 or 18. (5)

We just seem to be settling down when we have to move on. (5)

I think we should have to go to two schools only. What is the use of going to one school for three years and another for four years. Why can't we have a junior school for six years and a senior school for six years? (5)

Elaborating the same argument, one boy maintains:

I don't think it is a good idea leaving middle school at 13 because it often means you have to work harder to catch up with other children if you moved into another area and the children went straight up to comprehensive schools from primary. (5)

Others, perhaps, were repeating parental opinion when they wrote:

I think it is rather silly changing to another school. I have been to two already. It also costs a lot of money for my uniform. (5)

I don't think we should change three times like we do because its a waste of time and money. (5)

When the same pupils write from their respective high schools, there is not a single reference to the age of transfer question. Understandably most pupils see their transfer from one school to another as a very important stage in their school career, and it is not surprising to find personal aspirations and anxieties are central in nearly every essay, irrespective of the pupil's age.

Material resources

Several authors have noted the institutional characteristics of schools, and Becker (1968) and Jackson (1968) in particular have emphasized the power of institutions to structure the realities of their members. The physical structure of the building, the allocation of space, and the use of time are significant features of life in institutions, and these features provide recurring themes in many pupils' essays. The present writer has commented elsewhere (Bryan and Hardcastle, 1977) on the educational significance of the space which is formally allocated to pupils according to their age. (See also chapters by Wallace and by Ginsburg and Meyenn in this volume.) Many children have referred to this association, although the direction of their opinion is not consistent.

I have seen the school from the outside. It looks very big and exciting. (1)

I am looking forward to my new school because there are lots of facilities such as squash courts and badminton . . . cooking rooms and science rooms and lots of space. . . . (1)

Meanwhile the twelve-plus group in the eight–twelve middle school, which it should be remembered was formerly a secondary modern school for over five hundred children, were more cautious. Comments such as:

I am looking forward to going to a much bigger school than I am in now. (3)

were expressed far less often than the contrary opinion:

It's easy to get around in St. Michael's school. It will be harder to find the right classroom in the High School. (3)

I will be frightened because there are more people and more teachers than at St. Michael's. (3)

Very similar opinions were expressed by the thirteen-year-old pupils at the Rowland Hutty Middle School.

I've seen my new school and its very big there's corridors everywhere you look and an endless supply of classrooms and its very easy to get lost in a school like this. (5)

I've seen my school and its giant size. (5)

Frequently pupils associated size with facilities, and this association was generally expressed in more positive terms.

I am glad there is a big library because I like reading a lot. (1)

I think there's a big library there and I will enjoy that. (5)

When we got a letter about the school I saw one thing in it, it said there would be a drama studio that's one good thing because I want to be an actor when I grow up. (1)

I believe Rowland Hutty can no longer train us sufficiently for future life. Our science labs are insufficiently equipped and our sports equipment is old and worn out. (5)

When writing from the secondary and third-tier schools after transfer, these same pupils return to the same issues.

I think the buildings are quite good and big enough. (2)

I think the new school is too small because if you compare it with other high schools like Waverbridge it is not very big. (2)

Chester High School is a very big place. Sometimes you get lost and sometimes your late for your lesson. (4)

I dislike the way the stairs are one way because if you lose something on the stairs you only have a small chance of getting back to it. (4)

I don't like it when you change lessons because when you go up the stairs you get squashed. (2)

The way the school is laid out is very confusing 1S- on the bottom floor, 1Z- on the first floor and some of the 1Z- on the top floor. . . . (4)

These recent data support a point made by Eggleston (1967) over a decade ago in his researches into the correlates of extended schooling, namely that pupils' material environment is a significant factor in their response to schooling.

Friendship

Friendship is a cherished ingredient in most people's lives, and there is overwhelming evidence to demonstrate that this is particularly important to pupils in the middle years of schooling (Meyenn, 1980). Many were sensitive to the effects which the change of schools might have upon their friendship patterns. For some this generated anxiety, while for others it held the potential of more satisfying relationships.

> I am looking forward to going to the new school a bit, but not a lot because I will have to loose my friend. (1)

> When I go to my new school I want to make new friends. (1)

> I think comprehensive schools are a good idea because you make more friends. (3)

> I will be glad to leave St. Michael's because I will be able to meet my friends which I used to no at my first school. (3)

> One thing I won't like is leaving all my old friends who are going to different schools. (5)

> I don't really like leaving because in this school I know my way around and all my friends and people I know are here. (5)

> I don't want to leave this school because I will be losing my friends. (5)

Several pupils expressed the view that if they had a *real* choice, in our theoretical terms if status passage was a voluntary act, they would prefer not to change school at all, although a minority position is reflected in the following words from a twelve-year-old girl:

> Although I am leaving every one of my friends I know that I will soon make new ones and I can go to my next school and get myself a better reputation. (5)

On balance, pupils in the Rowland Hutty Middle School were more concerned about the effects of transfer on their friendships than pupils in the primary and eight–twelve middle schools. To conclude that this reflects the fact that such ties are more developed at thirteen rather than at twelve or eleven and is a function of maturation, could be too simple. It may be a consequence of the realization that their friends could be going to one of five different third-tier schools, whereas most pupils from Oakbank and St. Michael's transfer to a single high or third-tier school. Alternatively, it may be that maturation is organizationally determined and the 'common sense' explanation that friendship ties are more developed at thirteen is a reification of the notion of maturation (Blyth and Derricott, 1977).

The extent to which these hopes and fears concerning friendship are realized after transfer is indicated in the following comments:

> I have got some friends in other classes from Oakbank School and some from other schools. (2)

When I first went into the school a teacher took me into the hall. I got there and could see all my friends. I was scared I might not be in the same class as some of my friends and be the only Oakbank person. (2)

I soon got to know people and children in our class after a couple of days. I soon got to know my way around school and made lots of friends. (4)

I think there is more facilates than in St. Michael's but I haven't broken any friendships yet. (4)

The use of the term 'friends' in this context probably embraces acquaintances. Pupils are looking for the security of familiar faces.

Status

References to friends are few and reassuring, suggesting that the apprehension expressed some five or six months previously had not materialized. But two related themes, above all others, emerge and capture the trauma of enforced status passage from one school to another: the 'demoted' status from 'top' to 'first' year, and the fear of being 'picked on' and bullied. These feelings cut across age, sex, ability, and social class and are described openly.

I don't like the thought of being babies in the High School after being eldest in the school. (1)

I feel sad about this (changing schools) because I had a great time being at the top of school. (3)

I am used to being top of the school and don't like to be bottom of it again. (5)

In the school I am going to I will be a third year and will be like a first year and I will not be very dig (sic) to all of the boys and girls there I will be very small and I will get bost around and picket on. (5)

A smaller proportion, particularly in St. Michael's, adopt a more optimistic, and even reflective stance:

I will be happy in Chester High School because I will feel much older. (3)

I do not mind being the youngest because in a few years you will be the eldest. (3)

It is, however, the fear of being ragged, picked on, or bullied which is expressed most intensely, as the following quotations show:

I am hoping that when it is someone's birthday some of the older pupils do not break eggs over that person's head like they do at Waverbridge. (1)

There is only one thing I am frightened of and that is older ones picking and hitting me. When I get to the top form I am not going to pick on 12+ because I know what it is like. (3)

I do not think large comprehensives are a good idea because . . . there will be a lot more bullying. (3)

I expect big boys and girls biger than me to pick on me and bully me. (5)

I have horrible thoughts of my next school which is Seacombe High. I think there is no disciplin from what my friends have told me. They also told me that groups of lads go around battering people up, they are supposed to be from the dreaded B.E.B.B., which stands for the Brightsea Estate Boot Boys. (5)

Yet, perhaps the intensity of apprehension which transfer between schools brings for many pupils, as well as its more generalized focus, is conveyed most effectively by this thirteen-year-old boy:

If I go to my new school some big lads will bully me and if they so I will tell my teter and they will tell the Hed master and the Hedmaster will give them the cane so I wont want to go to anover scol yet I cant spell or read all that moth I will have to lon to read and spell. (5)

Much more than the issue of friendship, the question of physical intimidation recurs in several essays written after transfer. Although the majority of pupils reported that their fears had been overstated, as these extracts indicate:

I always had the feeling that you were bullied by older boys and girls, but no its been alright. (2)

Before I set foot in this school I heard some rumers about all the hard knocks, steeling your dinner money and all that . . . but now I feel its just like any other school. (4)

My thoughts on Chester High School are totally different than I thought they were. Because I thougt the bigger kids would hit us but they didn't. (4)

A minority complain that this is not the full story and that:

A lot of bullying goes on in this school and their are at least three big fights a week. (4)

Organization of time and school rules

That regulation of time and dress are important institutional characteristics in the lives of pupils, particularly at points of transfer from one institution to another, is made manifestly clear by the unsolicited observations on the organization of lesson time, homework, the use of detention, and the requirement to wear some kind of school uniform. If only one criterion is permitted to distinguish between 'primary' and 'secondary' school practices, the differential allocation of time in the two types of institution would be worthy of consideration. The extent to which a middle school is deemed primary rather than secondary, pedagogically rather than administratively speaking, could well be decided on this criterion. In the unstreamed primary school of this survey, all pupils were taught in a class teacher situation; at St. Michael's Middle School most of the lessons were of this kind, but the teaching of French, music, and most of the English was undertaken by a specialist teacher, with the exception of music in the group's classroom. At the Rowland Hutty Middle School, the following additional subjects were taught by specialists – maths, science, German, and PE. Science was taught in both the laboratory and classroom, while all PE was undertaken in the gymnasium. In the first year all classes, with the exception of the remedial group, 1S, were mixed-ability ones and with very minor variations followed a common curriculum. For the second and third years the remedial group was retained and the remainder of the classes divided into two broad bands on the basis of attainment in mathematics and English. One form only in each of the second and third years, 2R and 3L respectively, had the opportunity to study German. Otherwise the time-tables were very similar. In the two high schools where pupils' opinions were sought, all subjects were taught on a specialist basis with most pupils moving to the teachers' rooms. Thus a comparison of pupil responses to new time-table patterns should provide an important perspective on life in schools from behind the desk.

As a result of formal visits to their next school and through the informal communication networks, most pupils realized that their school day would be organized differently after they had left their present schools. Overall opinion was divided fairly evenly between those who welcomed more specialist lessons and those who were apprehensive. In the primary school most pupils were looking forward to the high school and this girl's comment is typical of those transferring at eleven plus:

> . . . and the teachers that are their to teach us will probably know more about the one subject that they will be teaching us about. (1)

There is, though, more uncertainty in the minds of pupils at St. Michael's about these impending changes.

> When you split up into groups I think it is confusing. Having different teachers all the time does not improve your work because you cannot guarantee that they are all good teachers. (3)

> I am not sorry about leaving this school because in the next school there is a lot to look forward to like Art and Craft and science with more experienced teachers. (3)

> It would be more exciting at Chester High School than it is at St. Michael's because you do metal work and wood work. (3)

> It will be confusing changing lessons all the time. (3)

Although the pupils at the Rowland Hutty Middle School have already experienced much more specialist teaching than pupils at St. Michael's, their comments reflect similar feelings:

> One thing I do like about it (the third-tier school) is that it seems to have teachers who just do their own special subjects. There also seems to be quite a lot of special rooms for subjects. (5)

> I wish though we wouldn't have so many sections in science, e.g. Biology and Physics in the next school. (5)

> In the nexed school you can learn better things like Chemistry and Physics. (5)

> In this school we have physics, chemistry and biology all under the same subject, science. . . . In my next school these subjects will be done in separate periods. I am pleased about this. (5)

After three months in the high schools, fewer pupils made reference to the structure of the time-table or to the labelling of school subjects, but those that do comment appear less than enthusiastic.

> I've got used to it now (changing lessons) and I know all the teachers that take me for lessons quite well. (2)

> And we never had a time-table in the old school (middle) . . . we just did what our old teacher wanted to do. (4)

> We also have 35 mins lessons which are very boring because as soon as you

have settled down the bell goes again for you to change lessons. (4)

One boy was clearly writing in a similar vein from personal experience:

> The half hour lessons which we have are daft because some teachers tell you off for being late when you have come from a mobile or the games field and you have to go to the top floor. (4)

Perhaps the majority who make no comment on time-tabling are quite happy with their new routine and, in one pupil's words, 'have taken it in their stride'. One further and related issue does emerge from the second essays; all pupils in the primary and middle schools have been taught in mixed-ability classes, and for between six and eight years this has been the only teaching environment they have known. Yet several pupils concur with the boy who wrote:

> Another thing I like is that you are streamed for French Maths and Science. In the middle school we went to lessons in one class and some pupils were not as good as others so you could not get on fast. (4)

And this view is not confined to the able pupils who feel that they are not being 'stretched':

> I think the idea of being split into vereus groups for your owne cape a bility is a good one as well. (4)

Homework and uniform

Homework and the wearing of school uniform are consistent themes in the initial essays. Pupils comment on both the principle and the detail, with favourable and contrary opinion being divided approximately equally.

> I am looking forward to doing homework, but not too much. (1)

> I am not looking forward to doing homework all the while. (1)

> I think homework should be stopped unless it is unfinished work because it is the kind of thing we should do in school. (5)

> I am looking forward to my first day so I can wear my new uniform. (1)

> I don't like the High School uniform much. (3)

> I think you should have a uniform. (5)

> When we come to school I think we should wear our ordinary clothes. (5)

Only one boy, however, referred directly to control:

> I think teachers should wear a uniform as well because they are always telling us to straighten our ties or comb our hair. (5)

Within the three-tier systems several pupils explained their objection to the detail of school uniform in terms of the unnecessary expense incurred:

> My Mum just can't afford the new uniform every three years or so. (5)

After transfer, the relative importance of these two issues diverges considerably. The wearing of uniform appears to be taken for granted and relatively few comments are made. Homework, on the other hand, becomes a greater constraint on a pupil's use of his time, as the following extracts demonstrate:

> I think homework should not be aloud because we do all our work at school and homework stops us from watching the telly at night. (2)

> I think that we should have homework but I don't think we should have it at weekend because you always have to worry about how much homework you have to do and sometimes you can't go out on family trips because you have to much homework to do. (2)

> My thoughts about Deebanks High when I was at my old school were that there would be very little homework to do but that was totally wrong. (2)

Pupils who transferred from St. Michael's to Chester High School made similar complaints about the intrusiveness of homework, 'even near Christmas'. Homework was set for the oldest age-group in both primary and middle schools, but this made fewer demands on pupils' time. When this is increased in all types of high school it is consistently resented, irrespective of pupils' age in the first year. Another consequence of the allocation of time in the high schools was unexpected to many pupils. We have seen that pupils were concerned about physical intimidation, but very few commented on the sanctions which they expected that schools might use to control nonapproved behaviour. Although many pupils thought that their new schools would be strict, the use of detention after school was considered to be unreasonable and unjust.

Discussion

This researcher's expectation that pupils would evaluate their new school in terms of their personal response to teachers was amply fulfilled. Some of the phrases used by pupils to describe their teachers were not in the conventional reference form, but only a few were derogatory. A small number of pupils felt dispossessed in terms of being 'lockerless' with the consequence that they had 'to cart all their kit about', and they certainly felt that this demeaned their status in the new school. More significantly, the majority of pupils felt that in their new schools they were 'treated more like adults', and whatever their initial reservations about their impending change in status, in retrospect they found the experience of transfer a desirable stage in their pupil careers, if only because 'I am now in the last school I'll have to go to.'

The above data have shown clearly that the aspirations and anxieties which pupils express are not particular to a given age, sex, or geographical location, and they are consistent with other findings (Piggott, 1977). Thus it would seem that such feelings exist in terms of the passagees' definition of the situation. Certainly it is worth noting that according to the responses in this study, no pupil was consciously aware of preparation for transfer beyond the allocation of a day or a half-day visit to the receiving school, and this occurred no earlier than three weeks before they left the feeder school. Perhaps the schools actually did prepare their pupils for transfer in other ways and, either the pupils omitted to mention them because they did not see them as significant, or they were unaware of the processes. In either event this is surprising. When the staff of both feeder and receiving schools were discussing the problems of transfer with the present author, as part of a more extensive study than is reported here, they stressed the need for continuity. Indeed, many of the teachers in the survey schools have been members of working parties and study groups convened to facilitate curricular continuity. Yet the evidence for anticipatory socialization is clear; pupils expected to be treated in a more adult way and for the next stage of schooling to be more demanding (Ginsburg and Meyenn, 1979). Although both St. Michael's and the Rowland Hutty Middle School were former secondary modern schools for more than six hundred pupils before reorganization, and both retained their equipment and laboratories when they became middle schools, pupils in these two schools expected 'better' facilities in the third-tier schools in a similar way to the eleven-year-old pupils at Oakbank Primary.

For several pupils, the prospect of transfer did provoke thoughts on the purpose of schooling, and predictably these covered a spectrum including:

I would like if you could learn about the job you are going to do. (5)

I want to get my A levels and my O levels at the High School. (3)

School is a waiste of time. (5)

Furthermore these reflections on a potential career path are not confined to the strictly instrumental aspects of schooling as the following quotation, which has been cited previously, indicates:

I can go to my next school and get myself a better reputation. (5)

Piggott (1977) similarly reported that those who had experienced 'trouble' in their middle schools looked to the high schools as an opportunity to start with 'a clean sheet'.

That there appears to be no set of pupil perceptions associated with particular forms of comprehensive schooling is reassuring in one sense. Whatever the specific circumstances which persuade a local authority to adopt either a two-tier system with transfer at eleven plus or a three-tier model with middle schools of the eight–twelve type, from what the pupils say there would appear to be no significant social consequences. It is less certain that there are no differences in pupils' attainment (Bryan and Hardcastle, 1978; Bryan, forthcoming). Whether transfer at thirteen plus does actually result in an undue disruption of friendship patterns will require more sensitive analysis.

To describe pupil perceptions is a relatively easy matter; to explain them satisfactorily calls for an understanding of social processes at the interactional and structural level. The evidence of these pupils confirms that the institutional processes which have been identified in a wider context (Goffman, 1961; Dale, 1972) are present to some considerable extent in schools. Also, it may well be that the data presented here in an interactional context reflect some general issues of schooling at a structural level. The assertion by some educationalists that middle schools are unique in identity is called into question. If the above quotations from pupils in the middle years of schooling represent their views fairly, then in the pupils' eyes they are schools like any other. The question of which interest group has the power to impose its definition of the situation upon others is a familiar one in the contemporary sociology of education and, in particular, is very pertinent to the study of middle schools.

Notes

1. The contrasting emphases of structural-functionalist and interactionist approaches within sociology generally can be clearly identified within the more specific area of the sociology of education. When these two broad theoretical perspectives are used to analyse the school as an organization, their different assumptions and methodologies are evident. On the one hand Blau and Scott

(1963) and Etzioni (1964), for example, adopt an essentially functionalist position which maintains that different responses of members, whether they are workers, patients, inmates, or pupils, can largely be explained in terms of the structural characteristics of the organization to which they belong. This type of analysis tends to focus upon the intended and unintended outcomes of the impersonal processes which are considered to be intrinsic to the organization in question, and it is through these processes that the organization maintains itself and adapts to its environment. In this perspective, the concept of school structure implies the existence of organizational arrangements that distinguish one type of school from another and schools as a class set apart from other formal institutions. The argument is that the structural differences between schools are important to the extent that they influence the process and product of education. Thus the school is part of the pupils' environment and, to quote McLuhan and Fiore (1967, p.68), 'Environments are not passive wrappings, but are rather, active processes which are invisible'. A structural-functional analysis is usually associated with a positivist methodology, but it is worth emphasizing that Talcott Parsons, who is frequently cited as the arch-functionalist, described his perspective as a 'theory of action'.

On the other hand, the interactionist perspective insists that social action must be explained in terms of the actors' motives and 'definitions of the situation'. Schutz was one of the seminal writers in this tradition. Dale (1972, pp.14–15), drawing extensively on the work of Silverman (1970), emphasizes the limitations of the functionalist approach, particularly when applied to the study of schools. He says that it directs attention to the consequences rather than the causes of social phenomena, it assumes that causes are inherent in the consequences, and, most importantly, it 'neglects the subjectively meaningful nature of social life'. Those who adopt the interactionist perspective contend that 'it is possible to come to grips with the subjective meaning attached to typical actions and to their intended and unintended consequences for the involvement of the actors, for their perceived place within the organisation, and for the stability of the common set of expectations within which they interact' (Dale, op.cit., p.13). Interactionists claim that social structures derive from the interaction between the participants, and that the degree of consensus or conflict depends on the individual's perception of means and ends. Methodologically, according to Schutz, the social scientist must 'step out' of the social world of practical interests and explain the social world as he sees it. This is done through a process of ideal type reconstruction which is judged in terms of the restraining postulates of relevance, adequacy, consistency, and compatibility. Parsons saw this 'as at best philosophy'. Recent research (Grathoff, 1978) suggests that Parsons and Schutz saw little relevance of each other's work to their own.

2. From an interactionist stance, an institution is defined as a place where a given activity occurs.

3. E. C. Hughes (1937), an influential member of the Chicago School of Sociologists who have developed a distinctive analysis of the 'self' in society and promoted the symbolic interactionist perspective, has defined career as follows: 'Subjectively, career is the moving perspective in which a person sees his life as a whole,

interprets his attitudes, actions and things which happen to him. Objectively, it is a series of statuses and clearly defined offices . . . typical sequences of position, responsibility and even adventure' (1937, pp.409–410). Hughes considers the concept particularly useful because it facilitates a link between the individual and organizational levels of analysis. Career is 'personal' in that it focuses on individual identity and 'organizational' in that it describes both a person's occupational path in the conventional sense, as well as 'any strand of any person's course through life', to use Goffman's phrase. Because many individuals can share aspects of their history in common, the term can equally well be applied to groups as well as to individuals.

The related concept of 'status passage' is also pertinent to our understanding of how pupils perceive the process of transfer between schools. The notion of status passage has been developed by Strauss (1971) and Glaser and Strauss (1971) from the original work on stratification theory by Weber. Although Glaser and Strauss 'prefer not to define status passages, but to let the full range of meanings for the concept emerge . . . through the combined references of the data analysed and the analyses themselves' (1971, p.6), the concept can be described simply as 'the moves which individuals make in and out of various social positions during the course of a career'.

4. The frankness, obvious sincerity, and absence of stereotyped format in these essays support the belief that the researcher's instructions were carried out to the letter and in the spirit by teachers and pupils. The feelings expressed range from 'I am sorry about leaving this school because the teachers have put a lot of hard work in for our school' to the terse 'This school is crap'.

CHAPTER FOURTEEN

PEER NETWORKS AMONG MIDDLE SCHOOL PUPILS

R. J. Meyenn

Introduction

The social relationships among pupils attending middle schools is an area which as yet has received very little attention from those writing about or researching into this new organizational phenomenon. As any teacher knows, the relationship that pupils have with each other has a crucial bearing on a pupil's adjustment, happiness, success, and orientation to school. In a recent study, Lomax (1978) concludes that irrespective of a child's orientation to the school, whether he/she is happy or not, doing well academically or not, peers are still the *most* important feature of a child's school experience. A pupil spends far more time with peers than with teachers, and yet the importance and influence of these peer relationships and networks is very rarely emphasized. The question of just what effect the new middle school organization is having on the pupils and their relationships with each other is very rarely asked, especially from the point of view of the pupils.

In researching and exploring the social relationships of middle school pupils, one is left to rely on work done in other types of school. As the nine–thirteen middle school spans two years of the primary school age-range and two years of the secondary school age-range, it is research in these areas that provides the reference points. The major work on primary school pupils conducted in this country is by Blyth (1960) who, when discussing research into the social relationships of pupils in their final year of primary school (eleven plus), found that boys tended to form larger groups than girls and that these boys' groups tended to dominate and were the focal point of social relationships of this age-group.

There is considerably more research into the social relationships of pupils of the secondary age-range. However, these studies have tended to focus on boys (Hargreaves, 1967; Lacey, 1970; Reynolds, 1976; Willis, 1977), and only in a very few cases on girls (Lambart, 1976; Furlong, 1976). This raises considerable doubts about the generalizability of such findings to the way girls organize their social relationships. Additionally these studies have been conducted in single-sex institutions, usually secondary modern or grammar schools, and so their applicability to the coeducational middle school is questionable. A common characteristic of these studies tends to be the focus on the upper age-range – boys and girls who are about to leave school or reach the statutory minimum leaving age. However there are indications, particularly in the work of Willis (1976, 1977) and also in the works of Lacey (1970) and Hargreaves (1967), that many of the features and outcomes that are observed and so vividly described at the end of a school career have their direct antecedents much earlier on in the school.

The majority of these studies of peer groups present a polarized picture with some groups accepting the definitions of them offered by the school (the pro-school, conformist, passive 'ear 'oles') and other groups rejecting these definitions (the anti-school, nonconformist, delinquescent 'lads'). There seems to be an additional tendency to concentrate on, or even celebrate, the most extreme of the anti-school groups. These groups are only one part of the total picture and if one is concerned to present more complete pictures, then these studies must be complemented by other studies which attempt to present cross-sections.

The usefulness and adequacy of peer groups as a concept, in terms of explaining and accounting for what goes on in classrooms, has recently been challenged (Furlong, 1976; Delamont, 1976). Furlong questions the approaches that see informal peer groups as the basis of pupils' social relationships. He argues for much more fluid groupings which he describes as *interaction sets*. The point that a certain degree of fluidity is present is taken, and must be included in a model of pupils' social relationships, as is the point that groups or more particularly individuals within groups are not always consistent in their behaviour and do not consistently adhere to group norms. Nor is it invalid to state that interaction takes place between individuals of different peer-group networks. However, for *this* age-group of pupils in the organizational setting of a middle school, peer-group networks were the dominant and obvious way that these middle school pupils organized their social relationships.

My field notes are replete with observations of girls and boys in groups in class, in the playground, coming to and going home from school, in the corridors, at the weekly lunch-time disco, at sporting events, and in the dining hall. These groups, organized differently for the boys and girls, were consistently similar in their compositions. In the staffrooms there was a lot of conversation among the teachers which indicated that they were aware of the girls' groupings in particular. Comments like 'you know, Josephine's mob', 'the science lab lot', and 'Betty and her lot' were commonly made in conversation or when recounting incidents.

The research reported and discussed here was conducted over a two-year period (1977–78) of intensive study of one cohort (four mixed-ability classes) of pupils in their final two years in a midlands, nine–thirteen middle school. The research has been conducted using a variety of techniques including participant observation, semistructured and informal interviewing, sociometry, and attitude surveys. Additionally data were collected from school records and transfer to high-school tests on the entire cohort, and an intensive study was carried out on one of these four classes, 4F, which consisted of fifteen boys and sixteen girls. This chapter attempts to explore both the formation and nature of this group of middle school pupils' social relationships. Simply, how do these boys and girls organize their social lives at school?

The school and its pupils

The school served a predominantly working-class, new town estate. Eighty percent of the pupils in the cohort were from rented, corporation accommodation. The bulk of the people living on the estate were settled there as a result of inner-city redevelopment/clearance schemes. Houses were new and modern and the estate was well served with shopping and other facilities, and there was a bus service to the nearest town. Many of the residents when interviewed claimed that they enjoyed living on the estate but did feel somewhat isolated. Employment was available in the many local light industries. Sixty-seven percent of the mothers in the sample were in paid employment – most worked in local factories, often on the 'twilight' shift.

The school itself was a county middle school. This particular part of the county reorganized its schools into a three-tier system as part of their comprehensive reorganization policy, so middle schools in the area catered for the nine–thirteen age-range. The school, new (seven years old) and purpose-built, was a four-form entry one. The four forms in each year group were mixed-ability ones, although the school was trying to operate a gradual transition model (see the chapter by Meyenn and Tickle) which meant that the organization changed to a largely secondary approach in the final year. This meant that, in the fourth year, the pupils were set for their maths, English, French, and some science, and so did not remain as a stable form/class group throughout the school day.

The peer networks

What became obvious from very early on in the research was that while in some ways one could say that the boys and girls formed peer networks, these networks were very different for boys and girls and this prevented anything but the broadest of generalizations when discussing pupil peer networks as a unitary category.

The following two sociograms illustrate this point quite clearly. These sociograms are drawn up from the sociometric choices of the boys and girls of the class group that was studied intensively, but are typical of those for the other class groups. Five sociometric questions were administered at three points in time, six months apart over the two-year period. Of the five questions administered, three indicated actual association patterns and two preferences (or not) for associates.

1 Who do you play with after school? (evenings and week-ends)
2 Who would you most like to be friends with at school?
3 Who would you least like to be friends with at school?
4 Who do you usually play with in the playground? (at breaks and lunch-times)
5 Who do you usually work with in class?

For the purposes of the sociograms illustrated here, the data sets for questions 1, 4, and 5 were combined and a reciprocated choice across or within any of the three data sets was plotted.

The sociograms here illustrate quite starkly the differences between the boys and girls. The girls formed tight cliques which were in many ways quite separate from each other. On the other hand the boys formed one largely undifferentiated class group which did contain some much more loosely formed smaller groups. The predominant form of organization for the boys was the class group. The one boy (No. 56) who was somewhat of an exception to this had been in a different class in the third year, and by and large maintained his links with that class.

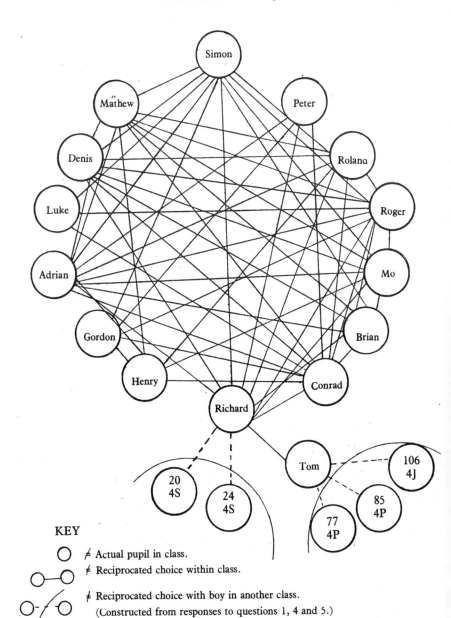

KEY

○   ≠ Actual pupil in class.

○—○   ≠ Reciprocated choice within class.

○–/–○   ≠ Reciprocated choice with boy in another class.

(Constructed from responses to questions 1, 4 and 5.)

Fig 14.2

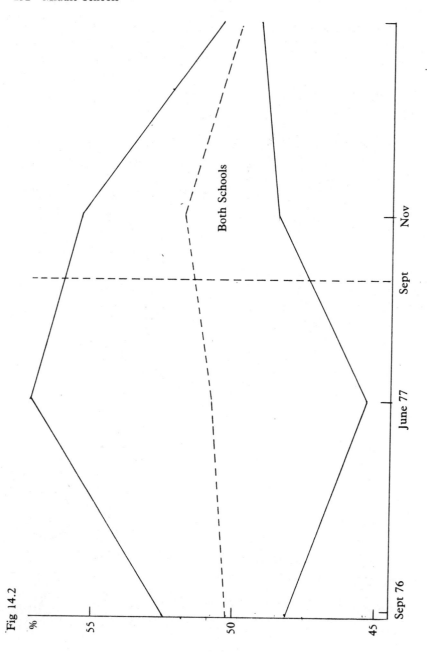

Both Schools

Both the girls and the boys emphasized continually the importance of these mates at school; for the girls this meant a very specific group of friends while for the boys this tended to be 'the kids in me class'.

Character and culture of peer networks

The girls

The girls of 4F formed four groups named for the purposes of differentiation the 'PE' girls, the 'science lab' girls, the 'nice' girls, and the 'quiet' girls (for a much fuller discussion of the nature of these groups see Meyenn (1980)). There were no other girls outside of the four groups and all of the groups, except the 'science lab' girls, contained additional members outside of this class group. For all the girls these groupings remained constant for school activities wherever possible, and for some this grouping extended to out of school social life. While it was possible to sit in the classroom and observe interaction sets which crossed the boundaries of these friendship groups (and which sometimes included the boys), the great majority of the interaction would take place within the peer network. For these girls it was groups rather than pairs that were the dominant form of social organization (cf., McRobbie and Garber, 1976).

For the girls their group of friends was vitally important and there were constant manoeuvres to make sure their group was together whenever possible.

Diane:	'If we had to say somebody who was our best friend you wouldn't say one person. It would be all this lot.'
Jennifer:	'We always stick in a group.'
R.M.:	'What do the teachers think of your group?'
Elizabeth:	'We always . . . um . . . sort of . . . if we have to do a job it will be all of us to do the job.'
Diane:	'Like if two of us are picked we go to the teacher and say "*please* let's do it together".'
Jennifer:	'I had to go to the post office to get 50p worth of stamps and I asked if Diane and them could go too.'

It can be seen from Diane's comment that the group is so important to the girls that it is inconceivable to just have one best friend. Any attempts to break up the group by other girls are resisted. The greatest 'disaster' that can befall a group is for another girl, or group, to take one of 'their' girls away from them. This fear is the source of much argument and causes a considerable amount of internal friction within groups. Accusations that 'you are taking her off us' are common. The following group of girls explain to me how they dealt with a threat such as this the previous year.

R.M.:   'Could there be anyone else in your group . . .?'
Diane: 'If they want to be in the group they've got to stop there and not try splitting us up. 'Cause sometimes. . . . We did have . . . in our group once.'
Jennifer: 'Yes we did once.'
Diane: 'And she tried splitting Jennifer away from us. So we said out she had to go.'

Contrary to the findings of McRobbie and Garber (1976) and of Henry (1963), girls in all of the four groups seem convinced that it is better to be in a group rather than to just have one friend.

Val: 'We all three of us sit on the same table in class.'
Natalie: 'We just go in a group.'
Val: 'We're just friends.'
Christine: 'We're always in a group.'
R.M.:   'So it's important to have friends.'
All: 'Yeah.'
Val: 'You're not supposed to have just one friend. It's best to have more than one friend 'cause you get on better like that.'
All: 'Yeah.'

At the very end of the year when the prospect of going to the high school with its setting and streaming organization loomed large, many of the girls were somewhat concerned as to what might happen to their groups. Three of the four groups felt that they would still be friends and remain as a group, but that it might be much harder as they could be split up a lot more and mixed with pupils from the other feeder school.

These girls felt that if their group was broken up then it would be as a result of the pressures placed on it by the organization in the new, bigger high school. If this happened, other groups would form to take its place.

One group though, felt that the upheavals caused by the new organization would probably lead to a change in the way their social relations were organized, and that the breaking up of the groups would lead to girls 'going round' in pairs rather than in a group.

R.M.:	'So you think your group might start to. . . .'
Jennifer:	'Yes. I don't think there will be another group anyway . . . and I think people will pair off then.'
R.M.:	'Pairs rather than groups? Why is that?'
Jennifer:	'I just think three is a crowd and all this business. If you have a group and everybody's in a different group (school subject groupings) you never see them.'
R.M.:	'What do you think Mary? Do you think there will be groups still at the high school?'
Mary:	'I think there might be the odd few groups but I think mainly one or two people together. I think the boys will go in groups. They are not in groups at the moment except for a few.'
R.M.:	'You think it will be in pairs then. Why do you think that?'
Mary:	'I think it will be casual groups. Because you can't see each other when you are in groups. If you have just one mate you are going to stick with them most of the time aren't you? You are not going to split off with them just to go in your normal group. To play at playtimes you probably will want to stay with the friend you stay with all the time in the lessons.'
Jennifer:	'Unless you have got more than one friend in your group. And it is impossible to get back if you go off with another friend.'

The comments of these girls, which were taken from an interview at the very end of the year, and which on the part of the girls are very much speculation and conjecture, do perhaps suggest that there may be a change in the nature of their social relationships when they move on to the high school. If indeed there was a movement from groups to pairs, this would tie in with the research findings of McRobbie and Garber (1976). This possibility at this stage can only be tentative, and would need to be explored by further research as would possible explanation of why girls feel it necessary to make these changes. It may well be that there is something in the nature of middle schools which encourages and develops this particular form of social organization among girls. Clearly, though, the possibility would need to be tested through a comparative study of the peer-group relations among girls of this age in other kinds of schools.

There was some interaction between the four groups but this tended to be limited. One group in particular (the 'quiet' girls) had very little contact at all with the others. Group boundaries were not rigid but remained relatively consistent throughout the final year of the middle school. There was considerable internal fighting. In the case of one group, this was often physical, with the girls 'breaking friends' with surprising (to me, at least) frequency and usually within a very short time making friends again. This appeared to be an ongoing feature of each of the girls' groups.

While each of the four groups had features in common, they also exhibited distinct and different patterns of behaviour, attitudes, and orientation to school (culture). Each of the groups readily saw itself as being different and distinct, and was identified by the teachers as being different.

For girls of this age-range, a dimension at least equally significant to that of pro-/anti-orientation to school would seem to be the degree of commitment to and involvement in teenage culture, elements of which, for these girls, were the wearing of make-up and jewellery, 'modern' dress, and boyfriends. This dimension seemed to be salient in distinguishing one group from another, but certainly did not run parallel to anti-school attitudes and postures as were the findings of Sugarman (1967) with boys. So, for example, the girls most likely to be described as pro-school express similar attitudes to the girls most likely to be described as anti-school in their opposition to the school's policy over the wearing of make-up.

The 'quiet' girls

This was an extremely quiet group of girls who were physically less mature than the 'PE' or 'science lab' girls and were socially unsure and uncertain. If they were sought out they would be very friendly, but they would initiate contact only in very rare circumstances. The three girls, Vera, Anne, and Judy, were in 4F and they were often joined by Roz from 4A. The girls were in bottom sets for most subjects, except for Vera who was in a top set for English. These girls, like the 'nice' girls, did not seem to be interested in make-up or fashion. They spent their time in the playground talking and playing their own games, always near to the school building where they were 'protected' by the teacher or playground staff from interference by other groups of girls or the boys. This is in marked contrast to the 'PE' girls who endeavoured to get as far away as possible from supervision. Mr. Fisher, their teacher, described the girls in the following way:

They're a very quiet group. They stick together and I think they're very happy now that they've found sort of mutual friends because they could all be loners very easily but they all seem happy working together and they stick together and seem to go round quite a lot together.

For these girls, virtually their entire social life at school is conducted within the bounds of the peer group. They are certainly a very good example of the effectiveness of the peer group in making the situation tolerable, even fun (Willis, 1977; Cusick, 1973). They show no interest in teenage fashion, clothes, or make-up, and seem to have accepted and, indeed, made light of their placement in the bottom groups. The acceptance of their 'thickness', even to the extent of playing games about it, has led to a complete inversion of official school attitudes towards academic learning. For these girls, it is more fun when you are not clever. Despite this inversion, these girls could hardly be described as anti-school or at least they do not fit that picture in the literature of anti-school groups. They certainly provide each other with considerable practical and moral support in coping with the demands of school work.

The 'science lab' girls

This was a group of four girls who looked after the science laboratory, particularly the animals, and who were all in 4F. They were a confident, outgoing group of physically and socially more mature girls and were seen by the staff as being popular and reliable. One girl, Diane, was in the top set for all subjects and the other three, Mary, Jennifer, and Elizabeth, were in a mixture of top and middle sets. They were seen by the staff as being very academically orientated and pro-school. Like the 'PE' girls they were certainly fashion-conscious and liked to wear make-up and jewellery. Most of their spare time was spent in the science lab as the officially designated science monitors. This involved the care and feeding of the laboratory animals. An interesting way in which they combined school duties with pleasure and their interest in animals and boys was the period when they were able to persuade several boys to dig worms for them in the lunch hour to provide food for the toads! Normally these boys were passionately involved in lunch-time football games.

These girls present us with an example of a very tight group who do many things together, rely on each other for support, and who are very much involved in school and school activities. While they often help each other with the work, they have taken on the school's definitions of the value of learning and of individual competence, and do not help each other in tests.

Similarly, they are very much involved in teenage culture with dress, make-up, records, and boys playing an important part in their lives. They are aware of their good relationship with the teachers and the fact that they are treated like 'grown-ups'. This relationship and their obvious (to the teachers) positive attitude to school enables them to avoid or not be subjected to some school rules.

The 'nice' girls

This group consisted of three girls, with two girls from 4D often joining in the group. The girls were of mixed ability with one girl, Christine, in top sets for most subjects while the other two, Val and Natalie, were in middle and lower sets. The girls were quiet and friendly and somewhat unobtrusive. In the classroom they did not seem to intrude, nor were they conspicuous, and would hardly be noticed around the school. The girls did not seem to be interested in fashion or make-up, and were physically less mature than the 'PE' or 'science lab' girls. They always met up in the playground where the main activity was standing around in their group and talking.

The 'nice' girls were primarily concerned with making their school lives as easy and pleasant as possible. They cooperate with homework and in school lessons but do not seem to be concerned to break the school rules and are certainly being 'well behaved'. Their attitude to their class teacher is one of acceptance of him as an authority figure – to be talked about and laughed about, but in no way is his authority challenged nor is he seen in any way as an equal.

The 'PE' girls

The group was given this name by the PE mistress as many of the girls in the group were good at, and interested in, PE and games. This was the biggest of the groups with six of the girls coming from 4F and one girl from 4E. There were two other girls from 4A who were often, but not always, part of the group. Two of the girls were in top sets, the others were in the middle sets (none were in the bottom sets).

All the girls were physically more mature than the average fourth-year girl, and as a group they were lively and friendly. They were a very noisy group and seemed to be somewhat conspicuous both in lessons and around the school generally. They were very conscious and concerned with their dress and experimented with the school uniform. Dresses had to be of a 'fashionable' mid-calf length. I was particularly intrigued by the shoes worn by the girls. The type of shoes worn changed three times during the fourth year. At the beginning of the year, they all wore black wedges, and when I asked Josephine why they had to be black, she replied 'I wouldn't be seen dead in brown shoes, sir!'

For this group of 'PE' girls, fashionable dress, make-up, and jewellery are important. There is an emphasis on having a good time and playing practical jokes, and it is important to be able to 'look after' yourself. Continuous attempts are made to 'get round' the school rules and there is much cooperation in helping each other cope with academic aspects of school life. There are indications of the girls' dominance over the boys in the area of fighting, and also the need for some girls, at least, to avoid parents in order to subscribe to peer-group norms concerning the wearing of make-up.

The boys

In many ways the 4F boys were themselves 'one big group' with the exception of Tom who had been transferred from another class, and spent most of his available time with boys from this class, and Peter who did not join in the football games. The following is an interview with two boys, Luke and Adrian, discussing their friendship group.

R.M.:	'Tell me then who your group of best friends are, Luke?'
Luke:	'You mean who's in our gang? It's nearly all the kids in our class except for Tom, Peter, and Richard and that's it. It's nearly all the boys in our classroom in one gang.'
R.M.:	'Are there any that you're specially friendly with?'
Luke:	'Most of the time it's me, Mathew, Adrian, Simon, and Roger. Sometimes we go up to the top field and sometimes we meet Roland up the top field and we play football over there.'
R.M.:	'What about you Adrian?'
Adrian:	'All of them, I like all the boys in the class.'
R.M.:	'You like them all but which are in your gang?'
Adrian:	'Luke, Mathew, Denis, Roland, Mo, Conrad, Richard . . . (pause).'
Luke:	'Just say all the boys except for Richard, Tom, and Peter.'
Adrian:	'I like Richard, he usually plays there. . . .'
Luke:	'Not usually, he just comes when he feels like it.'

It can be seen in this interview that it seems easier for the boys to define their group by saying who is definitely not in it. Another of the boys, Henry, defines his group by saying 'Well, it's all the boys in our class except for the girls'. On the other hand they do recognize and acknowledge that there are subgroups within this larger grouping. These subgroups are nowhere near as tight as the girls' peer groups described earlier (in no way did the girls in 4F see themselves as one big group), and there is a considerable amount of movement between them. When discussing further the groupings within the 'big group' of boys, several boys tried to explain these groupings within a group.

R.M.:	'Can you just tell me then who are the other groups in your class as you see them?'
Roland:	'Well they're all starting to bunch together apart from us three now ain't they?'
Mo:	'Yeah.'
Conrad:	'Well . . . what do you mean in the class itself or socially, 'cause its hard to tell, in the class you can tell easily but otherwise it's a bit hard to tell.'
R.M.:	'Both I think.'
Roland:	'I'd say Simon and Roger . . . for definitely.'
Mo:	'Yeah.'
Conrad:	'And Mathew and Denis and they join forces on and off. . . .'
Roland:	'Gordon and Henry, they're friends in school time, but when it comes to home time they don't play with each other much.'
R.M.:	'Who else?'
Conrad:	'Richard and Peter and I think they do because . . . in the class for design they get together, so they're friends in school and out of school.'
R.M.:	'Who else?'
Conrad:	'Tom, he's come into the class and I think he's probably got friends out of the class. . . .'
Mo:	'You see Adrian is on his own a bit now.'
R.M.:	'Is he?'
Roland:	'He's a good kid Adrian is.'
Mo:	'Yeah.'
Roland:	'Well he sort of drifts . . . he's the sort of kid that could join into our group I reckon.'

R.M.:	'And are you friendly with him now?'
Conrad:	'Yes except sometimes we have a joke.'
Roland:	'You know Irish jokes.'
R.M.:	'Does he get cross about Irish jokes?'
Conrad:	'It depends on what sort of mood he's in.'
Roland:	'He's a good kid.'

. . .

| Roland: | 'They sort of mix round a bit really.' |
| Conrad: | 'Well you're mixing really but you still got your own independent group . . . you know what I mean.' |

The fluid nature of the boys' groups becomes apparent as the boys, particularly Conrad and Roland, try to explain to me how their friendship groups and social relationships are organized. In the following extract Roger attempts to explain the nature of the subgroups and their relationship to the larger group.

Roger:	'We're all a big group but me, Mathew, and Simon are a sort of subgroup . . . so we can talk freely as our subgroup.'
Mathew:	'You're all part of a big group . . . but then there are sort of smaller groups.'
Roger:	'You've got to make subgroups to suit your friends. Say one friend could live way up – or somewhere, so you've got to make a subgroup.'

The two boys who are exceptions and are seen as somewhat outside the big corporate class group, Tom and Peter, are described as follows:

| Conrad: | 'We don't know Tom really, but still, nobody picks on him or anything really.' |

and when commenting on Peter, Denis and Simon say 'We play football, *everyone* in the class plays football except Peter'.

Even though they are regarded as being somewhat outside the larger group, mainly because they do not play football at breaks and lunch-time, they are still part of it and in the following discussion Luke explains how Tom has 'proved' his loyalty and allegiance to the class group.

| R.M.: | 'What sort of things do you share?' |
| Luke: | 'Sweets, pens. . . . Like Tom, this is where he comes friendly because what he does is . . . Robin (boy from |

another class) was picking on me and he just came up and he goes "What are you picking on my friend for?". He knew he couldn't beat Robin but he started acting tough on him. Robin just went away then.'

Peter's friend Richard proves somewhat difficult for the boys to understand because of his intermittent commitment to the playground football matches. Sometimes he would play and Peter would stand and watch, and at other times the pair would wander around the playground together. The rest of the boys found this sort of behaviour difficult to understand.

Luke: 'He doesn't even play football with you either.'
Mathew: 'Richard he said he'll play with you . . . he plays with you at one playtime and then he goes off with someone else.'
Denis: 'When we ask him if he wants to play football all he does is walk away and don't say nothing.'

The importance of having friends was expressed by many of the boys, as it was by the girls, and for many the opportunity to meet and make friends was 'the best thing' about school.

R.M.:   'So what's the best part of school then?'
Mathew: 'Friendships.'
. . . :   'Yeah.'
. . . :   'Yeah.'
Simon: 'Playtime!'
Roger: 'Hometime!'
Denis: 'Because school is like a meeting place really, you have to be playing, like when you play football.'

By far the most dominant concern and preoccupation of the boys was football. This was what they enjoyed doing more than anything else. It was the dominant theme in their conversations and they spent every possible moment playing football.

For a short period (referred to earlier), three of the boys started spending their free time talking to the 'science lab' girls. The other boys in the class found this absolutely incomprehensible and just could not understand how or why these boys preferred to spend their lunch hours with the girls rather than playing football. In a somewhat similar way the staff found it difficult to understand when, after having spent a considerable amount of time and energy organizing a Christmas party for the fourth year, they discovered half-way through the afternoon that some of the boys had slipped away from the party and were in the playground playing football.

In the classroom a lot of the casual conversation that was not directed towards the classroom task at hand was about football – the relative merits of the various football clubs they supported, discussions about the previous week-end's football matches, and very often discussions and arguments about their own lunch-time and break-time football matches.

R.M.:	'I'll ask you again, how do you behave in class?'
Adrian:	'Argue.'
Luke:	'Always . . . like when we've finished the game . . . like sometimes there's so many goals scored like today it was around 6–5.'
Adrian:	'Should be five each.'
Luke:	'We argue about the score. Roland always says it is something different and we start arguing. It's the way it is.'

It became apparent in some of the interviews that ability at, interest in, and devotion to football was the main dimension by which peers were evaluated by many of the boys. In the following interview we obtain hints of how ability and commitment to the playground football matches is in many ways equated with the 'worth' of the individual, and how any interruptions (e.g., one boy going home for his lunch) or anything less than total commitment is seen as a real problem and a reflection on the individual concerned.

R.M.:	'What's important to you about being in a group?'
Luke:	'Because we're all friends and we rely on each other, that's the main thing. There's one person you can't rely on and that's Henry, most of the time he keeps walking off and that. He walks off and says "I'm not playing with you" and then about ten minutes later he comes back. Brian's just the same. If Gordon can't play then Henry won't play.'
R.M.:	'Why can't Gordon play?'
Adrian:	'He's rubbish.'
Luke:	'Half the time he gets in the way and half of the time he doesn't want to play, he goes home.'
Adrian:	'He goes home dinners, that's the real problem.'

As well as the interest and involvement in football and sport more generally, the boys identified several other characteristics as features of their group or perhaps more particularly of the way in which their group behaved. Sharing was seen as important. The sharing of books, pencils, sweets, and more important the sharing of homework and helping each other with the demands of school work.

R.M.:	'What about in school, do you help each other with your school work?'
. . . :	'Homework!'
. . . :	'Yes!'
. . . :	'Maths!'
Denis:	'Me and Mathew there's only one group that we're not in together, that's maths.'
Mathew:	'Give each other ideas about questions.'
Denis:	'In English me and Mathew are doing exactly the same thing.'
R.M.:	'What about you Simon?'
Simon:	'Yes we help each other all the time.'
R.M.:	'What about homework?'
. . . :	'Yes.'
. . . :	'Yes.'
R.M.:	'Do you help each other in tests?'
All:	'No!!'
Roger:	'You can't.'
Denis:	'That's cheating that is.'
Mathew:	'If you get caught you get nought.'
Denis:	'I don't cheat, I work on my own.'
Simon:	'What about the time you got sent by yourself for copying me in French?'
R.M.:	'And you think it's wrong to copy in tests do you?'
Simon:	'Yes you cheat yourself.'
R.M.:	'But you help each other with homework and work in school?'
. . . :	'Yes.'
. . . :	'Yes.'
Denis:	'It's not worth it cheating in tests 'cause if someone says do this and you can't do it, well they say you did it easy enough in the test, so then you cheated.'

So helping each other in class and with homework, especially when someone has forgotten to do it, is an important part of belonging to the group, but helping each other in tests was not seen as a function of the group.

Being able to take a joke was stressed as an important characteristic of group members and seen as an important feature of the group.

R.M.:   'Tell me about this group. Tell me what this group of friends that you play with is like.'

Adrian: 'They're good.'

Luke: 'There's one thing you'll never be able to do. In the group if they make a joke about you you've got to take the joke. If you don't they all call you a cissy or something like that.'

Adrian: 'An' you've got to stick up for your friends like . . .!'

Denis: 'You gotta be able to take a joke.'

Simon: 'Don't lose your temper.'

Not only is it important that group members 'take a joke' but they must also be loyal to and stick up for their friends, and this means that you should never 'drop your mates in it'. The boys recount to me an example of the way in which mates should be protected at all times, especially from teachers.

Roger: 'Say Simon and Peter were having a fight in class and (teacher) walked in and she said "What's going on then?" and she asked what happened and we all said nothing.

Luke: 'She goes to me "What did happen Luke?" and I said nothing, and she said Jennifer wouldn't bring me here for nothing.'

Denis: 'Jennifer she's the one though.'

Adrian: 'You can't drop your mate in it.'

Boys who 'think they're a bit good' or 'like acting big' are either not seen as appropriate group members or else need to be 'cut down to size'. This category tends to be one that is applied most often to boys in other classes. 'Most of them are big heads.'

Academic ability, attitude to school, or set placement did not seem to be important distinguishing dimensions of this class group of boys. It was of course a mixed-ability class and boys were in different sets for maths and English. Some appeared to be more academically inclined but this did not seem to be of any major importance in terms of group formation. Football ruled.

R.M.:   'Does your group usually do well at school?'

Mathew: 'No.'

Denis: 'Not really I suppose.'

Roger:	'I do quite well.'
	. . .
R.M.:	'Does it make any difference to you whether someone is clever at school or works hard at school?'
. . . :	'No.'
. . . :	'It doesn't matter at all.'
R.M.:	'That's not an important thing at all?'
Denis:	'It doesn't matter if it's science or French or maths. . . .'
Simon:	'Because otherwise you always get someone coming round and saying that I'm better than you at this, and I'm better than you at that – it's *crap*.'

As mentioned earlier, the main benefit of school for most of the boys is that it provides a meeting place for friends. The academic aspects of school are seen as something that has to be 'put up with', usually because it is felt that school is important in helping you get a good job. The following interview with three of the most academic boys in the class illustrated this point.

R.M.:	'Well tell me how you like school.'
Conrad:	'You must go. We need a good education for when you leave school and get a good job.'
R.M.:	'That's not the question I asked. How do you *like* school?'
Roland:	'It's all right. I can't see anything wrong with it. You have your good days, you have your bad days, most of them are normal really.'
R.M.:	'What about you Mo?'
Mo:	'Same I reckon.'
Conrad:	'I wouldn't criticize it to a great length, saying you shouldn't go to school and things like that.'
R.M.:	'So you're not mad about school?'
. . . :	'Not really.'
. . . :	'No.'
Conrad:	'It's a thing you have to put up with. We tend to accept it anyway.'
R.M.:	'Why do you tend to accept it?'
Conrad:	'Well you have to don't you, and you need good education anyway if you want to get a good job.'
Mo:	'Yeah.'

Apart from the dominance of the influence of sport and particularly football, there does not seem to be any great peer influence towards conformity to peer-group norms and values. This is perhaps because of the size and constitution of the group i.e., most of the boys are in a randomly assigned mixed-ability class group which encompasses a wide range of attitudes and abilities. When questioned specifically about this peer conformity/influence, the boys tended to treat it as almost a 'non-question' compared to the girls, who were very much aware of and able to describe the way in which they influenced and were influenced by each other. The following are responses from several of the boys.

R.M.:	'. . . do you all try to do the same things as each other?'
Luke:	'No.'
Adrian:	'No, I don't think so.'
R.M.:	'Do you find that your friends influence you?'
Mathew:	'I don't think they've got an influence on me.'
R.M.:	'What about you Denis?'
Denis:	'No not really.'

One may attempt to explain this by concluding that the boys did not influence each other to any great extent, or alternatively by concluding that the boys did influence each other but were very much unaware of this. The actual position is probably somewhere between the two possibilities. Differences did not seem to matter within the boys group except in relation to football; whether you did your homework or not, what clothes you wore, and how conscientious you were in class seemed to matter little in terms of acceptance or rejection by the rest of the group. The overriding norm seemed to be that if you wanted to play football then you were 'in'.

Very few of the boys had any definite plans or ambitions for the future. This was very noticeable in comparison with the girls, many of whom had very definite, and perhaps romantic, future plans in terms of career and life styles. In the following transcript the boys' concern with the here-and-now and (except for Denis) their lack of interest in the future except in a very generalized way is apparent.

R.M.:	'What are your plans for the future then?'
Mathew:	'Go to the pictures with me girl friend.'
R.M.:	'Do you think about the future?'
. . . :	'No.'
. . . :	'No.'

. . . :	'Not really.'
Roger:	'We just take it as it comes.'
R.M.:	'Do you think about what sort of job you'd like?'
Denis:	'Oh I got a job already. . . .'
R.M.:	'What's your job?'
Denis:	'Game keeping.'
R.M.:	'And you want to do that?'
Denis:	Yes. My Dad's a gamekeeper.'
R.M.:	'What about you Simon?'
Simon:	'Anything with good pay.'
Luke:	'My Dad says he wants me to do carpentry all over Europe and the world, and you can get a job qualifying for anything.'
Mathew:	'Don't think about it much really.'
Roger:	'At high school there's a bloke that tells me about jobs so you can think about it then.'

The boys here obviously feel themselves a long way from the world of work. This may well be because they are still 'one school' away from having to face such decisions, and if they had been in the second year of a comprehensive school instead of the fourth year of a middle school these boys' attitudes may well have been different. Clearly, there are implications here for the specific effects of middle schools as such on peer-group relations, this time for boys, which require further study. By contrast, many of the girls had quite definite ideas about the jobs they wanted when they left school.

At least some of the boys saw education and staying on at school as a possible part of their future. These possibilities tended to be expressed in somewhat generalized terms.

R.M.:	'What sort of, I mean do you have plans for the future?'
Conrad:	'What together or . . . (pause).'
Conrad:	'Well I want to do well.'
Mo/Roland:	'We all do.'
R.M.:	'Well . . . yes . . . what sort of things do you want to do?'
Conrad:	'I want to do well at school and get as far as I can, probably in education.'
R.M.:	'What does that mean to you? As far as you can, how far would you like to go?'
Roland:	'College.'

Conrad/Mo:	'Yeah.'
Conrad:	'University too if I can – that's a long way off.'
R.M.:	'And what other plans for your life have you got?'
Conrad:	'Just to live a happy life I suppose.'
R.M.:	'Do you think you'll be friends?'
Conrad:	'Probably.'
R.M.:	'Do you ever talk about what you'd like to do?'
Conrad:	'It's hard to tell really.'
R.M.:	'What about getting married?'
Conrad:	'It depends if the right girl comes along.'
Roland:	'If I could hold the girl friend I've got now yeah – but I'm not sure 'cause I save the numbers of trains and I want to finish them off first!!!'

This sort of general commitment to education does not come through when talking to the girls, and is perhaps significant in terms of the future differences in educational ambitions and life plans between boys and girls as they progress through school. It may also be possible that once the boys reach the high school and are confronted with the setting and streaming patterns of organization, that there may well be a considerable development and polarization in terms of pro- and anti-academic attitudes.

Perhaps because of the flexible nature of the boys' groups, arguments and making and breaking friends, which were such a dominant feature of the girls' groups, were not a striking feature of the boys' group. When there are arguments they tended to centre almost exclusively on the playground football matches. This is in direct contrast with the girls.

R.M.:	'Do you sometimes fall out?'
Roger:	'Not very often no.'
Mathew:	'We fall out but then we make friends again.'
	. . .
Roland:	'Last year, it was really bad. This year at the beginning it started badly as well, but recently the arguments have been cut down quite a lot.'
Conrad:	'Me and Mo don't really seem to fall out.'

For those boys who perhaps would rather not play football *all* the time, this can be a potential source of 'breaking friends'. Two of the boys, Henry and Gordon, discuss this.

R.M.:	'Why do you break friends?'

Henry:	'Mostly over football, 'cause if we don't play they break friends with me, and they want me to play but sometimes I don't want to play.'
R.M.:	'Over football or over other things?'
Gordon:	'If they say a goal was off-side, then if it's a goal they shout at each other, and there are F's and B's and then they start calling each other names, they say "shit head" or "long legs", they just don't call them proper names.'

Leadership was not seen by the boys as an important feature of or within the group. To the observer the only indication of leadership was the captains of the two sides in the playground football games – Mathew and Roland. Situations where leadership in decision making could be exercised or observed were rare. As Gordon said: 'We always play football so there's no decision.' When the boys were pushed on the question of leadership they usually came up with the names of the football captains, but were quick to add that this did not mean that they 'bossed' them around or decided what to do.

R.M.:	'Who decides what you're going to do?'
Denis:	'Mathew usually is the leader, he's usually in charge of the gang, he doesn't boss you about though.'
Luke:	'No. He doesn't boss you about.'
R.M.:	'So who decides what you're going to do?'
Adrian:	'No one really, we decide for ourselves.'

Relationships between the boys and girls of 4F

The boys in 4F were very much dominated by the 'PE' girls. Where there were friendships it was with the girls from the 'science lab' group and there tended to be very little contact with the other two groups of girls, except for Vera who was often teased mercilessly by some of the boys, particularly Tom.

'The boys in this class are a bunch o' weeds, I could do the lot o' them', Josephine announced to the class one registration period while they were waiting for Mr. Fisher to arrive. The boys chose to ignore the challenge.

The majority of the boys in 4F, while perhaps not publicly acknowledging the superior toughness of the girls, certainly did so by their actions. In the following interview the boys acknowledge the superiority of the girls, and describe the way they always get what they want and how they can interfere with relative impunity with their sacred playground football matches.

R.M.:	'Do you get on with the girls alright?'
Adrian:	'Yes.'
Luke:	'Yes as long as they can borrow your things they're all right.'
R.M.:	'They borrow your things do they?'
Adrian:	'Yeah.'
R.M.:	'Do you borrow their things sometimes?'
Adrian:	'No.'
Luke:	'The only thing I've borrowed is a pen off Josephine. Everyone borrows things off her because she's the only one that will let you borrow anything and she *knows* that you will give it back anyway.'
R.M.:	'Why's that?'
Luke:	'She'd have you if you didn't give it her back. There's one thing though when she's outside, that's when she's at her worst because she'll try and grab hold of your football and run away with it.'
Adrian:	'And then pass it to all her friends.'
Luke:	'Like Betty and Barbara.'
Adrian:	'And Lorraine.'

Many of the boys, especially the physically smaller ones, found the 'PE' girls in particular somewhat intimidating. They were 'picked on', teased, and called names. The following transcripts express the boys' feelings.

R.M.:	'And how do you get on with the girls in your class?'
Henry:	'Not well! We don't like no girls in our class.'
R.M.:	'Oh. Do you like girls in other classes?'
Henry:	'We don't like any of them!'
	. . .
R.M.:	'And the girls in your class, do you have much to do with them?'
Henry:	'Sometimes Betty comes and calls me names.'
R.M.:	'What sort of names?'
Gordon:	'Like scruff. They call Brian that as well. He used to wear a really big flashy tie, not a school tie, and they used to say he's going to a wedding.'

R.M.:	'What about the girls in your class? Do you have much to do with them?'
Brian:	'No.'
R.M.:	'Why not?'
Brian:	'Just don't. Argue with 'em.'
R.M.:	'What do you argue about?'
Brian:	'Just argue, calling each other scruff and that.'
R.M.:	'What about you Tom?'
Tom:	'Don't get on with them much. Don't like girls that much.'
R.M.:	'Don't you? Why not?'
Tom:	'They're big heads, they think they're better all the time. Keep calling you names.'
R.M.:	'What sort of names?'
Tom:	'Scruff and weed an' tramp an' that.'

The 'big-headedness' of the girls was often remarked upon by the boys. In this case it is the 'science lab' girls who are 'attacked' as being teacher's pets and big-headed.

Luke:	'There's only one person in our class who everyone doesn't like except for Conrad and Roger – Diane's the teacher's pet isn't she?'
Adrian:	'Yeah.' (Adrian and Diane became boyfriend and girlfriend later in the year!)
Luke:	'There isn't a single mark that she has had below A. She hasn't had a B plus even, she usually gets A or A- all the time.'
Adrian:	'Yeah.'
Luke:	'She's a snob. She thinks that she's too good for everyone like Jennifer does. Jennifer is one of the most common people in our class and yet she thinks she is the best person in the whole world. She goes round saying "Oh you little shrimp".'
Adrian:	'She thinks she's fantastic.'
Luke:	'I know. She used to be Mathew's girlfriend for three years and then he jacked her in.'
Adrian:	'It wasn't three years.'
R.M.:	'Why did he do that?'

Luke: 'It was two then. He just didn't like her, she was acting too big-headed.'

It was felt by at least some of the boys that the girls were responsible for 'getting them into trouble'.

R.M.:   'What about Betty and Josephine and that lot?'
Mathew: 'They're all right but we don't play with them.'
Roger: 'They can be a bit spiteful.'
Simon: 'If you go anywhere near them and you start talking and then they start talking really loud and the teacher blames the boys and it's really the girls.'
Denis: 'Yeah that's true.'

It is perhaps important to note that Mathew, the only boy to comment that the tough 'PE' girls are all right is probably the most physically mature boy in the class.

The 'quiet' and 'nice' girls appear to play very little part in the social lives of the 4F boys. The following is the response when I tentatively raise the names of these girls:

R.M.:   'What about the other groups in your class then – Vera and . . . .'
Denis: 'Oh my God.'
Mathew: 'We don't have anything to do with them.'
Roger: 'They're a private group.'
Simon: 'They keep to themselves.'

One of the 'quiet' girls, Vera, often receives attention from some of the boys, especially Tom, in the form of teasing (she is also teased by the 'PE' girls). Peter explains what often happens.

Peter: 'Tom is the worst for getting Vera, he keeps getting her bag and running round with it.'
R.M.:   'Why does he do that?'
Peter: 'Just to get her aggravated.'
R.M.:   'Why don't you like them?'
Peter: 'Nobody ever talks to them.'

The only group of girls where positive relationships with the boys does sometimes occur is the 'science lab' group of girls. In a general way there seems agreement among the boys that they 'like' the 'science lab' girls best. This was not the case with boys from outside the class who found the 'PE' girls as most attractive. This is perhaps only to be expected in view of the comments made by the 'PE' girls about the boys in their class. Tom and Brian illustrate the general 'liking' for the 'science lab' girls.

R.M.: 'What about the girls in your class, what do you think about them?'

Tom: 'There's only one group that I like, that's Jennifer's group I think.'

Brian: 'Yeah.'

R.M.: 'And why do you like them?'

Tom: 'Because they're quiet and Josephine's group ('PE') shout about and that, though Jennifer's got a big head though. She thinks she's tough and everything.'

R.M.: 'You quite like that group though?'

Brian: 'They're all right yes. The best group out of the girls.'

Usually there was very little interaction or contact between the boys and the girls in the class except for the few classroom 'romances'.

R.M.: 'How do you get on with the girls in your class?'

Mo: 'We leave them alone.'

R.M.: 'You have nothing to do with them?'

Conrad: 'Nothing.'

R.M.: 'Do you get on with them but just don't have much to do with them?'

Conrad: 'Nothing whatsoever. Some people have but we haven't.'

Mo: 'Yeah.'

Roland: 'Yeah, yeah.'

Mo: 'It's mainly Mathew and Simon and Roger joining in with the girls.'

Roland: 'Mathew really not so much, Simon really not so much. Simon hasn't got a chance with Jennifer.'

R.M.: 'Why not?'

Mo: 'She's as stubborn as a cow she is.'

Conrad: 'Got a big mouth as well ain't she?'

The three boys with girl friends were causing a certain amount of disruption to the football matches, much to the annoyance of the rest of the boys.

Denis: 'This business with their three girlfriends is causing a bit of trouble in the playground.'

Adrian:	'Lot of aggro.'
Mathew:	'So why shouldn't we be with our girlfriends, sir?'
Denis:	'When we play football, say we were winning, they go off at any time and then we have to lose 'cause they go off.'

Conclusions

Among this cohort of middle school pupils there would certainly appear to be considerable differences between the ways in which boys and girls organize their school social lives. The girls' school peer networks were much more clearly delineated than those of the boys, and there was little doubt about the membership of the different girls' groups. These groups were clearly identified by the girls themselves, the boys, and the teachers. Contrary to previous research, girls of this age and in the organizational setting of a middle school felt that groups rather than pairs were the best form of social organization, although some felt that this may change when they go up to the high school. Any attempts to 'break up' the peer groups were strongly resisted and this was often the cause of much friction within the groups.

The different girls' groups exhibited many features in common, but saw themselves as being different from each other and were identified by the teachers as being different. Commitment to and involvement in elements of teenage culture were an important distinguishing feature between groups which did not run parallel to pro- and anti-attitudes and orientation to school.

The boys spent most of their time and certainly saw themselves as one big class group. Their school lives remained within the bounds of this class group, and boys in other classes were classed as almost strangers. Football was the dominant concern, interest, and activity, and for most of the boys the reason for having a network of friends. Where there was friction within the group, football was the major cause. Individual boys tended to be evaluated in terms of their commitment to the playground football matches.

The two most obvious features of these pupils' peer networks were that they were formed largely within class-group boundaries and were almost entirely of the same gender. The class-group boundary appeared to be a much greater barrier for the boys than for the girls. For both sexes there was an increase in the number of friendship choices which crossed class-group boundaries over the two-year period, probably due to the effects of the increasing setting procedures. Peer networks were almost exclusively single-sex in character and there tended to be very little interaction between the boys and girls. This should not be interpreted as the boys having no influence on the girls or vice versa. On the contrary, the presence of boys considerably affected the girls and the presence of girls considerably affected the boys in this coeducational establishment. The girls tended to be dominant in their social relations with boys. This is in many ways not surprising as the girls of this age were physically and socially more mature than the boys. Many of the boys found at least some of the girls intimidating, and adopted deliberate strategies to avoid them whenever possible.

In general terms the girls seemed to be far more engaged with and aware of what school was about and what was going on in school. They had made definite responses to the school, and adopted orientations towards school, and in some cases employed deliberate strategies to help them cope with the demands made upon them by the school. On the other hand, the boys, at this age, tended to be almost unaware of what school meant and of the sorting and processing that was taking place. They were far more concerned with meeting their mates and playing football and any commitment to academic school learning was almost incidental.

CHAPTER FIFTEEN

IN THE MIDDLE: FIRST AND UPPER SCHOOL TEACHERS' RELATIONS WITH MIDDLE SCHOOL COLLEAGUES

M. B. Ginsburg and R. J. Meyenn

The nature and extent of the relationships of first and upper school teachers with the middle school teachers involved with them in a three-tier pattern, can be seen as an important element in the continuity of a child's educational experience. A number of important issues need to be addressed. How are the organization and practices in middle schools viewed by teachers in first and upper schools? How do first and upper school teachers view the extent and nature of their contact with middle school teachers? What adaptations (if any) have first and upper school teachers made in their own practice as a result of their schools' connection with (in this case, nine–thirteen age-range) middle schools? Finally, what are the implications of middle school teachers' relations with colleagues 'above' and 'below' for the nature and continuity of pupils' school experiences from age five to sixteen plus?

To explore these and other issues, the authors conducted semi-structured, individual, and small group interviews during the spring and summer terms of 1978. In all, the interviews involved sixty-two teachers who were members of staff of six first schools and three upper schools. These nine institutions – along with three of the five nine–thirteen age-range middle schools involved in previously reported research (Ginsburg et al., 1977) – constituted three 'pyramids' or three-tier feeder patterns of schools in one LEA. In the first schools, all or most of the staff were involved in interviews, while in the upper schools those involved were the heads, staff with formal responsibilities for pastoral care, staff responsible for various subject areas, and those with designated responsibility for liaison with middle schools and the transfer of pupils from middle to upper schools.

Middle schools as seen from outside

When first and upper school teachers were asked about their impressions of middle school organization and practice, a number of interesting issues emerged. First, it was apparent that in a large number of cases, these teachers did not have a clear picture of what, in fact, was occurring in middle schools. Phrases such as 'this is pure assumption' or 'I've never really been in a middle school' were frequently used by these teachers to qualify their remarks. Nevertheless, perceptions and attitudes were expressed, and it seems likely that these are what teachers rely on when commenting upon or discussing middle schools.

The teachers' perceptions of middle schools are remarkable in the sharp contrast shown between the views of first and upper school teachers. If previous primary and secondary experience is not an important source of division for teachers within the middle school, it certainly would seem to be between teachers in different schools. Many of the first school teachers involved in the interviews thought that middle schools have *not* followed the Plowden Report's (Plowden, 1967, p.146, para. 383) encouragement to 'develop further the curriculum, methods and attitudes which exist . . . in junior schools'. Rather, middle schools were seen as introducing secondary practices earlier than eleven plus.

> . . . I feel as though sometimes – and this is pure assumption, having never been in a middle school and seen it in a working situation – that they seem to me to be like mini-high schools . . . they are divided up, say, in subjects, so they have a different teacher for a different subject; whereas, I think, perhaps they would be better having a class teacher for general subjects, say up to eleven. . . .' (First school teacher)

Although the above quotation represents how many first school teachers view the operation of middle schools, not all teachers reacted negatively to the situation.

> They [middle schools] are less like a primary school, in my opinion. I think they have to be. Having two daughters in the high school, knowing that they have so little time once they get to high school to prepare for 'O' levels and CSEs . . . the junior stage seems to have disappeared. . . . Not so much in their first year [of the middle school] because they still have their class teacher for everything . . . but it [subject-based versus class teacher-based teaching] has to come sooner than it would have had it been a junior school. (First school teacher)

The head of one first school, and it is perhaps significant that she was head of a school in the pyramid where contact and liaison between the *three* tiers was most extensive, indicated that she felt middle schools should be 'something different', neither primary nor secondary, when she said:

> . . . one would hope that it would be neither but it would be a mingling of the two. It's a new conception and so it really should not be a high school or a primary school – it has got to be a mingling of the two. . . . (First school head)

This head goes on to add that from her experience, so much is likely to depend on the previous experience of the head.

> . . . but again, I think it depends on who's appointed as head, because if you get a primary school teacher appointed as head, and I've seen this in one nearby middle school where a primary person has been appointed as head, and certainly it is more primary-based and orientated whereas if a high school teacher comes in to take a middle school, then it is much more high school orientated. (First school head)

In contrast, upper school teachers interviewed tended to see the middle school as extending primary practice and organization, or at least delaying pupils' exposure to a secondary form of teaching organization. Although there were some comments on how middle schools varied in this regard, and other remarks indicating that the transition from primary, class-based to secondary, subject-based teaching had remained at eleven plus, most upper school teachers interviewed seemed to agree with the following viewpoint:

> I think they're remaining in a primary situation until they're thirteen. (Upper school teacher)

This and similar perceptions were amplified in terms of the middle school *not* tending to be organized with specialists teaching subjects in which they were specifically trained.[1]

> The whole ethos is rather different from the ethos which they would have had as eleven-year-olds in the secondary school. They are basically still in the class teaching situation; we have to get them used to the subject teaching situation in the high school. (Upper school teacher)

For others, it was also a question of the differential intensity of the work demands on pupils in primary and secondary forms of schooling.

> As far as I can make out – I'm not an expert on middle schools, it's only what I've seen – the middle school is an extension, or tends to be an extension, of the primary school instead of getting down to the work of the secondary school. In other words, they play for two extra years. (Upper school teacher)

As with the first school teachers, those in the upper school varied in their evaluation of the perceived state of affairs in middle schools. Some were wholly or partially satisfied and others were very negatively disposed to middle schools. However, compared to those in first schools, the upper school teachers interviewed were much more likely to be critical of the practice and organization in middle schools. Such criticisms were *not* directed at middle school teachers personally, but at the system which provides inadequate facilities, few attractive (salary-wise) posts for subject specialists, as well as no formal 'end product', i.e., external exams.[2]

Upper school teachers often went to great lengths to point out that their criticisms were directed at the system and not at individual middle schools or teachers.

> I think we are very lucky; we may be giving an impression that says we are a bit dissatisfied but I think we are not dissatisfied with the two feeder schools that we have got at all. We may be a little bit dissatisfied with the system. (Upper school teacher)

The lack of equipment and facilities, particularly in the practical subjects, is seen by many upper school teachers as an inhibiting factor in middle schools. This factor, so often argued in our interviews, is a very good example of the difference between what upper school staff perceive to be the situation in middle schools and what is, in fact, the case. The following is typical:

> A lot of middle schools are so designed that the science room is a bench and a sink – behind it is a cooker and in the corner there is the sewing machine. I am not exaggerating – the situation is like this. When you get someone at an eleven–eighteen and she goes to her first cookery lesson she goes into a room full of cookers and sinks, and deep freezes and this kind of thing. If she does it at another school and a modern designed middle school, there is probably one cooker and, again, this does make a difference. This makes a difference to the child's attitude. (Upper school head)

One subject which was often cited when discussing middle school facilities was science. The researchers have, in fact, been in well-equipped middle school science laboratories and observed stimulating science lessons with a high degree of pupil involvement in practical work. So why is it that the bulk of upper school staff hold the impressions that they do? There are, perhaps, two main reasons. One, mentioned above, is that upper school teachers have very few insights as to what actually goes on inside middle schools and, secondly, because of the pressure of exams faced by the upper schools and hence their desire to 'get on and do separate sciences' earlier, there is a dismissal of much of the middle school science curriculum as interesting but not especially relevant.

The perceived lack of equipment and facilities is seen as affecting all subjects.

And our money – I get as much in some ways for my department (English) as they get in a middle school for a whole year – you know, for books and things, and I think they look at us and think, well, you have got all the facilities and everything. (Upper school teacher)

Many of the upper school teachers saw the inadequacies of the middle school system being particularly obvious in the area of subject specialisms and the availability of scale posts.

The other problem is that these people are not specialists. This is my problem, as well. That all the teachers in the middle schools are doing, except for a bit of specialization, all subjects. How can you expect them to be a specialist in every subject they take? (Upper school teacher)

Another commented:

It is very largely at the root of all this, it is this system which we have built up whereby if you've got somebody with a qualification in French so that he could really teach it going into a high school, keeping his or her head above water doing a good job, she is going to be knocking on a Scale 2 fairly soon, a Scale 3 is well within her reach in the foreseeable future where not so many of those scales are around in a middle school. You take your French qualification into a middle school, however good you are, you are going to have to wait a certain time before you can get any scaling at all because the scaling is not there. (Upper school head)

Most upper school teachers saw the lack of public examinations as a considerable disadvantage of the middle school system. This is in direct contrast with the majority of middle school teachers who felt this to be a 'liberating factor' and something that enabled them to get on with 'proper education' and not simply become 'exam factories'.

I get the feeling that in the middle school there is no end-product. They're just sort of drifting along and don't know exactly where they're going. . . . (Upper school teacher)

Another upper school teacher saw an important role for the upper school to act as an 'examining board' for middle schools.

The old junior school had the 11+ and we have got the examinations at the end of our course. But they have got no sort of examinations to know how they have done. . . . I think it is good to have the pressure of exams. If we can act more or less as the examining board for the middle schools and say I don't think you are up to the standard, it doesn't hurt and they might take it as a dreadful criticism if I say to Dingleside I am sorry but you are not up to the standard of Lodge Farm, but surely it is going to make them work harder to improve. And to get a bit of competition is a good thing.

It would appear that the differences in the perceptions and evaluations of middle schools by teachers 'above' and 'below' have implications for the nature of the contact between teachers in these different schools.

Teacher contact between schools

All staff interviewed acknowledged the importance of contact between middle school teachers and colleagues in associated first and upper schools. Such contact was seen to be helpful, particularly on an annual basis to make arrangements for and pass on information about pupils transferring from one tier to another. More frequent contact involving a larger proportion of teachers was also considered very important by many of those interviewed, because it was thought to promote a greater understanding of what teachers in other tiers were doing and of the constraints under which they were operating. This in turn might have ensured greater continuity and less repetition in pupils' curricular experience. A substantial number of both first and upper school teachers also expressed enthusiasm for some arrangement by which a teacher exchanged places with a colleague in a middle school for a specified period of time, either on a full-time or part-time basis. Strong support was also given to the idea of arranging interschool staff, informal, social occasions. Such activity was seen as having pay-offs in terms of facilitating subsequent, more formal interaction focused on curricular, organizational, and pupil transfer matters. (See also Blyth and Derricott, 1977, p.77.)

> I think it would be invaluable because it would break down what sometimes are resentments. And if we have contacts where people met each other as people rather than as teachers from another school that relationship would sometimes break down. (Upper school teacher)

There is some indication in the interviews that, once established, good informal relations facilitate liaison between schools.[3] On numerous occasions those interviewed referred to extensive liaison with middle school colleagues whom they had known over a period of years and in a variety of contexts. One department head in an upper school explained his difficulty in trying to establish links with the middle school because he lacked such informal contacts.

> Well I am happy with the way the relationship is growing and I think that the fact that some of my teachers were at college with the . . . teachers has helped because they have something in common and they mix more. (First school head)

However, while there was much support for extensive formal and informal contact between teachers, the frequency of this contact was less than what many desired. Many of our respondents suggested that time constraints[4] both in and out of school hours were a major factor – one that is reinforced for schools at some distance from each other. This was especially important for first school teachers who had little, if any, nonteaching time during the school day. For some teachers, time constraints were exacerbated by the LEA's practice regarding the provision of 'supply' or substitute teachers, which meant that not infrequently (and especially since recent cutbacks in educational expenditure) staff would lose their nonteaching periods in order to cover for absent colleagues. One respondent, while recognizing the financial implications, went as far as to suggest:

> What I feel is . . . that the number of teachers who are out of jobs at the moment and the number of part-timers that are hanging on for a job, that in the summer term it would be an ideal opportunity for perhaps two or three part-timers to be employed to just go out in the schools to allow the permanent staff to go up to make this kind of link (to visit the other schools). (First school teacher)

Another factor which reduces the amount of between-school contact, especially that which is focused on curricular and organization of teaching issues, is a concern about being perceived as infringing upon another school staff's autonomy.[5]

> If they (middle school teachers) want anything, it's their job to ask me. . . . I don't want to tread on anyone's toes. (First school teacher)

> Liaison with the middle schools is essentially our business. We need to know what the kids are like, what's happening to them before we get them . . . the staff who teach them have got to be well informed about what we want. . . . It could help us if we could say that we would like things done this way . . . it would make our job easier. (But) we haven't got the right to do that. (Upper school teacher)

Apparently, middle school teachers' perceptions of their relations with upper school colleagues had been communicated clearly enough so that upper school teachers could recognize and perhaps empathize with middle school teachers' situation.[6]

> It's up to them to decide how they're going to run, as it's up to us to decide how we're going to run the school. I would hate the middle school to come here and tell me how I'm going to run this school. (Upper school teacher)

However, although this factor was recognized by both first and upper school staff as inhibiting contact, it presented less of a problem to first school teachers, who could refrain from initiating contact with middle school staff because this was not seen as their responsibility.

> I'm sure if they thought that there were problems with regard to any particular aspect, they would have been in contact with us by now. And there certainly hasn't been anything like that. (First school teacher)

It is obviously also a question of the curricular and teaching practices in the middle school having a much greater bearing on upper school teachers, because they work with middle school 'products'.

> I'll get people from the department saying, you know, so and so is not doing very well. . . . Can't we do something about this? Can't we tell them (middle school teachers) to pull their fingers out! (Upper school teacher)

Perhaps for these and other reasons, contact seems most often to be initiated from colleagues in the school dealing with older pupils – a point that was noted, for example, by two teachers involved in the same interview.

> I always feel that it is us going down to them telling them what to do and I don't like that. (Upper school teacher)

> I think it's fair to say that except by specific invitation we don't often see them coming to us. I think that they probably have a lot more contact in the same sort of way with the first schools and they tend to go to the first schools rather than vice versa. (Another upper school teacher)

The upper school teacher frequently experiences a dilemma; not wanting to appear to interfere and yet desiring to influence what goes on in middle schools (either for pupils' and/or upper school teachers' benefit and often discussed in terms of demands of external exams). As one respondent expressed this dilemma:

> I don't want to dictate, but I guess I really do! (Upper school teacher)

Another upper school teacher comments:

> I see the problem as being again part of the system – I see it in terms of the break at thirteen having been, having the effect that we no longer have an influence, we only have an influence I should say. We don't have any control over the type of work that they do. . . . We have got no control over what they do, we can influence them but it would be a massive undertaking for them to take on the course which we would like them to have.

There is, however, probably largely due to the relative positions in the educational system, a feeling which comes through in the interviews of institutional superiority. This does not mean that upper school teachers see themselves personally as better teachers, and many acknowledge that in some ways middle school teachers probably work a lot harder. It is simply that they are higher up in the education system and it is they who are ultimately responsible for preparing pupils for *public examinations.* An upper school head explains:

> To be frank about this I think if when we called a meeting and we all came together we would be a little wary of each other to start with. I think our colleagues in the middle schools might well come with slight inferiority complexes because they think we would be looking down on them. One hard fact from which you cannot escape is that, and this is not a criticism it is a statement of fact I keep saying, but one mustn't hedge facts, but if you actually took the paper qualifications of the people in the school, add them up, we are a much better paper qualified lot. I am not saying we are better teachers or worse teachers. All I am saying is that there are far more university degrees in this place than there are in a middle school because this again for reasons best known. Well it tends to make you feel a little bit inferior. . . .'

In coping with this dilemma, upper school teachers have developed a variety of strategies. In discussing these we will also look more broadly how (if at all) upper and first school teachers have adapted their practice and organization of teaching because of their schools' connections with middle schools.

Adaptations by first and upper school teachers

One general strategy developed by upper school teachers involves continuing to attempt to exert influence on middle schools, but attempting to minimize the perceived threatening nature of such contact. Reference was made to being 'tactful' not 'pontificating', and going about it 'very, very carefully'. This might involve holding meetings at the middle school or making a conscious effort not to chair meetings. In some cases the strategy involved disguising upper school influence as efforts to coordinate the curricular and organization patterns across middle schools in a pyramid.[7]

> We have regular meetings. They (teachers from the two middle schools in the pyramid) just come here and we meet once a term to discuss their coordination, ostensibly, though . . . what we really discuss is what we (the upper school) want them to do. (Upper school teacher)

Another teacher commented somewhat similarly:

> We try to do all we can to demonstrate that we are not trying to run everybody else's school. We simply want to be in a situation together and make it continuous and fruitful, and above all avoid the silly squabbling between one school and another which doesn't do anybody any good. I think we've

succeeded, it took an awful long time, though, it took years to break down the idea. (Upper school teacher)

Another strategy aims to overcome this dilemma by attempting to define common goals, in terms of examinations, with the middle school staff.

. . . I said to them look you don't even see the examination papers and yet you are preparing those children for their exams just as much as I am. They really should know what an 'O' level and CSE and 16 paper look like. So they came in and they looked at them and we have got a lot of books which we never use, sets of books, so I gave them those. (Upper school teacher)

In some circumstances, but not all, teachers perceived enlisting the support of county advisers as a fruitful strategy.

You are stuck if you don't get cooperation from . . . the middle schools. There's nothing you can do to force them . . . (except) to get hold of the County Adviser and say 'you've got to do something'. (Upper school teacher)

Another strategy involved reducing attempts to influence middle schools to a bare minimum, to occasions when the situation was in drastic need of repair.

Well, I don't believe in interfering unless things are going very, very badly. (Upper school teacher)

It would seem that such a strategy would tend to exacerbate the situation, although it might reduce the number of confrontations, since middle school teachers would become aware that any contact was because they were seen to be doing something 'very badly'.

Interestingly, in terms of our own previous research (Ginsburg et al., 1977, pp. 38–40), some upper school teachers seemed to opt to adapt their own teaching rather than, or as well as, to attempt to influence middle schools' curricular and teaching organization. Allusions were made to 'having to start further back.'

We just take what we get and what we get we work with. (Upper school teacher)

But in no way have we tried to say to them (middle school teachers): 'Will you do this, this and this so we can carry on?' 'You teach what you think you ought to teach and then we take it from there.' (Another upper school teacher)

The respondent who made the latter comment (above) indicated that his department went even further in adapting to the exigencies of the three-tier system.

. . . we devised . . . a particular system for doing this, in that we do hardly any formal teaching in the first year. I ask them (the pupils) to work, if possible, from worksheets and do investigations, do practical work. . . . They do a full year, pretty much, of practical work, working from a worksheet. Then when they get to the end of a section there's usually a bit of formal teaching and they all work together. But we do hardly any formal teaching. It's up to individual members of staff, some do more formal teaching than others but we try, you know, so that it marries the two schools together. I've found it works quite well. (Upper school teacher)·

Another teacher who felt that the school did 'miss the enthusiasm of the eleven- and twelve-year-olds' comments on the speed with which the incoming pupils are expected to settle into the upper school routine.

They will wander around which is something that perhaps in some high schools this is accepted anyway – but they are used to getting up in the middle school situation and wandering round and finding what they want and going and asking somebody if they want a rubber. Whereas we tend, I think to expect them to say, put their hand up, and ask for whatever they want. Which is something they just have to get trained to in a very quick time. We just have a year before they start on their examination work as far as English is concerned – the beginning of the fourth year. Whereas before we had three years to get them used to the system.

Thus, although there is evidence of a 'top-down determined educational system' (Hargreaves, 1977, p.38, footnote 24), there is also, but to a much lesser extent, evidence of the upper school adapting 'its courses to cater for the needs and capacities of the pupils it receives' (Culling, 1973, p.93). It should be noted, of course, that it is the existence of such examples of upper school adaptations that help to sustain the ideology of the autonomous middle school extending the best of primary practice into pupils' later school experience.

To the extent that middle school teachers experience a dilemma similar to upper school teachers (i.e., wanting to influence first school practice and organization and yet desiring not to be seen as interfering), and to the extent that middle school teachers develop similar strategies for coping with the dilemma, it may explain another somewhat surprising finding emerging from the interviews. Assuming a top-down influence model in a three-tier system, one would expect first school teachers frequently to refer to being pressured into changing by middle school teachers. Such pressure is sometimes reported, although what was striking was the number of first school staff members who did not perceive any such pressures. In first schools where no such pressures were perceived it was not easy to probe beyond the disclaimers; the response was just that it did not occur.[8] It was noted, however, that the lack of pressure was seen as an indication of no problems.

> Most of our children have reached a satisfactory-plus standard when they start (in middle school). We've had no complaint about anything of that nature or even down to the actual schemes of work we use. . . . The first year coordinator . . . knows exactly what we're doing and I know exactly what they want. (First school teacher)

At times the lack of problems was attributed not only to first school teachers' skill and efforts, but also to the type of child (implicitly in terms of social class background) that attended the first school.

In the above quoted comment one begins to see how a lack of perceived pressure does not necessarily indicate a lack of desire to influence or even a lack of previous, and subtly effective, efforts to influence. As one upper school teacher remarked, in explaining why extensive contact with middle schools was not necessary:

> I can't see any need for – we have got everything from the middle schools that we have asked for. They have been extremely helpful. (Upper school teacher)

Thus, influence or a desired state of affairs can exist without colleagues 'above' having to exert pressure openly on colleagues 'below'. This is also indicated by interview data pointing to specific examples of adaptations which first school teachers have made due to their connection with middle schools. For example, one first school teacher noted that middle school teachers 'said that writing is to be standardized and we started to do it', but added moments later:

> I think we'd rather do what was helpful to the child. . . . Well in that way, perhaps if we discovered that the transition was a great problem to our children, perhaps we'd have to alter our last year slightly.

Another first school teacher commented:

> . . . you don't want to interfere with the other party at all but you want to do the best for the children. So usually what happens is that we have discussions and rather than change or alter the whole of our system to fit in with somebody else's, we have our system they have theirs and we try and between us build bridges that make the passage from one to the other as easy as possible.

For the first school teacher there is a related kind of dilemma; desiring to maintain autonomy and yet not wanting to disadvantage their pupils' future school careers. As one first school teacher put it: 'We need freedom, but it would be better if there was consensus.' And given the problems of making contact with, let alone influencing the practice of, middle school teachers, first school staff may find adapting to the perceived or real pressures from the middle school less difficult than other alternatives.

In this regard it is important to note that some first school teachers adapt their teaching to what they perceive to be the requirements of the middle school, even though, because of limited contact with middle schools, they are only guessing what those requirements in fact are. One respondent discussed how he:

> . . . does quite a lot of work in these last two terms (before pupils transfer to the middle school) to prepare them for the different system of working in the middle school, . . . giving them set duties, like a programme of work for each day. But it's only a guess, you see, (that) they're expected to do a . . . certain amount of work each day.

This may be another mechanism operating (perhaps effectively in terms of continuity) to produce adaptations in the practice/organization in first schools without staff viewing it as an unreasonable violation of autonomy. In a sense, they are not being pressured to change or unduly influenced; rather they are 'voluntarily' adapting their practice on the basis of judgements informed by experience and expertise.

Implications for the nature and continuity of pupils' school experience

In looking at the discussion above on first and upper schools teachers' perceptions of middle schools, the nature and frequency of interschool liaison/contact, and adaptations by first and upper school teachers, as well as other data collected in our interviews, a number of implications became apparent. First, although some abrupt changes in organization, teaching style, and curricular emphasis may be experienced by pupils as they move through a three-tier system, most first and upper school staff view the interschool transfer of pupils as generally smooth.

During the period of the research, considerable variation was observed in the frequency of the interschool contact which was directed towards the transfer of pupils. The pyramid where this transfer from first to middle and middle to upper was seen to be most satisfactory was the one with fewest schools. Here, the first-year middle school team visited the first school on several occasions, first-year middle school pupils conducted an assembly at the first school, teachers of the final-year first school pupils visited the middle school, final-year first school pupils visited the middle school, a parents' evening was held at the middle school for the parents of the new intake, teachers from the first and middle schools met and discussed each child's record, and there was considerable contact between the first school and first-year middle school coordinators. The transfer from the fourth year of the middle schools to the upper school was impressive, painstaking, and meticulous. School records and assessments were supplemented by further high school administered tests in English and maths, as well as nonverbal IQ tests. This was supplemented by a discussion of each child, between the head and fourth-year coordinator of the middle school and the head of year and assistant from the high school. The middle school pupils visited the upper school and the upper school conducted a parents' evening for parents of the new intake.

Transfer between schools may also be seen as relatively smooth because of the policy of many middle schools to operate a 'transition' model, where much of the transition in organization and teaching approaches takes place within rather than between tiers. (See also the chapter by Meyenn and Tickle in this book.)

It is important as well to point out the variation among schools in any one tier, even within the same pyramid. For example, in discussing what had transpired with previous junior and/or infant schools when they were redesignated as first schools, one respondent commented:

> It certainly doesn't happen in this school, but I can see how it can happen in other first schools, where you've got infant-biased heads and staff: you could have nine-year-old infants. . . . I think that's very bad. I think at seven, eight, and nine they (the pupils) have got to start being made to be a bit more mature. (First school teacher)

Upper school teachers similarly remarked about the differences (some of which they would like to eradicate) among middle schools in orientation to discipline, testing, organization, and instruction. Thus, for some pupils in a pyramid, there may be more or less discontinuity experienced when transferring between tiers in the system, because not all middle schools or first schools are the same.

If first schools and middle schools have varied because of the different backgrounds of teachers assuming positions in them, upper schools in our sample (despite important differences potentially stemming from secondary modern and grammar school background differences among teachers) seem to have one major characteristic in common. References were made by the upper school to the domination of and their 'preoccupation' with examinations, with emphasis on 'getting people through CSE and 'O' levels'. Because of being connected with a nine–thirteen middle school, teaching in an upper school meant (as one upper school teacher remarked):

> . . . having to start a bit further back. You've really got to have your eye on examinations from the time that people come here. And it means that there's not much time available for doing the other things on the periphery, things which are worth following up. . . .

The domination of the examination system occurs time and time again.

> And in a way I think some people say that you are far too examination-minded and I think perhaps the middle schools might say that to us, but that is ultimately what these kids want and what they have got to have when they leave. (Upper school teacher)

And another teacher:

> I think that this is our main concern, we are rushed and consequently although one doesn't want to delay an examination machine, you end up by being an examination machine because there is not time to spread your education as wide as you would like. Because this is on you and all the idealism about teaching and exams are not the be all and end all it becomes that to a large extent even though you try not to. You just find that you are bound by them. (Upper school teacher)

This situation was a source of dissatisfaction for many upper school teachers, who preferred a broader role for themselves.

Such discussion, of course, raises the question of the most appropriate age of transfer. In this regard it is interesting to note how little agreement there was amongst those teachers we interviewed as to the best age of transfer from either first to middle school, middle to upper school, or primary to secondary level. For many teachers, transfer would occur ideally when individual pupils had acquired the skills and knowledge provided in one school and had developed physically, cognitively, and socially to a point where they were ready to cope with the demands of the next school. However, when focusing on a (perhaps) more realistic situation of pupils transferring en masse from one tier to another, the first and upper school teachers interviewed expressed preferences for transfers occuring at ages ranging from seven to fourteen. Reasons given for preferring a certain age normally centred on the pupils' stage of physical, cognitive, and social development as well as on the time required for course offerings.

Interestingly, however, using similar arguments one teacher could promote age eight, while another teacher could promote age ten or eleven as most appropriate for transfer from the first school.

> I think eight was better myself, because we used to keep them until eight you

see, and I found that most of them had mastered their reading. (First school teacher)

. . . with the system we have at the moment, the teachers who are teaching in the system haven't necessarily been trained for the system. . . . You've got people who are dealing with children who come to middle school at nine with reading disabilities and staff who do not know how to teach children to read. (Another first school teacher)

And a similar situation exists with regard to the most appropriate age of transfer to the upper school.

I think it (twelve) might be better for transfer, because at the present stage I think the trend, as I say, physical and mental maturity, the third year is the problem. We would have a year of settling and then the problems would come to light. So you'd know a lot better the background of the people you've got. (Upper school teacher)

I . . . think thirteen is most probably a very good year for change. . . . Problems in schools that used to run from eleven to sixteen; the majority of your problems start at this age (i.e., thirteen). I think that is why the age of thirteen was decided upon in the first place in the idea of the three-tier system. . . . I'm not saying it overcomes all of them but it does tend to. . . . They haven't had, you see, the two years in a known environment. So that when they start to become adolescent, they . . . know what the establishment is like to become awkward against. (With transfer at thirteen) they've got to find out (about a new school) and by that time they're getting over that problem. (Another upper school teacher)

These and other differing interpretations as to the best age for pupils' transfer between schools undoubtedly reflect the experience of at least some pupils in at least some types of school situation. The preferred age of transfer is therefore influenced by the teacher's previous and current experience. As one respondent remarked in discussing the age of transfer:

Well, it's a very difficult question to answer, because like any teacher I'm conservative and what you get used to over the years seems best to you, doesn't it? It's human nature. I try to be objective about this. (Upper school teacher)

It is also apparent that although such views are not totally inaccurate, they are also not totally accurate for all pupils – a point many of the teachers acknowledge. More importantly, however, one must be aware of how the diversity of common-sense views connects up with ideologies of middle schools (see Hargreaves, 1977(c)). For example, in Ginsburg et al. (1977, p.7) we argue that:

Middle schools may become less prominent as part of an economically expedient strategy for comprehensivization with existing school buildings. We even speculate that the age of transfer from primary to secondary schools will depend more on the number of students that can be accommodated in existing school buildings, than it will depend on psychological and developmental arguments. Nevertheless, it is likely that psychological and developmental and other educational arguments will be proffered as a rationale for what is primarily an economic decision.

If this prophecy turns out to be accurate and there is a move away from having ages of transfer at nine and thirteen, some people will be disgruntled but another set will potentially be greatly satisfied. This latter group's views and experience would also provide support for the ideology used to deflect attention from the economic and administrative basis for the decision to alter the ages of transfer.

Conclusions

In this chapter we have attempted to explore the views of first and upper school teachers on the organization and practices of middle schools. In general, first school teachers saw the middle school as introducing secondary practices at an earlier age than was the case in the two-tier system. Upper school teachers, on the contrary, saw middle schools as an extension of the former primary schools.

Contact between the teachers in the different schools was seen as important but was, in many cases, less than that seen as desirable. It was argued by many teachers that informal, social contact facilitated the necessary formal contact. Several reasons were put forward as to why the amount of contact was often less than desirable. Time constraints were seen as an important factor, especially by first school teachers, although the major factor would appear to be a concern not to infringe upon the autonomy of the staff of another school. This posed a dilemma especially for upper school staffs who on the one hand did not want to infringe upon this autonomy, and on the other wanted to influence what is taught because of their overriding concern and responsibility in preparing pupils for exams.

While upper school teachers did attempt in various ways to influence what went on in the middle schools, they also adapted and employed different strategies in the upper schools to cope with being part of a three-tier system. First school teachers claimed on the whole to experience very little pressure from the middle school to change what they were doing.

However, most could give examples of how they had changed their existing practices as a result of a comment or suggestion from the middle school, or in an attempt to prepare their pupils for the perceived practices of the middle school.

Most teachers view the transfer between schools as being satisfactory. The degree of satisfaction, and indeed the degree of smoothness of transfer, varied quite widely. The amount of time and effort devoted by staff to liaison, especially in terms of 'passing up' information on pupils prior to transfer, is seen as an important factor. Additionally this process may be aided by the fact that a considerable amount of 'within school transition' takes place.

Opinions, among our teachers, on the 'best' age of transfer, varied from seven to fourteen, and it is interesting to speculate that if the age of transfer were to change, there would be one set of teachers who would be greatly satisfied. This group of teachers is a potential source and may be 'used' to provide the developmental and other educational arguments to 'justify' this change, even though economic or political or more pragmatic reasons like population changes are the basis of the decision to change.

Notes

1. In order to ensure confidentiality, the interviews are only distinguished in terms of the level of school in which teachers work. Thus, all respondents are labelled (first or upper school) teachers regardless of their formal school status (e.g., head).

2. It is important to note that a first school and an upper school teacher, both of whom had considerable formal and informal contact with middle school teachers, viewed middle schools as 'something different', neither primary nor secondary. As the first school teacher explained:

   > . . . one would hope that it would be neither but it would be a mingling of the two. It's a new conception and so it really should not be a high school or a primary school – it has got to be a mingling of the two. . . .

   Having extensive contact with middle school teachers may make these teachers more aware of the complex resolution of primary- and secondary-orientated practices in middle schools. Alternately, it may make these teachers more likely to incorporate elements of the ideology of middle schools – in particular the element which purports 'an emphasis on an institutional uniqueness which would transcend preexistent educational categories' (Hargreaves, 1977, p.15).

3. It is important to note that (at least in one teacher's comments) the desire to see more teaching in middle schools done by individuals specifically trained in a

given subject, is matched with a cynical questioning of the subject specialists' motives for taking a middle school position.

> Being rather a cynic, I would perhaps ask: why do people transfer to a middle school? . . . For anyone to move from a high school to a middle school, unless for promotion, being a cynic, I would perhaps suggest they're going there for an easy life. Because it's no doubt it's getting increasingly more difficult to teach the adolescent. (Upper school teacher)

4. Interestingly, one teacher, although recognizing that upper schools put pressure on middle schools (see subsequent discussion) and even when discussing his own personal part in this, seemed to view the absence of external exams as equivalent to being 'completely free of external restraints'. (For a discussion of the ideological roots and implications of such a view see Hargreaves, 1977(b), pp.18–19.)

5. It is worth noting that one upper school teacher, although identifying the benefits of informal contacts, would react negatively if those staff below him in the upper school hierarchy made use of informal associations to bypass him in establishing contact with a middle school.

> I think any friendship that does occur is useful . . . rather than go through all the official channels . . . I would frown upon any member . . . phoning up about a particular pupil without me. I would prefer it came from me. . . .

6. Many of those interviewed did not explicitly link up time constraints and the question of economic and political factors, which can be seen to produce the time constraints. Although teachers may, in fact, normally consider time constraints in this regard, it is interesting to speculate that time functions ideologically as a focus of blame in place of the economic and political context.

7. Blyth and Derricott (1977, p.77) similarly indicate that first, middle, and upper school teachers in their relations with each other 'are almost by definition mutually on guard, each with their own interests to maintain'.

8. There is some indication that ex-secondary teachers working in middle schools are perceived to be more resentful of infringements of autonomy.

> When the change-over (three-tier reorganization) took place I think you got in middle schools a lot of people who had been in secondary schools who had perhaps felt that they wanted to rule their own down there. (Upper school teacher)

9. Relatedly, one first school teacher said that middle school teachers' efforts to influence what occurred in first schools were welcome if they were done in the 'right way', the 'proper way', with 'good manners' and without being critical.

10. Such a top-down influence strategy might be less successful if teachers in different middle schools in a feeder pattern interacted frequently, and coordinated their own middle school form of curricular and teaching organization. The minimal evidence available, however, indicates that middle school col-

league contact is even less extensive than the contact between middle school and upper school teachers or middle school and first school teachers (Ginsburg et al., 1977, p.38).

11. At the same time a similar phenomenon of middle school teachers adapting their practice to cope with the demands presented by the type of pupil transferring from first schools (Ginsburg et al., 1977, p.19) might be seen to detract from the image of middle schools' autonomy.

12. In some cases, although middle school teachers were not seen to be trying to change the first school, parents were described as making such efforts in anticipation of potential problems for their children when they transferred to the middle school.

13. It is possible, of course, that in the context of the interviews some first school staff members felt (perhaps for self-impression/management reasons) that they needed to avoid references to being pressured or influenced by middle school teachers.

14. This does not necessarily mean that they saw the three-tier system as desirable.

CONCLUSION

This book has provided the first collection of research papers on middle schools and middle schooling. Its scope, like that of the field of research it reflects, is modest. We hope it constitutes a beginning, a starting point of systematic and rigorous research into the organization and practice of middle schooling and into its relationship to political, economic, and demographic changes. This issues raised in this book, whether they concern staff relations and career structures, pupil relations and their experiences of transfer, the structure of the middle school curriculum, and so on, all require further study. In addition, there are many aspects of middle schooling about which there is virtually no knowledge, though some of these gaps are beginning to be filled. Recent additions to the pool of middle school research include an analysis of teacher participation in curriculum decision-making (Hargreaves, 1980); a study of the effects of contemporary educational issues, such as the demands for standards, accountability, and a more specialist curriculum, on teachers' classroom practice (Wallace, 1980); and investigations of patterns of sex-role stereotyping and their effects in middle schools (Delamont, 1980; Jones, 1980).

Research of this kind is particularly urgent at a time when rapid contraction in the education service is exerting severe pressure on the organization of middle schooling. As Bornett (Chapter 11) pointed out, promotion opportunities in middle schools have never been great, there being few posts available at Scale 3 level and very few indeed beyond that point. With the onset of falling rolls and reductions in middle school staffing numbers, these already restricted avenues for career advancement are being limited still further. It is not inconceivable to suggest that, in the absense of any compensating action at LEA or school level, the result may well be one of disappointment and disillusionment among middle school teachers as they envisage little prospect of movement from their present positions. Indeed, on the basis of some small-scale research, Hunter (1980) has stated that such reductions in staff morale are already occurring, and may well carry with them a measure of stagnation in teaching practice and act as a brake upon curriculum reform. The claimed need for 'the conversion of views and expectations suited to expansion, and based on the important assumption that expansion would always be sustained, to a wholly new set of cicum-stances' (Dennison, 1979, p. 39) seems particularly apposite for middle schools (see also Bainbridge, 1979; Briault, 1979).

The implications of contraction for middle schools are, of course, even greater than this. The very existence of middle schools is threatened by increasing pressures for the provision of more specialist types of curricula in the eleven–thirteen range (a demand which middle schools will have diffi-culty in satisfying) and by an interest on the part of many policy-makers in rationalizing educational provision for the sixteen-plus age group in order to protect curriculum choice at A-level. Where such rationalization leads to the setting up of sixth-form education in separate colleges, nine–thirteen middle schools will very likely be phased out as a result, due to the unpopularity and consequent lack of support for thirteen–sixteen schools. Because of these twin pressures, the fate of middle schools already hangs in the balance in several LEAs (Bryan and Hardcastle, 1980).

In the context of such changes, some might view this book as a defence of middle schools by those who wish them well. Such an interpretation would not be justified. Whether or not middle schools deserve, on balance, to be received and evaluated favourably must remain an open question for the moment. Our concern as editors, one which we share with at least some of our contributors, is about the terms in which the question is posed and the grounds on which it is answered. The fate of middle schools should not be subject solely to the vagaries of demographic change and economic reces-sion as well as the ideological themes of standards, accountability, and giftedness which have accompanied such changes in the years following the Great Debate. Instead, the future of middle schools ought to be discussed in the context of a rationally planned and democratically formulated system of educational change which takes into account existing, relevant research in different disciplines and traditions. This book, we hope, makes a small contribution to that large project. Of course, such research has not and indeed will not throw up consistent and irrefutable 'findings' about middle schools. In this book alone, the differences between the conclusions reached in different chapters (e.g., the ones by Hargreaves and Nias, respectively) are often considerable. We do not see research as an arbitration device, as a sort of ACAS or Clegg Commission for the settling of unresolved educational disputes. Rather we deem it important that policy-relevant debates and discussions should be conducted in the knowledge of, and with the degree of rigour usual in, educational research. In short, the grounds for answering questions about middle schools should include careful study and research in middle schools.

The way in which the pertinent questions are posed is also of crucial importance. When middle schools or other schools are evaluated in terms of their accountability, their capacity to maintain educational standards, and their ability to contribute to curriculum continuity, these themes ought not to be interpreted in the rather restricted fashion that has been usual to date. They should themselves be treated as problematic. Continuity of curricular experience, for example, is not the same thing as the subordination of the curriculum of one school to that of another, though that is the more conventional interpretation. Similarly, the call for standards should spread beyond the well-worn paths of literacy and numeracy to include standards of political literacy which one would think to be of paramount importance in a self-professed democratic society where rates of political participation are, paradoxically, exceedingly low. And accountability should embrace not only the school but also the LEAs and the DES so that they too are held to be accountable for their policies and can demonstrate that those policies have been rationally produced in full cognisance of relevant research.

The widest possible interpretation of and debate upon these questions is called for. As the categories of standards, accountability, and curriculum continuity are currently defined, middle schools are coming to be expected to perform tasks for which they were never designed. There is, therefore, a need for policy to be based on a *detailed* understanding and assessment of middle schools as well as for *detailed* study and assessment of the demands which are made upon middle schools and the context in which those demands are generated. Whether the outcome will be one of vindication or invalidation of the middle school concept is uncertain. The important point is that the judgement should not be made prematurely.

As part of their claimed ability to effect a smooth transition between primary and secondary work, middle schools have been credited with the strategic significance of a bridge in the educational system. The bridge metaphor has, in the main, held positive connotations in the middle school literature. One perceptive commentator, however, has seen quite a different possibility contained in the 'bridge' metaphor. He remarks that:

> A metaphor not infrequently used about the middle school is that it is a bridge. The trouble with the use of metaphor in educational discourse is that it suspends thought at the level of simple analogy. A bridge is an inanimate contrivance which links two or more places, its sole purpose being to speed communications between them, lending of itself no development to the traffic. (Miles, 1979, p. 1)

Whichever interpretation of the metaphor is the most appropriate, the matter can be resolved only if reference is made to available research on middle schools. The future of middle schools will be determined by policy-makers. At the same time their destiny can be influenced by educational research. It is to be hoped that the contribution of research will not be pre-empted by over-hasty implementation of policy changes.

BIBLIOGRAPHY

Ader, J. (1975) *Building Implications of the Multi-Option School*, Paris, OECD.

Alexander, R. and Wormald, E. (1980) *Professional Studies for Teaching*, London, Society for Research into Higher Education.

Assistant Masters' Association (1976) *The Middle School System: An AMA survey*, London, AMA.

Bainbridge, J. W. (1979) 'Falling Rolls: Teachers and shrinking schools', *Durham and Newcastle Research Review*, vol.IX, no.43.

Baron, D. G. (1974) 'The Shrink Factor in the Classroom', *Education*, vol. 144.

Baron, D. G. and Howell, D. E. (1974) *The Government and Management of Schools*, London, Athlone Press.

Bassey, M. (1978) *Nine Hundred Primary School Teachers*, Slough, NFER Publishing Company.

Bauman, Z. (1978) *Hermeneutics and Social Science: Approaches to understanding*, London, Hutchinson.

Becker, H. (1968) *Making the Grade*, New York, Wiley.

Beetham, R. et al. (1973) *Report on the Organisation of 9–13 Middle Schools: With particular reference to the role of the year group leader and the subject head*, University of London Institute of Education, University Centre for Teachers Research Club.

Bellaby, P. (1977) *The Sociology of Comprehensive Schooling*, London, Methuen.

Bennett, S. N. (1976) *Teaching Styles and Pupil Progress*, London, Open Books.

Benn, C. and Simon, B. (1972) *Half Way There*, Harmondsworth, Penguin.

Benton, T. (1974) 'Education and Politics' in Holly, D. (ed.) *Education or Domination*, London, Arrow Books.

Bernstein, B. (1971) 'On the Classification and Framing of Educational Knowledge' in Young, M. F. D. (ed.) *Knowledge and Control: New directions for the sociology of education*, London, Collier-Macmillan.

Bernstein, B. (1975) 'Class and Pedagogies: Visible and Invisible' in *Class, Codes and Control Volume 3: Towards a theory of educational transmissions*, London, Routledge and Kegan Paul.

302 Middle Schools

Blau, P. M. and Scott, W. R. (1963) *Formal Organisation: A comparative approach*, London, Routledge and Kegan Paul.

Blyth, W. A. L. (1960) 'The Sociometric Study of Children's Groups in English Schools', *British Journal of Educational Studies*, vol.8, pp.127–147.

Blyth, W. A. L. (1978) 'The Curriculum in the Middle Years of Schooling'', *Education 3–13*, vol.6, no.2, pp.26–27.

Blyth, W. A. L. (1979) 'The Middle School Curriculum' in Marsden, W. E. (ed.) *Post-War Curriculum Development: An historical appraisal*, Proceedings of the 1978 Annual Conference of the History of Education Society of Great Britain.

Blyth, W. A. L. and Derricott, R. (1977) *The Social Significance of Middle Schools*, London, Batsford

Blyth, W. A. L., Cooper, M. R., Derricott, R., Elliott, G., Sumner, H., and Waplington, A. (1976) *Curriculum Planning in History, Geography and Social Science*, Bristol, Collins-ESL.

Blyth, W. A. L. et al. (1977) 'Aspects of Power in the Genesis and Development of One Curriculum Project' in Richards, C. (ed.) *Power and the Curriculum: Issues in curriculum studies*, Driffield, Nafferton Books.

Board of Education (1926) *Report of the Consultative Committee on the Education of the Adolescent* (Hadow Report), London, HMSO.

Bornett, C. R. (1976) *The Social Relations of the Middle School Curriculum: Some preliminary observations*, M.Ed. dissertation, School of Education, University of Bath.

Bourdieu, P. (1977) 'Symbolic Power' in Gleeson, D. (ed.) *Identity and Structure*, Driffield, Nafferton Books.

Boyle, E. (1972) 'The Politics of Secondary School Reorganisation: Some reflections', *Journal of Educational Administration and History*, vol.4, no.2.

Boyle, E. and Crosland, A. (1971) *The Politics of Education*, Harmondsworth, Penguin Education.

Bowles, S. and Gintis, H. (1976) *Schooling in Capitalist America*, London, Routledge and Kegan Paul.

Briault, E. (1979) 'The Politics of Primary Contraction', *Education 3–13*, vol.7, no.1

Bryan, K. A. (1979) *Some Empirical Evidence Concerning Pupils' Achievement in the Middle Years of Schooling*, unpublished paper, Chester College, Chester.

Bryan, K. A. and Hardcastle, K. W. (1977) 'The Growth of Middle Schools: Educational rhetoric and economic reality', *British Journal of Educational Administration and History*, January, pp.49–55.

Bryan K. A. and Hardcastle, K. W. (1978) 'Middle Years and Middle Schools: An analysis of national policy', *Education 3–13*, vol.6, no.1, pp.5–10.

Bryan, K. A. and Hardcastle, K. W. (1980) 'Reflections on Recent Developments within the Middle Years of Schooling', paper delivered to the Middle Schools Research Group Conference, Maryland College, Woburn, April 1980.

Bruner, J. S. (1966) *Towards a Theory of Instruction*, Cambridge, Massachusetts, Harvard University Press.

Building Performance Research Unit (1972) *Building Performance*, School of Architecture, University of Strathclyde, London, Applied Science Publishers.

Burrows, J. (1978) *Middle Schools: High road or dead end?*, London, Woburn Press.

Carr, E. H. (1964) *What is History?*, Harmondsworth, Penguin.

Central Advisory Council for Education (England) (1963) *Half our Future* (Newsom Report), London, HMSO.

Central Advisory Council for Education (England) (1967) *Children and Their Primary Schools* (Plowden Report), vols. 1 and 2, London, HMSO.

Charles, K. (1974) 'Aims, Organisation and Planning', *Education 3–13*, vol.2, no.1, April 1974.

Clarke, Sir F. (1940) *Education and Social Change*, London, Sheldon Press.

Clarke, J. et al. (1976) 'Subcultures, Cultures and Class' in Hall, S. and Jefferson, T. (eds.) *Resistance Through Rituals*, London, Hutchinson.

Clegg, A. et al. (1967) *The Middle School: A symposium*, London, Schoolmaster Publishing Company.

Cockburn, C. (1977) *The Local State: Management of cities and people*, London, Pluto Press.

Cohen, S. (1978), 'Survey Standards Plummet under Standstill Budgets', *The Times Educational Supplement*, 13th October, 1974.

Comber, L. D., Foster, A. W., and Whitfield, R. C. (1977) 'An Analysis of the Middle School Curriculum', paper presented to the British Association for the Advancement of Science, Aston, Birmingham, September 1977.

Cox, C. B. and Boyson, R. (1975) *Black Paper 1975*, London, Dent.

Culling, G. (1973) *Teaching in the Middle School*, London , Pitman.

Cusick, P. A. (1973) *Inside High School: The student world*, New York, Holt, Rinehart and Winston.

Dale, R. (1972) *The Culture of the School*, Open University Course E282, unit 3, Milton Keynes, Open University Press.

Dale, R. (1979) 'The Politicisation of School Deviance: Reactions to William Tyndale' in Barton, L. and Meighan, R. (eds.) *Schools, Pupils and Deviance*, Driffield, Nafferton Books.

Delamont, S. (1976) *Interaction in the Classroom*, London, Methuen.

Delamont, S. (1980) 'Sex Role Stereotyping in Two Middle Schools', paper delivered to the Middle Schools Research Group Conference, Maryland College, Woburn, April 1980

Dennison, W. F. (1979) 'Expenditure Planning in English Education: Recent developments in the relationship between central and local authorities', *Journal of Educational Administration and History*, vol.XI, no.1, January 1979.

Dennison, W. F. (1980) Falling Roles: Predictions and prospects', *Durham and Newcastle Research Review*, vol.IX, no.43.

Department of Education and Science (1962) *The School Building Survey 1962*, London, HMSO.

Department of Education and Science (1966) *Building Bulletin No. 35: Middle Schools*, London, HMSO.

Department of Education and Science (1970(a)) *Launching Middle Schools: An account of preparations and early experiences in Division No. 15 of the West Riding of Yorkshire*, Education Survey No. 8, London, HMSO.

Department of Education and Science (1970(b)) *Towards the Middle School*, Education Pamphlet No. 57, London, HMSO.

304 Middle Schools

Department of Education and Science (1976) *Statistics of Education: Teachers Vol.4*, London, HMSO.

Department of Education and Science (1977(a) *A New Partnership for Our Schools*, London, HMSO.

Department of Education and Science (1977(b)) *Education in Schools: A consultative document*, London, HMSO

Department of Education and Science (1977(c)) *Educating our Children: Four Subjects for debate*, London, HMSO.

Department of Education and Science (1977(d)) *Gifted Children in Middle and Comprehensive Secondary Schools*, London, HMSO.

Department of Education and Science (1977(e)), *Information for Parents* (Circular 15/77), London, HMSO.

Department of Education and Science (1978) *Primary Education in England*, survey by HM Inspectors of Schools, London, HMSO.

Department of Education and Science (1979(a)), *Statistical Bulletin 3*, London, HMSO.

Department of Education and Science and Welsh Office (1977) *A New Partnership for our Schools*, London, HMSO.

Derricott, R. and Blyth, W. A. L. (1979) 'Cognitive Development: The social dimension' in Floyd, A. (ed.) *Cognitive Development in the School Years*, London, Croom Helm.

Doe, B. (1976) 'The End of the Middle', *The Times Educational Supplement*, 26th November, 1976.

Douglas, J. W. B. et al. (1968) *All Our Future*, London, Panther.

Dressel, P. L. (1958) 'The Meaning and Significance of Integration' in Henry, N. B. (ed.) *The Integration of Educational Experiences*, 57th yearbook of the National Society for the Study of Education, Chicago, University of Chicago Press.

Edwards, R. (1972) *The Middle School Experiment*, London, Routledge and Kegan Paul.

Eggleston, S. J. (1967) 'Social Factors Associated with Decisions to "Stay on" in Non-selective Secondary Schools', *Educational Research*, 1967.

Eichorn, D. H. (1966) *The Middle School*, New York, Centre for Applied Educational Research Inc.

Ellis, T. et al. (1976) *William Tyndale: The teacher's story*, London, Anchor Press.

Entwistle, H. (1970) *Child-Centred Education*, London, Methuen.

Etzioni, A. (1961) quoted in Morphet, E. et al. (1974) *Educational Organisation and Administration*, Englewood Cliffs, New Jersey, Prentice Hall.

Etzioni, A. (1964) *Modern Organisations*, Englewood Cliffs, New Jersey, Prentice Hall.

Field, F. (1977) *Education and the Urban Crisis*, London, Routledge and Kegan Paul.

Fiske, D. (1979) 'Falling Numbers in Secondary Schools: Problems and possibilities', paper given to the North of England Education Conference, January 1979.

Ford, J. (1969) *Social Class and the Comprehensive School*, London, Routledge and Kegan Paul.

Foucault, M. (1977) *Discipline and Punishment*, London, Allen Lane.

Fowler, G., Morris, V., and Ozga, J. (eds.) (1973) *Decision Making in British Education*, London, Heinemann.

Freire, P. (1976) *Education: The Practice of Freedom*, London, Writers and Readers Publishing Co-operative.

Galton M., Simon, B., and Croll, P. (1980) *Inside the Primary Classroom*, London, Routledge and Kegan Paul.

Furlong, V. (1976) 'Interaction Sets in the Classroom: Towards a study of pupil knowledge', in Hammersley, M. and Woods, P. (eds.) *The Process of Schooling*, London, Routledge and Kegan Paul/Open University.

Gannon, T. and Whalley, A. (1975) *Middle Schools*, London, Heinemann.

Ginsburg, M. B., Meyenn, R. J., Miller, H. D. R., and Ranceford-Hadley, C. (1977) *The Role of the Middle School Teacher*, Aston Educational Monograph No. 7, Birmingham, University of Aston.

Ginsburg, M. B., Meyenn R. J., and Miller H. D. R. (1979) 'Teachers, the "Great Debate" and Education Cuts', *Westminster Studies in Education*, vol.2.

Glaser, B. G. and Straus, A. L. (1971) *Status Passage*, London, Routledge and Kegan Paul.

Godfrey, J. A. and Cleary, R. C. (1953) *School Design and Construction*, London, The Architectural Press.

Goffman, E. (1961) *Asylums*, Chicago, Aldine.

Gorwood, B. (1973) 'The Middle School Experiment?', *Forum*, vol.15, no.3.

Gorwood, B. (1978) '9–13 Middle Schools: A local view', *Education 3–13*, vol.6, no.1.

Gosden, P. H. J. H. and Sharp, P. R. (1978) *The Development of an Education Service: The West Riding 1889–1974*, Oxford, Martin Robertson.

Grathoff, R. (ed.) (1978) *The Theory of Social Action: The correspondence of Alfred Schutz and Talcott Parsons*, Bloomington, Indiana University Press.

Griffin-Beale, C. (1977) 'Plowden Plus Ten', *Education Guardian*, 11th January, 1977.

Griffith, J. A. (1966) 'The School Building Programme – The roles of central and local government' in Fowler, G. et al., op. cit.

Habermas, J. (1976) *Legitimation Crisis*, London, Heinemann.

Hadow Report (1926) *Report of the Consultative Committee on the Education of the Adolescent*, Board of Education, London, HMSO.

Haigh, G. (1975) *Integrate*, London, Allen and Unwin.

Halsey, A. H., Floud, J., and Martin, D. (1956) *Social Class and Educational Opportunity*, London, Heinemann.

Hardcastle, K. (1977) 'Teaching Methods and Teacher Progress', *Education 3–13*, vol.5, no.1.

Hargreaves, A. (1977(a)) 'Progressivism and Pupil Autonomy', *Sociological Review*, vol.25, no.3., Summer 1977.

Hargreaves, A. (1977(b)) 'The Ideology of the Middle School', paper circulated to Middle Schools Research Group following seminar, University of Liverpool.

Hargreaves, A. (1977(c)) 'Ideology and the Middle School', paper circulated to Middle Schools Research Group following seminar, University of Liverpool.

306   Middle Schools

Hargreaves, A. (1978) 'The Significance of Classroom Coping Strategies' in Barton, L. and Meighan, R. (eds.) *Sociological Interpretations of Schooling and Classrooms: A re-appraisal*, Driffield, Nafferton Books.

Hargreaves, A. (1979) 'Strategies, Decisions and Control: Interaction in a middle school classroom' in Eggleston, J. (ed) *Teacher Decision-making in the Classroom*, London, Routlage and Keegan Paul.

Hargreaves, A. (1980) 'Curriculum Decision-Making: Participation and control', paper delivered to the Middle Schools Research Group Conference, Maryland College, Woburn, April 1980.

Hargreaves, A. (forthcoming) *The Sociology of the Middle School*, London, Routledge and Kegan Paul.

Hargreaves, A. and Warwick, D. (1978) 'Attitudes to Middle Schools', *Education 3–13*, vol.6, no.1.

Hargreaves, D. (1967) *Social Relations in a Secondary School*, London, Routledge and Kegan Paul.

Hargreaves, D., Hestor, J., and Mellor, F. (1975) *Deviance in Classrooms*, London, Routledge and Kegan Paul.

Head of Clarendon School (1977–78), 'Changing a Secondary Modern into a Middle School: The head's viewpoint', *Educational Administration*, vol.6, no.1.

Henry, J. (1963) *Culture Against Man*, New York, Random House.

Higginson, J. H. (1973) 'Evolution of "Secondary Education" ', *British Journal of Educational Studies*, vol.XX, no.2, pp.165–177.

Hirst, P. H. (1975) *Knowledge and the Curriculum*, London, Routledge and Kegan Paul.

HMSO (1977) *Education in Schools: A consultative document* (Cmd. 6869), London, HMSO.

Holly, D. (1977) 'Education and the Social Relations of a Capitalist Society' in Young, M. and Whitty, G. (eds.) *Society, State and Schooling*, Brighton, Falmer Press.

Holness, D. (1973) *Policy and Expediency: The evolution of the middle school*, M.A. dissertation (Education), Institute of Education, University of London.

Hopkins, L. T. (1937) *Integration, its Meaning and Application*, New York, Appleton.

Howell, D. A. (1976) 'The Government and Management of Schools Reconsidered', *Research in Education*, no.16, November 1976.

Houghton Report (1974) *Report of the Committee of Inquiry into the Pay of Non-University Teachers*, London, HMSO.

Hughes, E. C. (1937) 'Institutional Office and the Person', *American Journal of Sociology*, 1937.

Humphrey, C. (1968) *The Re-organisation of Secondary Education in the County Borough of Wallasey*, M.Ed. dissertation, University of Durham.

Hunter, C. (1980) 'Falling Rolls and Morale in Schools: Some implications for career and management', paper delivered to the Middle Schools Research Group Conference, Maryland College, Woburn, April 1980.

Husen, T. (1974) *The School as an Institution*, London, Methuen.

Jacks, M. L. (1946) *Total Education*, London, Kegan Paul/Trench and Trubner.

Jackson, P. W. (1968) *Life in Classrooms*, New York, Holt, Rinehart and Winston.

Jackson, B. and Marsden, D. (1966) *Education and the Working Class*, Harmondsworth, Penguin.

Jenkins, D. and Shipman, M. (1976) *Curriculum: An introduction*, London, Open Books.

Jones, R. (1980) 'Fostering Femininity in Middle School Girls', paper delivered to the Middle Schools Research Group Conference, Maryland College, Woburn, April 1980.

Kirk, G. (1973) 'A Critique of Some of the Arguments in the Case for Integrated Studies', *Scottish Educational Studies*, April 1973, pp.95–102.

Kogan, M. (1971) *The Politics of Education*, Harmondsworth, Penguin.

Lacey, C. (1970) *Hightown Grammar*, Manchester, Manchester University Press.

Lambart, A. (1976) 'The Sisterhood', in Hammersley, M. and Woods, P. (eds.) *The Process of Schooling*, London, Routledge and Kegan Paul.

Lawton, D. (1973) *Social Change, Educational Theory and Curriculum Planning*, London, University of London Press.

Lee, T. (1976) *Psychology and the Environment*, Essential Psychology F.5 (General Editor: Herriott, P.), London, Methuen.

Lomax, P. (1978) 'The Attitudes of Girls to Different Aspects of their School Experience', *Educational Reviews*, vol.30, no.2.

Lynch, J. (1975) 'Legitimation of Innovation: An English path to open education', *International Review of Education*, vol.21, no.4.

Lynch, J. (1980) 'Lifelong Education and Teacher Education in Great Britain', in Jourdan, M. *Recurrent Education in Western Europe*, Slough, NFER Publishing Company.

Mack, J. (1978) 'What's the Point of Strong School Governors?', *New Society*, 7th September, 1978.

McLuhan, H. M. and Fiore, Q. (1967) *The Medium is the Massage*, New York, Bantam Books.

MacLure, S. (1975) 'In Search of the Best of Both Worlds – Middle schools for the middle way', *The Times Educational Supplement*, 18th April, 1975.

Marjoram, D. T. E. (1978) 'The APU and Assessment in the Middle Years', *Education 3–13*, vol.6, no.2.

Marsden, D. (1971) 'Politics, Equality and Comprehensives', *Fabian Tract No.411*, London, British Fabian Society.

Marsh, C. (1973) 'The Emergence of the English Middle School', *Dudley Educational Journal*, vol.1, no.3.

Mason, S. C. (1964) *The Leicestershire Experiment and Plan*, 3rd edition, revised, London, Councils and Education Press.

McRobbie, A. and Garber, J. (1976) 'Girls and Subcultures: An exploration' in Hall, S. and Jefferson, T. (eds.) *Resistance Through Rituals*, London, Hutchinson.

Measor, L. and Woods, P. (1979) 'Myths of Transfer', paper presented to SSRC seminar on ethnography, St. Hilda's College, Oxford.

Medd, M. (1976) 'Schools – Primary' in Mills, E. D. (ed.) *Planning: Buildings for education and science*, London, Newnes Butterworth.

Mercer, C. (1975) *Living in Cities: Psychology and the urban environment*, Harmondsworth, Penguin.

Meyenn, R. J. (1980) 'School Girls' Peer Groups', in Woods, P. (ed.) *Pupil Strategies*, London, Croom Helm.

Miles, R. (1979) 'The Educational Importance of the Middle School', paper delivered to the Middle Schools Research Group Conference, University of Leeds, November 1979.

National Union of Teachers (1964) *First Things First: A memorandum of evidence submitted to the Central Advisory Committee for Education under the chairmanship of Lady Plowden*, London, NUT.

National Union of Teachers (1969) *Plowden – The Union's comments on some of the major issues of the Plowden Report*, London, NUT.

National Union of Teachers (1979) *Middle Schools: Deemed or doomed?*, London, NUT.

Newsom Report (1963) *Half Our Future*, report of the Central Advisory Council for Education (England), London, HMSO.

Nicholson, J. S. (1970) 'Delf Hill Middle School, Bradford', in Halsall, E. (ed.) *Becoming Comprehensive: Case studies*, London, Pergamon.

Nisbet, J. D. and Entwistle, N. J. (1966) *The Age of Transfer to Secondary Education*, London, University of London Press.

Oddie, G. (1964) *School Building Resources and Their Effective Use*, Paris, OECD.

Oddie, G. (1975) *Industrial Building for Schools*, Paris, OECD.

Owen, R. (1974) *Middle Years at School*, London, BBC.

Oxfordshire County Council Communication Centre (1977) *The Child at 13: Expectations in the field of humanities*.

Pearson, E. (1972) *Trends in School Design*, London, Macmillan.

Pearson, E. (1975) *School Building and Educational Change*, Paris, OECD.

Peel, E. A. (1960) *The Pupil's Thinking*, London, Oldbourne.

Piggott, C. A. (1977) *Transfer from Primary to Secondary Education*, M.A. dissertation, University of Southampton.

Piggott, C. A. (1979) 'Childrens' Reactions Before and After Transfer to Middle Schools', paper presented to the 1979 Annual Conference of the British Educational Research Association.

Platten, D. E. (1978) *Curriculum Integration: A review of theory and problems of implementation*, M.Ed. thesis, University of Liverpool.

Plowden Report (1967) *Children and Their Primary Schools*, report of the Central Advisory Council for Education (England), London, HMSO.

Pollard, A. (1979) 'Negotiating Deviance and "Getting Done" in Primary School Classrooms' in Barton, L. and Meighan, R. (eds.) *Schools, Pupils and Deviance*, Driffield, Nafferton Books.

Pring, R. (1976) *Knowledge and Schooling*, London, Open Books.

Raggett, M. and Clarkson, M. (1974) *The Middle Years Curriculum*, London, Ward Lock Educational.

Raggett, M. and Clarkson, M. (1976) *Teaching the Eight to Thirteens*, London, Ward Lock Educational.

Razzell, A. (1976) 'The Effect is Neutral', *The Times Educational Supplement*, 26th November, 1976.

Razzell, A. (1978) 'Mixed Ability Teaching in the Middle School – A personal view', *Forum*, vol.20, no.2.

Reynolds, D. (1976) 'The Delinquent School' in Hammersley, M. and Woods, P. (eds.) *The Process of Schooling*, London, Routledge and Kegan Paul.

Richards, C. (1979) 'Primary Education: Myth, belief and practice', in Bloomer, M. and Shaw, K. (eds.) *Innovation and Constraint*, London, Pergamon.

Robinson, P. (1977) 'Poverty and Education: A pragmatic circle' in Gleeson, D. (ed.) *Identity and Structure*, Driffield, Nafferton Books.

Rochdale Education Committee (1969) *Report on Middle Schools*.

Rutter, M. et al. (1979) *Fifteen Thousand Hours*, London, Open Books.

Sallis, J. (1978) 'Current Practice in School Government', *Where*, 143, pp.295–300.

Satterly, D. J. H. (1970) *A Study of Cognitive Styles and Their Implications for Curriculum Development*, Ph.D. thesis, University of Bristol.

Schools Council (1969) *Working Paper No. 22, The Middle Years of Schooling from 8 to 13*, London, HMSO.

Schools Council (1972) *Working Paper No. 42, Education in the Middle Years*, London, Evans/Methuen.

Schools Council (1975) *Working Paper No. 55, The Curriculum for the Middle Years*, London, Evans/Methuen.

Seaborne, M. (1971) *The English School, its Architecture and Organisation, Volume I 1370–1870*, London, Routledge and Kegan Paul.

Seaborne, M. and Lowe, R. (1977) *The English School, its Architecture and Organisation, Volume II 1870–1970*, London, Routledge and Kegan Paul.

Sharp, R. and Green, A. (1975) *Education and Social Control*, London, Routledge and Kegan Paul.

Silverman, D. (1970) *The Theory of Organisations*, London, Heinemann.

Smith, P. (1973) *The Design of Learning Spaces*, London, Council for Educational Technology for the United Kingdom.

Spady, W. (1974) 'Authority and Empathy in the Classroom' in O'Shea, D. (ed.) *Sociology of the School and Schooling*, Proceedings of the Second Annual Conference of Sociology of Education Association, February 1974, Asilomer, California, National Institute of Education.

Staffordshire County Council Education Committee (1974) *Uttoxeter Three-Tier Reorganisation*, reports of working parties given limited circulation.

Stebbins, R. A. (1976) 'Physical Context Influences on Behaviour: The case of classroom disorderliness', in Hammersley, M. and Woods, P. (eds.) *The Process of Schooling*, London, Routledge and Kegan Paul

Stenhouse, L. (1975) *An Introduction to Curriculum Research and Development*, London, Heinemann.

Sugarman, B. (1967) 'Involvement in Youth Culture, Academic Achievement and Conformity in School', *British Journal of Sociology*, vol.18, pp.151–164.

Thompson, J. (1973) *Organisations in Action*, New York, McGraw-Hill.

Tickle, L. (1979) *Sociological Analysis and Case Study of the Organisation and Evaluation of Art and Design Subjects for 3rd and 4th Year Middle School Pupils*, M.A. (Ed.) thesis, University of Keele.

University of Exeter Institute of Education (1968) *Themes in Education, No.14, Middle Schools*.

Vaizey, J. and Sheehan, J. (1968) *Resources for Education*, London, Allen and Unwin.

Wallace, G. (1980) 'Paradox and Policy: The redefinition of the Middle School', paper delivered to the Middle Schools Research Group Conference, Maryland College, Woburn, April 1980.

Wallace, G. M. (1977) *Architectural Constraints on Educational Aims and Organisation: With reference to middle schools*, M.Sc. dissertation, University of Aston in Birmingham, Department of Educational Enquiry.

Wardle, A. (1974) *The Rise of the Schooled Society*, London, Routledge and Kegan Paul.

Warwick, David (1973) *Integrated Studies in the Secondary School*, London, University of London Press.

Warwick, David (1975) *Curriculum Structure and Design*, London, University of London Press Ltd.

Warwick, Dennis, (1974) 'Ideologies, Integration and Conflicts of Meaning' in Flude, M. and Ahier, J. (eds.) *Educability, Schools and Ideology*, London, Croom Helm.

West Riding Education Committee Reports (1963) *The Organisation of Education in Certain Areas of the West Riding*.

West Riding Education Committee Reports (1965) *The Organisation of Comprehensive Schools in Certain Areas of the West Riding*.

West Riding Education Committee Reports (1967) *The Middle School*.

Willis, P. (1976) 'The Class Significance of School Counter Culture' in Hammersley, M. and Woods, P. (eds.) *The Process of Schooling*, London, Routledge and Kegan Paul

Willis, P. (1977) *Learning to Labour*, London, Saxon House.

Worcestershire County Council Education Committee (1968) *Report of the Droitwich Working Party on Middle Schools*.

Young M. F. D. (ed.) (1971) *Knowledge and Control*, London, Collier-Macmillan.

Youngman, M. B. and Lunzer, E. A. (1977) *Adjustment to Secondary Schooling*, Nottingham, The School of Education.

AUTHOR INDEX

SUBJECT INDEX

The Harper Education Series has been designed to meet the needs of students following initial courses in teacher education at colleges and in University departments of education, as well as the interests of practising teachers.

All volumes in the series are based firmly in the practice of education and deal, in a multidisciplinary way, with practical classroom issues, school organisation and aspects of the curriculum.

Topics in the series are wide ranging, as the list of current titles indicates. In all cases the authors have set out to discuss current educational developments and show how practice is changing in the light of recent research and educational thinking. Theoretical discussions, supported by an examination of recent research and literature in the relevant fields, arise out of a consideration of classroom practice.

Care is taken to present specialist topics to the non-specialist reader in a style that is lucid and approachable. Extensive bibliographies are supplied to enable readers to pursue any given topic further.

Meriel Downey, General Editor